Phone #: 250-448 ~~

No Pretending

The Honest Journey of a Pastor's Wife

To Debbie:

Life has many challenges
with great blessings and
deep pain + loss.
   May you be encouraged
as you read "my story" to
trust Jesus MORE!

In His love,

Shirley Unrau

John 14:6

Copyright

Endorsements

Reading Shirley's memoire has been a privilege and a challenge. I have been formed spiritually in so many ways by her honesty regarding journey and mystery. I would recommend this book to anyone who is ready to "quit pretending" that a walk with God is easy. Her story is not formulaic, she shares a wild ride of faith that values honesty before God and others.

Susan Anquist, Friend, Co-worker at OASIS Ministries, Certified Spiritual Director, Masters of Spiritual Formation, Portland Seminary

Shirley Unrau will undoubtedly strike a chord in your heart as she has done in mine. Her humble and honest journey beautifully depicts the steadfast faithfulness of a godly wife, the protective love of a mother's heart, and the undeniable commitment to God and His church. I could not help but rejoice with her in all of her rejoicings and mourn with her in all of her mourning. Her wisdom is invaluable, her insights are timeless, her integrity through difficult times is commendable, and her persevering faith is endearing. This love story between Father and daughter contains a treasury of hidden gems and is well worth the read. I would, without hesitation, recommend it to all pastors' wives, but as well, to anyone who has experienced love, loss, heartache, or trial.

Lisa Elliott, Inspirational speaker and Award-winning author of *The Ben Ripple* and *Dancing in the Rain.*

Shirley reveals a side of ministry most never see. Her raw vulnerability and complete trust in God through all circumstances are both inspiring and faith building. This book will take you from the valleys to the mountaintops and show you how to keep your eyes on the One who leads the way.

Tandy Balson, Inspirational Speaker and Author at timewithtandy.com

We often struggle to find a reason for our pain, grief and wounding along our life's journey. What is God's plan when our world is suddenly turned upside down? God doesn't waste our pain. He used Pete and Shirley's wounding as a redemptive pulpit to help countless ministry people going through the dark night of their souls. We learned from them that our pain and confusion does not refute or contradict the promises of God. And that we were not alone in our pain. Let her words coax life and hope into the painful places in your story. Thank you, Shirley, for pouring out your soul for us to learn from you and to walk with you on your journey. With love, gratefulness and deep admiration,

Dianne Esau Porter, Author of *Not Abandoned*

Dedication

I dedicate this book to my best friend in life, my husband Pete for over 60 years. He has been the wind beneath my wings, my encourager, my helper, and editor. This is our story my dear. We are one. I couldn't have done this without you.

I also dedicate this story to my children by birth and by marriage:

To Bevan and Rebecca, Brent and Denise, Kim and Darlene and Kathy and Bruce. You have all been such a source of delight and blessing in my life. Special love and dedication to my ten grandchildren, and six great grandchildren. How you cheer my heart and help keep me young.

Special Thanks

Thank you to those who have come along side of me and helped me write, edit and complete this book. To my husband Pete who has without wavering, walked with me through all of life's experiences. You are my treasure. Tandy, my cousin, who I first trusted with this my new baby book, edited and led me to my wonderful publisher. To Serenity McLean, who went way beyond the call of duty to help me with all the publishing needs. You gave me confidence and assurance. To son Kim who helped me with the wild computer world and gave me hope. To Dianne who tirelessly and professionally edited my work and encouraged my heart. To Lisa who came alone side to give insight, editing and prayed for me in the work of writing a book. Finally, to Susan, who journeyed faithfully with me in the hardest part of my life and my book and on to victory in Jesus.

Table of Contents

Preface

I was adorned in the most beautiful bridal gown I had ever seen, handcrafted in love by my dear mother. As I walked down the aisle of my home church, on the arm of my special daddy, I wished that walk could go on for mile after mile. As I looked at the front of the church, my beloved's eyes were brimming with tears of joy, overwhelmed at the bride walking to meet him. I was excited and a little apprehensive about the future. I knew the moment I said, "I do" to becoming this handsome man's wife, I was also saying, "I do" to becoming a pastor's wife.

My soon to be husband who turned twenty one on the bus, on his way to his first church. He had pastored without me for one year; now I was joining him. My eyes were covered with imaginary rose tinted glasses that day. I was full of anticipation. My heart of innocence knew nothing of what lay ahead for us.

We chose a theme for our wedding: "United to Serve." This was on all our invitations, our programs, our place cards, our thank you, along with a big banner hanging in our reception hall. We wanted to be a team working for God side by side, hand in hand, and heart to heart. We both felt God's call to full time Christian ministry.

Now we are looking back on sixty years of Christian ministry. We have traveled a lot of miles. We have scaled amazing heights we would have never dared to dream attainable. We have also plunged to the depth of sorrow, betrayal, and loss that we didn't know was possible.

We have pastored large churches, and small ones. On the scale of experience, we have pioneered a church plant beginning with one other couple, and we have served as Senior Pastor to a congregation of over 1,400. My husband has held many positions of leadership in the Christian ministry. These include: senior pastor, youth pastor, music pastor, assistant pastor, church planter, camp director and speaker, Youth for Christ director, denominational president, Bible college professor, evangelist, missionary, and Oasis Retreat Founder and Director. We have traveled across Canada teaching Family Life Conferences together for seventeen years. We have had many opportunities to speak at missionary conferences in seventeen different countries. Each one was an honor, a challenge, and a time of untold blessings.

We have stood in awe as God has used our lives and testimony to bring people to know and trust in Jesus as their Savior and Lord. As 3 John 4 says, "There is no greater joy than to hear that my children walk in truth." We say that of our birth children and we say that of those we have had the privilege of assisting in their spiritual birth. No greater joy this side of heaven than to be in God's birthing room and then to travel with these new babes until they are mature followers of Jesus Christ, leading others to follow Jesus as well.

For many years we didn't know what it was like to have an enemy. Now we do. For many years we could not identify with the depth of despair and questioning that Job had of his God or David as he wept out his pain and confusion in many of the Psalms. Now we can.

We have felt so totally loved, accepted, and graced by our God and Savior, Jesus Christ. We have often cried out to Him, "Why me?" when the blessings were flowing upon us and around us. We have also cried out to our God, "Why me, why now," when we felt He had abandoned us, turned His back on us in our pain, and was silent to our prayers.

My story is one of God's presence in the face of joy and pain. It's a story of how the soul grows through difficulties. It's my personal story of God's strength infused into my weakness. If the telling of my story can encourage those of you who follow behind me, then that is another of God's unique purposes for the journey He has allowed me to travel.

For almost twenty years now I have felt the tug of God on my heart to write my story. I have written bits and pieces of it over the years, but never seemed to have the time to pull it all together. A friend keeps telling me, "Keep writing your unique story. It matters, tell it."

Carol Kent, author of the book, *When I Lay My Isaac Down* put it this way: "In telling our real life stories, we are no longer hiding behind the masks of denial, embarrassment, guilt or shame. We're just us, people who have had some good days in life and people who've had some very bad days. We've quit pretending that everything is fine and that life is always grand. We are finding ways of relating without the facade and without the need to impress. We can just be real. That brings tremendous freedom." Carol quotes a friend, Christine Caine: "God is able to take the mess of our past and turn it into a message. He takes the trials and tests and turns them into a testimony."

All of our stories matter. All need to be told. This is not just a book for pastors' wives, although I have written it with them in mind. There are very few books that address the problems unique to a pastor's wife. How I would have loved to have read a book like this when I was walking in the "dark night of my soul." It is also a story that can be of benefit for all who read it. The struggles I have had, the joys and pain I have experienced are common to all, regardless of call. It offers you encouragement on the road of life's random, unpredictable journey.

I have written my story as honestly and as real as I was able. I know it is a biased story. It is what I saw, experienced and vividly remember. *No pretending* has been a goal of mine throughout my life. I highly value integrity, authenticity and real truth speaking to those with whom I have journeyed. Putting on a mask allows us to live on the surface of life, but it robs us of the beauty of experiencing deep relationships that offer one another hope for all who have tasted the darkness.

Jesus said, "Go home to your friends, and tell them what wonderful things God has done for you; and how merciful He has been" (Mark 5:19 Voice). I write this book with a special desire that it may be of encouragement, help, and blessing to my four children, their spouses, their children and their grandchildren. "Let each generation tell its children of your mighty acts; let them proclaim your power." (Psalm 145:4 NLT)

The following words from Steve Saint, sum up my heart's desire as I write my story. "God writes great stories when common, ordinary people give Him their wills as His quill and their lives as His slate. Some of God's chapters are painful, but we are promised (Romans 8:28) that they all make sense in the end."

Jesus said, "In the world you shall have tribulation" (John 16:33). So it's a given that we will face physical, emotional, relational and spiritual suffering. Jesus doesn't end that verse with tribulation, but rather with "be of good cheer; I have overcome the world." It is that focus of good cheer and overcoming that I trust we can learn to live, even in the storms of life.

Travel with me. Learn with me. Be strengthened with the comfort and courage I have received from my God. So, here is my offering, my sacrifice, my story, written for you, WITHOUT PRETENDING.

Chapter One

THE ROOKIES SET OUT

Jamestown, North Dakota 1958-1960

"The future is a bright as the promises of God." Pete Unrau

The wedding and honeymoon were behind us. We were traveling thousands of miles from our parent's home to our first place of ministry. Pete had been invited to be the youth pastor of a thriving church, in the middle of the plains of North Dakota. This was very appealing to him. Alongside this call, was an opportunity to further his education at the local Jamestown College.

The trip was memorable. We were so poor, we slept in the car and ate picnic meals along the way. Nothing however, robbed us of our great optimism and enthusiasm for what lay ahead. We had both worked as missionaries under the Canadian Sunday School Mission, and had been on traveling teams, singing and speaking. However, we were not prepared for the enormity of the task that was before us. Pete loved to preach and had a natural gift for it but that is not all a youth pastor does.

We arrived in our small town only to find that the senior pastor was away. We received instructions to find our home that had been rented and furnished for us. It was a one-bedroom basement apartment. The only windows were one foot high, at the top of our walls. The view outside these windows was the dirt and grass of our landlord's yard. Our entrance was the same as the people who owned the house.

Greeting us at the door as we arrived at our first home was this very excited special needs son of our landlord. He enthusiastically said, "We've been waiting for you a long time. You're finally here." At first his exuberant mannerisms, strange speech and waving, shaking arms made me uneasy and somewhat fearful. Later we learned to laugh with him and to love him. Every time we came home he was always there to greet us with laughter, waving arms, and enthusiasm. He brought variety and unexpected joy to our lives.

The very first day Pete went to work at the church, the senior pastor met with him and told him, "You'll never get caught up in this calling. Don't let that bother you. Just do your best." We never forgot that. For those in Christian ministry this fact is often a point of pressure. No matter how hard you work, how many hours you put in a day, in a week, in a month or year, you never feel like you have done enough. People often get hurt because you didn't tend to their need when they wanted you to.

The second thing this senior pastor did was to ask Pete to pray with him. He got down on both of his knees on the hardwood floor where Pete joined him. There this beautiful, soft- hearted, Godly man poured out his heart on behalf of Pete as he began his new ministry in this church and in this community. He prayed, "Lord, help Pete to never feel that he is working under me but alongside of me." That act of humble, prayerful submission to God and full support of Pete's ministry alongside of him, stayed with Pete for the rest of his life. We have kept in touch with this precious couple, faithfully serving God until His recent call to Glory.

Our salary was $175.00 per month. Pete was youth pastor, music director, and assistant pastor. He hit the ground, running. Pete was also taking a full academic load at the private college in our town, seeking to get his Bachelor's degree. I was often left at home alone, wondering what I should do with myself? What did God have in mind for me? Pete's ministry was neatly cut out for him. Mine was not.

I have realized, during our sixty years of ministry, that the role of the pastor's spouse is ever changing. The seasons of a woman's life drastically change, as do the needs in each church. The call of God doesn't change, but I soon realized that in order to survive being in ministry I would need to learn to be flexible, realizing that I would never meet everyone's expectations in every church and in every situation. Pete's calling, giftedness, and ministry in the church has remained the same, throughout our years of pastoring.

I soon became involved with the choir and playing the piano for services. I also loved connecting with the youth of our church and interacting with them. Our youth group grew to over seventy. Our hands were full, and so were our hearts. What a joy to see these teens coming to know Christ as their Savior and forever friend. Sharing our love and our lives with these teens was what God had called us to do. We couldn't have been happier. We saw many of these teens taking huge steps of growth and commitment to Christ in their walk with God.

There was another crying need in our town. Youth for Christ needed a director for our city. He was a natural, so soon that was added to his already overloaded schedule. He has always had a hard time saying "no" to a great opportunity to share Christ. He battles this to this very day.

To augment our meager salary of $175.00 per month, I began working at the local Catholic hospital as a nurse's aid. I loved my work. I loved to make the very ill, elderly people happy. Often I sang for them as I bathed them, or made their bed. They began to look forward to my coming, thus I also looked forward to lifting their hearts. The Catholic sisters were especially kind to me. Often when there was a patient who was seriously ill, the sisters would ask me to go to that room and sing and pray with the patient. Others would do my assigned rooms. I could see that this was God's hand of blessing on my life and work.

We began our marriage living a very frugal life style. We found many ways to reuse, recycle and make do. We were green before we even knew what that meant. We never went out to eat, bought prepared food, or phoned home. Letters from home were a major highlight. We rented garden space and learned how to can produce.

At this time we bought our first piece of furniture. I decided I could also teach piano lessons in our little basement apartment. Getting the piano into the basement was the big problem. I enjoyed many hours of teaching from our little home. This opportunity blessed me financially, and socially.

We were married for four months when we discovered that we were going to have a baby. We were delighted. We never thought to ask ourselves if we could afford a baby. Of course we could not. We didn't even question if a baby could fit into our already overloaded schedule. We were totally unprepared for a baby. I had no one to talk to about my joys and my fears. There were no classes to attend to help us prepare. There were no books to read that we could find. We were thousands of miles from our families, and I had not established friends to whom I felt free to ask questions. The doctor kept telling us that I was doing very well. I felt great, excited and unprepared.

Our little rented apartment in the basement was proving not to be a healthy place to live. It was so damp down there that the walls were literally wet with moisture. Little rivers would flow down the walls, making puddles on the floor. When we got into bed at night, it felt like the sheets had just been taken from the washer and had never been dried. Pete got sick and the doctor ordered us out of this tiny basement home. We were told to move immediately before our baby came.

We had no money and we had no furniture. A kind friend from the church owned a mobile home dealership. Often people would upgrade to a new mobile home and leave their old furniture in on the deal. Well, it was a deal for us as well. We bought enough second hand furniture to equip our new two-bedroom apartment. After buying a washing machine, stove, fridge, kitchen table and chairs, sofa, rocking chair, lamps, double bed, crib, and desk for Pete, we were set. The total price for everything was $218.00. Many helped with the move. We were happy to be in a dry, warm place and totally on our own.

At this point in our lives I loved to entertain. Our home was not big or fancy. It didn't matter whether people were rich or poor, all were welcome. People were happy to come. It was clean and tidy, decorated with orange crates for end tables covered with linen table clothes and lamps. And then there was our eighteen-dollar sofa adorned with a lovely bedspread Pete's parents had given to us as a wedding gift. We had little to offer, but our love and friendship. To our surprise, that was exactly what our congregation needed. I enjoyed making hospitality simple, putting the emphasis on relationships rather than amazing decor and exotic foods. I realized in our culture people are not hungry but they are lonely. Throughout our ministry, this knowledge has given me the strength to use my gift of hospitality to the blessing and encouragement of many. However, there are times when I loved getting out my English bone China, making everything extra special.

The church ladies put on the biggest baby shower I had ever seen, I was thrilled with everything. My pregnancy was going well and I was happy. Our first-born son was born within two hours of being admitted to the hospital. He was beautiful. We named him Bevan James. I was thrilled of course, but also feeling apprehensive about looking after this new little human being. I had never been around babies, and had done no babysitting as a teen. I was too busy practicing the piano. I was literally clueless when it came to babies.

My mother came to help for the first two weeks. When she left I cried, and the baby continued crying. I often thought he was upset because I was upset. The doctor and nurses had an unwritten law that said you must wait four hours between feedings for the baby. They insisted that right from the beginning, the baby needed to know who was in charge. I know now that this was not a good plan. Bevan was a healthy eight pound two ounces baby, who didn't know about this law. He was hungry far before the four hours were up. Somehow we made it through and he was a healthy son. Now I watch our granddaughters feeding their baby so leisurely, when the baby is wanting to feed. How lovely and how natural. But I didn't know any better, but to obey my doctor and the nurses. I regret this.

The ministry was going so well. We were seeing God's blessing, in every area of our lives. Youth for Christ rallies were a highlight for the youth of our city. At our church, Pete loved and respected our senior pastor and learned much from him. What we came to find out however, was that this pastor was suffering from severe burnout and needed a break. So, Pete took on the full load of pastoring, which included preaching on Sundays, as well as caring for our congregation. He didn't find this hard. He has always had unbounded energy and passion with an ever positive attitude. I saw little of him at home. With his full-time studies at the college, and such a full load at church, what could I expect? We had, in fact believed that the ministry comes first and that God would reward our sacrifice as we gave Him first place in everything. I didn't share my deepest fears and thoughts with even Pete, let alone anyone else. This was a lonely, isolated time for me. I gave my loneliness to God and He met me in my place of need in loving and surprising ways.

I did continue teaching piano lessons. One day a week, on Saturdays, I got a babysitter and taught all of my students in that one day. This helped us with our meager salary and it also gave me a much needed change for one day out of the week.

One great highlight for me at this time was a trip we took with a group of our youth, to the Youth for Christ Capitol Teen Convention in Washington, DC. At first it looked impossible for me to go. We didn't have the money, and I had a young baby. To my total surprise my parents sent me the money to go with Pete, and a dear friend offered to look after our baby. We headed off with two busloads of ninety teens. We joined up with eight hundred teens in Minneapolis and rode the train to Washington, DC. Ten complete hotels were used to house all these teens. It was an amazing time.

When we got to the first rally in DC, the sight of ten thousand teens gathered in one spot singing "Christ for Me", was overwhelming. One of our teens started crying. Pete asked her what was wrong. Through her tears, she said, "Look at all these teens who love Jesus too, this lets me know that we are not alone." This was all a little taste of heaven. We heard great music, and great speakers, one being Billy Graham. Our group from North Dakota won the award for the most teens per capita. It was one of those mountain top experiences for us and for the youth we worked with.

When Bevan was five months old I discovered I was pregnant again. I was so totally shocked. This is not what I had in mind. How could I handle two babies, when I was just beginning to relax with one? I cried out my frustrations to God. In time, I adjusted to this new life growing within me. Never did I feel healthier than when I was pregnant. I knew, with God's help, we could work through this time.

Pete was a great husband and father when he was home, often changing the baby and helping me in every way. We were seeking to love and serve God with all our heart, soul, mind and strength, and to love and serve each other as well. United to Serve was our heart's desire but it was quite a balancing act.

I was beginning to feel more and more at home in our new place of calling. I had made some special friends. I felt like I finally fit in and had areas of ministry that I could contribute. Our little baby was growing into a beautiful healthy boy. Life was good. God was good.

And then...the phone rang! This was my first experience of how one phone call can change a person's life forever.

Chapter Two

CHURCH PLANTING

North Park Bible Church, Saskatoon, Saskatchewan
1960-1964

"Life is just a schoolroom with a glorious opportunity to prepare us for eternity." Billy Graham

The outrageous phone call came from a group of men from churches in the farm areas surrounding Saskatoon, Saskatchewan, Canada. They had been dreaming and praying about starting a new church in a largely unchurched area of this city. They were seeing a lot of their young people moving to the city and were wanting to establish a church of their denomination in Saskatoon. They were wondering if Pete would come and meet with them and consider pastoring this new church plant.

I was stunned. I could not believe this could be God's will for us. I had settled myself into at least four years in North Dakota because I knew by then Pete would have completed his Bachelor's degree. This is what made perfect sense to me. Moving in the middle of college years did not. I cried at the thought of leaving these good new friends. The ministry at the church was going so well. Why couldn't Pete be content and just stay put until college was over? And then, to top it all off, I was very pregnant with our second child. This was a difficult time and I was feeling sidelined and confused.

Pete, however, felt he needed to check into the opportunity and see if this was the hand of God or not. He took the long trip to Saskatoon alone, to talk to the men who had this vision of a new church. I stayed home and prayed, and cried, and read God's word, and fretted some more. We were miles apart physically as well as in our thinking and feelings.

Pete met with the men, prayed about it and felt God was asking him to accept their invitation. He read in his normal Bible reading a verse that confirmed his decision that this was the plan of God for us. He phoned me at home to tell me he had accepted the call and we would be moving to Saskatoon in the summer. Up to this point, my life had been pretty predictable. This was a new challenge for me, a young wife and a young pastor's wife. I had committed myself to say, "Yes" to God whatever the cost and wherever God would lead me. I remembered kneeling with Pete during our wedding ceremony and singing together, "Savior like a shepherd lead us. Much we need thy tender care." I had asked God to give me a Godly spiritual leader as a husband and now I was fighting his decision in my heart. This I needed to resolve with God and with Pete. I was learning that the sweetest music to my ears was, "Let's do it my way."

I knew the verses in Isaiah 55:8-9, "For my thoughts are not your thoughts, neither are your ways my ways declares the Lord. As the heavens are higher than the earth, so are my ways higher than your ways and my thoughts than you thoughts." I needed to do a radical rearranging of my heart attitude. As I wept out my commitment to follow God's plan and Pete's heart, God poured His peace into my heart. I knew the path ahead of me would not be easy, but I knew the best place for our little family was to be in the center of God's plan for us.

My fear of being out of the will of God was always present in my mind, throughout my life. I knew God's will and way were the best for our little family but I often struggled to know for sure that this decision or move was God's leading, not our own reasoning. Before long we were packing up our meager belongings into an old farm truck, saying farewell to a church body who had loved us so well. Now we were heading off to a whole new adventure in trusting our God. I had made the decision to obey God's leading but it took a while for my emotions to catch up with my obedience. Saying goodbye was hard.

We arrived in a strange city that was to be our home. We had no place to stay so we bunked in with a pastor and his family who lived out in the country. I felt like we were imposing terribly with a small toddler and a very pregnant wife. Pete and the men were off to look for a home in the city for us to rent. We had no money at all. Finally, a little home was found for us. Our salary of $215.00 a month was little more than half the rent for this home. We moved all our old furniture into this little two bedroom home. Even our old $18.00 couch fit in.

We felt ready for this new ministry, with only one couple committed to joining us, we embarked upon planting a church. We went to a prayer meeting at one of the country supporting churches. After Pete had shared, the men and women divided into two groups to share prayer requests and pray. I was shocked when the mother of one of my friends from Bible college, got up and asked prayer for her son who was dating an English girl. She asked the group to pray that his eyes would be opened and that he would end this relationship. Here I sat in a strange church, among strange women, hearing an indictment on my own soul. Did they not know that I was an English girl who couldn't speak a word of the German language? How would they respond when they would eventually find out? How would they support this new pastor when they found out he had married an English girl?

I had faced some opposition from Pete's parents before our marriage. They would have been much happier if I had come from a German Mennonite background. My mother in law had the idea that English girls knew nothing about baking, cleaning house or raising children. I didn't blame her, as this was the mindset in which she was brought up, a very strict Old Colony Mennonite one. Pete was very supportive of me, telling me that he didn't want to marry a Mennonite girl. He wanted me, just as I was.

He had no hesitation that in time I would not only win over his mother's heart, but these folks from the country as well. They needed to see our kind of marriage work. They needed to get to know English wives that were functional. There was no hiding the fact that I was on display. Pete had a desire to make this new church, in the city, a church where "everyone" would be truly welcome. We named the church, North Park Bible Church. It was the first church in this denomination that did not have the word Mennonite in it. Pete was making a statement that "all" would be included. It wasn't long before my heart settled into this new ministry. As we look back over sixty years, it was one of the most exciting ministries of our lives.

We rented a school auditorium and with the help of some folk from the country we started our first meetings in an area of the city where there was little gospel witness. All the weekday meetings were held at our house. Before the folks would go out on visitation, or door-to-door evangelism, they would meet in our home for prayer, and then gather later for fellowship. Our weekly prayer meetings were also held at our home. Our place became like Grand Central Station. Sometimes a kind woman would look after our son so I could get out for a few exhilarating hours. I loved talking to people about their lives and the hope Jesus could give them. English people did come to our baby church. If there was anyone who spoke German, the English folk would all look at me for my reaction of a smile and a nod of understanding. I knew God had placed both Pete and me in the exact spot He had designed for us, and it was good.

Two months into this ministry, our second son was born. He came faster than the first one had. In fact, my labor was only twenty minutes from start to finish. The nurse had just told me she didn't know why I had come into the hospital so early, and that it would be a long wait before the baby would be born. She had just closed my door to let me sleep, and then the baby was on his way. The nurse on duty was filled with panic. She hollered at me and told me to stop pushing. I would have loved to obey her, but I could not. This baby was on his way and I could do nothing to stop him. The nurse became more and more upset with me. I thought Pete was going to have to deliver this baby. Of course, my doctor didn't make it. The intern sleeping down the hall made it just in time to catch the baby. I heard the next day that my nurse had quit that night and said, "I can't take this. You never know what's going to happen in this job." Because we didn't have any hospital or health insurance, I was allowed to go home with only one night in the hospital. The doctor allowed this because my mother was on her way once again, taking the train the many miles, to be by my side to help and support me.

This new baby boy, Brent Timothy, was born with a very contented nature. He slept well, ate well, and played well. He was blessed with a more relaxed mom than our first child. He was a perfect playmate for his big brother. God knew what he was doing in giving us two boys, just fourteen months apart. I often dressed them alike and was constantly asked if they were twins. Now, my hands were really full, both at home and at church. At church there was no nursery. We had rented the one big room of the school for our meetings and two classrooms for Sunday School. That meant I was pretty exposed to the concerns of everyone in the school gym church! Pete couldn't help because he was doing everything from the front, while I was doing my own balancing act at the back.

To get the boys and myself ready for church was a challenge. Some Sundays, I just wanted to stay home. I learned the importance to make the effort to go to church. Once I was there I found I had put myself in a position to receive blessings from the worship time and the parts of the message I would hear. Instead of counting what I was missing, I started counting what things I had gained by going. It was good for me to get out and to meet the people and give a smile or a word of encouragement to someone. The people were considerate and often helpful to me with our small boys. They loved seeing these precious babies and their pastor's wife. The more I went, the more excited I got about what God was doing.

This church plant was every young pastor couple's dream. Every Sunday we saw our numbers increase. We attracted a lot of young couples, who were excited about our vision and emphasis. In six months, the church had grown so much that we knew it was time to build our own church building. What an exciting time this was. Pete contacted his father, who was a retired carpenter, to see if he would come to superintend the building. He agreed to come. Pete's parents moved in with us for the five and a half months it took to build the church building. Our tiny two bedroom home was too small for us all to fit into comfortably. Pete built a small bedroom in the basement for his parents to sleep in. It was not an ideal situation, but we all made it work.

For the men this was like old times. How they enjoyed working and building together. Most of this new church building was erected by volunteer labor. People from the mother churches in the surrounding farm communities came to help. It was like a huge, five-month barn raising, with lots of good will, excitement, and relationship building.

Back at our little home, however, things were very different. While the men worked on building the church, my mother-in-law and I worked on building our relationship. It had, up to this point, been superficial. Now we were stuck together in a very small house, with two very small children, for a very long time. We had no escape. We would have to work things out. Mom was great with the new baby, now five months old. He was content with anyone and Mom loved rocking and holding him.

I think my mother in law looked upon this time as an opportunity to change me. It was a good time to show me how to do things the right way, the German way! I was just as determined to show Mom that the English knew a few things and that my ways were also good, maybe even in some cases superior. And so the contest began. Our arguments were often about how to peel potatoes, knead the dough, cut up chicken and so forth.

One lunchtime, when the men came home from work, they found our little home draped in relational ice. It didn't take long for the men to discover that Mom and I had had a conflict. We began to share our problems with them. Each husband took his wife's side. In no time at all we had four people upset with each other. My father-in-law was a very quiet, soft-spoken man. During the meal, he did something he had never done before. In anger, he got up from the table, left his meal and went to his bedroom in the basement. The rest of us tried to eat but the silence was so deafening we could not. In ten minutes, dad came up the stairs in tears, went to his young son and said, "Pete, I was wrong, will you forgive me?" This quiet older man led the way. Soon we were all confessing, making things right and in each other's arms. That day broke the heart of conflict in our home. The patriarch had led the way in confession and brokenness.

I eventually began to realize that I would not change my over sixty-year-old mother-in-law. Why could I not love and accept her and let her teach me some of her ways? The more I loved and honored her, the more I saw our relationship change. These five and a half months turned out to be God's gift in our relationship building.

The church building was complete. The dedication was such an awesome time of giving God praise and counting our blessings. That same weekend Pete went through the ordination procedure and became an ordained minister. The Reverend Pete Unrau was now my titled husband He always preferred to be called, "Pastor Pete".

A funny thing happened on this ordination Sunday. There were lots of ministers attending this momentous occasion. We had them all over to our home for a snack. Four preachers were sitting on our North Dakota eighteen-dollar couch, when very gradually, the legs on one end of the couch gave way and all the preachers slid to the floor. Lots of laughter and a few bricks later, the couch was as good as new.

The year was 1962. For some reason I kept a calendar of the people we had over and the amount we paid for groceries each month. When I look at that little calendar now, I can hardly believe it to be true. During that year we entertained and gave a meal, a snack or a dessert to seven hundred people. Our home after all was "the meeting place" for our growing baby church. Many of the families from the farm communities would come to the city and drop in to see us. They would often bring produce from their farms. Little by little they started to accept and then love this English pastor's wife. Our salary remained very low. We could hardly make it from one month to the next. We did everything to augment our meager salary. We rented plots of ground to grow gardens. We canned, froze, and prepared produce for the winter like squirrels in fall.

One time we were asked by a farmer if we'd like some chickens? We said we would love some chickens. What a delightful change that would be from hamburger, bologna and wieners. The farmer promised he would bring us fifty chickens. We could not believe how wonderful that would be. The farmer and the chickens arrived while we were away. I opened that back door to find a big box filled with fifty chickens with only their heads cut off. The farmer had forgotten to inform us of that small detail, that we would have to get the feathers off and the innards out ourselves. Pete said he knew how to get the feathers off. I knew how to clean the insides out. We thought we were set, but we ended up with a huge stinking mess. That night was visitation night. When a dear farm lady came to our home and saw the mess we were in, she stayed to help me. Oh what a blessing she was. She laughed with me and worked with me. Before the others were back from visitation, the chickens were nicely packed in the new deep freeze. We never tried that again even though it was a good bargain. We learned how to be very frugal and careful. I could write a book on the ways we made a dollar stretch. As I look back, I am amazed at God's blessing on our lives and our labors.

I am awed at how He used us and brought needy people into our lives. One such needy person stands out.

One day I was listening to the radio while working in the kitchen. A new talk show host had come to our city. He was the talk of the town. He had been an important man in Toronto life, the religion editor of one our nation's most prestigious newspapers. He was also a former minister of a large church in our city. While I was listened to him, this Monday morning, I was stunned and exercised by the topic being discussed. His question was, "Do people really go to church to worship God or do they just go to show off their latest hat?" I was alarmed that everyone who phoned in said church meant nothing to them. They said it was just a social engagement, or something that was expected of them. The more I listened, the more I wished some brave Christian would call in and share what true church and a relationship with God really meant.

Just then Pete walked in to get his books for university. I told him who was on the radio and asked him to make a call. He said he had classes in five minutes. As he left, he encouraged me to call. That was the push I needed. I put my two little boys in their cribs, each with a little bag of candy. While they sat in shocked silence, I dialed the number. To my surprise, I got on right away and was told this would be the last call of the day. I then shared my faith and told the host how wonderful it was to know Jesus, to be born again and to worship Him at church. I said my relationship with Jesus means the same to me as I sit in church on Sunday as it does on Monday morning when my wash line has broken and all my clean clothes are in the mud.

The host closed the morning with saying, "Very interesting conversation. Who knows, maybe I'll be born again as soon as I'm off the air." I was so excited and thankful that I had gotten on the air and was able to share my testimony. I began praying for him and could hardly wait until I could hear him on the air again. The next day he was not on the radio as scheduled. For the next couple of weeks, the regular host was not on the air and no explanation was made. I began to wonder if he had become a Christian and was fired from his job. I tried phoning the station and all they would say was he had been in the hospital and was not well.

Finally, in desperation I called the operator to see if I could get the radio hosts home phone number. To my amazement she gave it to me and, in no time, I was talking to him. Yes, he did remember me. He recounted the whole conversation we had had on the last radio show. Then he said, "Since that day I talked to you I have been on a steady drunk." I asked him if my husband could come and see him. He said, "Yes."

Pete called on him the next day. There he sat, a former prominent wealthy man who had owned a home with a three-car garage and a swimming pool, now in a little hovel of a motel room with empty beer bottles surrounding him. After Pete shared about Jesus, this formerly proud, man knelt to receive Christ. He then said, "I won't need this any more", as he poured the rest of his booze down the sink.

The radio host was now our friend. He lived with us for a while after that, until we could find him a job on a friend's farm. He had his ups and downs, but years later we heard he was going back into pastoral ministry. Unfortunately, he suffered a heart attack and went home to Heaven before he got to his new ministry. I knew it was the Spirit of God that had drawn our show host to himself. It was an awesome privilege to be part of God's plan in that one man's life. How wonderful to be the last link in the chain of God's events that brings a person to saving faith.

We were aware of God's unique blessing on us and on our ministry. Pete was continuing his studies at the University of Saskatchewan. He was beginning to find himself in places of leadership with our denomination. Our boys were growing and were a delight to our hearts. Our church was continuing to be healthy in spirit and growing in numbers. Life was good. God was good. We were content...and then sickness struck!

Chapter Three

IN GOD'S WAITING ROOM

Saskatoon, Saskatchewan, 1962

"Pain is inevitable, but misery is optional." Tim Hansel

I had heard about a new vaccine that had just been approved for the public to receive. It was a little drink called "Oral Polio Vaccine." Since I had polio as a teenager, I thought I must get this for my little boys, who were now two and three. When I took them to the Health Unit to get the vaccine the nurse said to me, "You should also take this vaccine." When I questioned her further she said, "Everyone is to have this vaccine." In obedience, I took the little drink as well.

That night, at home, I became extremely sick and my heart was gripped with a terrible fear. I told Pete, "I feel just like I did when I had polio as a teen in 1949." My whole body ached and I felt nauseated. I went to bed early, hoping that this aching dread would pass over me. I did feel some better the next day, but in a few days I began to feel like I was getting the flu.

My body was unable to absorb my food. It seemed to travel right through me. I began to have constant diarrhea. In time, I was alarmed. I went to the doctor who had no idea what I was dealing with. I told him about the time I had colitis when I was only eight months old. The colitis was so severe, I went down to eleven pounds. My mother said I was so thin she could pick the skin up off my bones. My mother had rushed me to the Baby Hospital in Vancouver, BC. The doctor told my mother, "If you had come five minutes later, your baby would have been dead." I now wondered if this disease had returned.

The doctor decided to put me on a 7-Up and cracker diet for a whole month, to see if my system could be cleaned out and the diarrhea stopped. Nothing worked. I continued to be very sick and to lose weight rapidly. I lost twenty pounds in one month, dipping as low as eighty-five pounds.

The doctor was alarmed enough to put me into the hospital to receive a number of tests. These are the kind of tests that you wonder when you are having them, if your sickness might not be better than having these terrible tests.

I was finally back into my hospital bed, awaiting my test results. I really was very, very ill. I was also beginning to get worried and anxious. I could not look after my family or myself. It seemed I was constantly in one waiting room after another. Waiting to see a doctor. Waiting for the phone to ring. Waiting in the hospital to get my test done. And now waiting in my hospital room for the test results. Waiting is especially hard when you are very weak and sick and are in the land between. The children of Israel, God's people, experienced this land between on their journey from Egypt to the Promised Land of Canaan. This land is full of mystery, turmoil, confusion, and forever waiting and wandering. God leads us into the land between to teach us valuable lessons, and to grow our character and our trust in Him, but I had no knowledge of this land or what my God was up to. We had little teaching on suffering and waiting. Few books had been written that addressed this difficult journey of God's children. Of course, the Bible is full of examples of this land between but I was in my own world and sinking fast.

One day my nurse came into the room with a sad look on her face. She began with, "Mrs. Unrau, we are so sorry." I immediately thought that they had discovered some terminal disease. Instead the nurse said, "We have just lost all your test results. We will have to repeat them."

"Lost?", I cried out, "how can you lose tests results in a hospital?" These people are professional, how could this have happened, I wondered, silently? Within me rose a spirit of anger toward the nurse and the hospital staff. Now these terrible, agonizing tests would have to be repeated, and they were. The tests showed nothing. I was finally sent home, as sick as ever, and very uncertain as to what the future held. The doctor eventually asked me to come back into the hospital for more observation. I was getting weaker and weaker and more concerned in my spirit.

Of course we were praying much. Yes, we had many people praying for me. We were claiming God's promise of healing. We were crying out to God for His mercy. But nothing seemed to be happening, either in my body, or with the doctor's ability to assess my situation. One day the doctor came into my hospital room and told me I would have to go home. The doctors in the province of Saskatchewan were going on strike. Socialized medicine was now coming to Saskatchewan and the doctors were opposed to it. The strike was their way of showing their opposition. I felt caught in the middle of a problem that wasn't mine, but had huge ramifications for me. Once again anger arose in my heart. How could these doctors just leave me and tell me to go home when I was so sick and needed them?

When I arrived home and was in my own bed, I began to cry out my frustrations with the nurses, the doctors, and the government. Pete sat on my bed, concerned but also alarmed at the anger he sensed boiling up from within my heart. Finally he said, "Honey, if God asked it of you, would you be willing to be on this bed of sickness for the rest of your life?" Now I was angry with Pete. I reminded him how many months I had been so very sick, and how hard the waiting and mystery had been. I told him of my disappointment to have hoped again and again only to have no answers and no remedy. Pete said he understood all of this, but he told me he had sensed a spirit of anger within me and he knew that was not pleasing to God. He prayed with me and tried to comfort me. With that, he left me to wrestle that long terrible night with God.

Tim Hansel says, "God has given us such immense freedom that he will allow us to be as miserable as we want to be. We can choose joy or we can choose misery. We cannot avoid pain, but we can avoid joy. Joy is a choice!" I was choosing the attitude of anger and misery. I wouldn't have been able to verbalize it then, but my real anger was centered in my God. I felt like he had forsaken me. Had God not promised to supply all my needs? (Philippians 4:19) Had he not said, "Call unto me and I will answer and show you great and mighty things that you know not?" Jeremiah 33:3 (KJV) Had he not said, "Wait on the Lord, be of good courage and He shall strengthen your heart, wait I say, on the Lord" Psalm 27:14 (KJV).

Waiting? That is what I had been doing for months now. I had been waiting on God, waiting for His voice, as I prayed and read the scriptures, waiting on doctors, in waiting rooms, at offices, hospitals and by the phone at our home. I felt God had not kept His promises to me. I felt His silence in a profound way.

What I really wanted was for God to take away the mystery and the waiting and to heal my body so life could once again be normal, healthy, and happy. We want to be in control and often God puts us in a situation of confusion. I was living in mystery just where God wanted me to be, off balance just enough to lean on Him and Him alone.

I wasn't learning the lessons very fast. I wasn't experiencing "the peace that passes all understanding" Philippians 4:7 (KJV). That lonely night, I cried and I prayed and finally I yielded. I told God I was willing for Him to take my life, or He could answer my prayer and make me whole again or he could leave me with this sickness. I handed over the controls of my life to my God, my Master. I was telling God, that my answer to the waiting, the confusions, the mystery, and pain of life was an unconditional "Yes" to God. I had made my choice to let God be God.

I had nowhere else to turn and I did want to surrender all to Him. I remembered the verse I had taken as my life verse when I was in my late teens. "As for God His way is perfect; the word of the Lord is flawless. He is a shield for all who take refuge in Him" (Psalm 18:30). I would take refuge in my God, believing His way was perfect although I could not see what He had in mind.

Well, God did a miracle work that night. He healed me instantaneously. Oh, isn't that what we always want, to be a miracle, to experience healing, to be done with waiting and mystery? But wait a moment. God healed me but not the physical healing that I was looking for, God healed me of the demand to be healed. God healed my angry, anxious spirit. In place of the anger, God granted me His peace that passes understanding. For the first time in many months I felt my body, my spirit and my soul relax. I was at peace. I was at rest. I was done with the choice of misery. I was choosing the attitude of JOY! I had once again put my life into God's hands. I was going to trust Him no matter what.

It took months before my physical body got better. I put myself on a very soft diet. I rested a lot. I gave God and my body time. Little by little my strength came back. To this day, we are not sure what that sickness was all about. Some doctors have thought it was a severe reaction to taking the polio vaccine. I should have never taken the vaccine, because I had had the real disease years earlier. I will never be sure what caused that severe reaction in my body, but I will always be sure of the peace of heart that comes when Jesus is invited into the waiting rooms of life and given the keys as to when that door will be opened, if ever.

I have never forgotten the lesson I learned in the darkness of that night. I had said, "Yes to God, when times were good and life seemed to be full of promise and opportunity." Now I was saying a big "Yes to God, when the road looked uncertain and I had no idea where the hand of God would take me."

Each of us, day-by-day, has the choice as to whether we are going to be miserable and complaining or choose the attitude of joy, as we place our trust in God. Of course I have never found this easy. Yielding my will into God's hands for His will to be done has been a lifelong, moment-by-moment challenge. I know God's way is best, but at times I cannot imagine that what I am going through could be God's will.

One of my all time favorite songs, Pete and I used to sing, continues to give me reason to turn to trust in God grace, over and over again. How often I have sung this song as I lay on a bed of sickness or recovery, letting this truth sink deep into my soul:

He Giveth More Grace

He giveth more grace when the burdens grow greater,

He sendeth more strength when the labors increase;

To added afflictions He addeth His mercy,

To multiplied trials, His multiplied peace.

Chorus:

His love has no limits, His grace has no measure,

His power no boundary known unto men;

For out of His infinite riches in Jesus

He giveth, and giveth, and giveth again.

When we have exhausted our store of endurance,

When our strength has failed ere the day is half done,

When we reach the end of our hoarded resources

Our Father's full giving is only begun.

Annie Johnson Flint

I have spent my life discovering that God's grace has no limit, and no measure. He gives His grace to us when we humble ourselves, stop insisting on our own way, and yield our all into His loving hands.

My blind mother, on her ninety first birthday shared with me her life verse. It was beautiful to see that even in advanced years, with much hardship, my mother had learned the truth of Philippians 4:9, "In whatever circumstances I find myself in, I am learning to be content". I smiled as I realized my mother had given me an example of choosing to say, "Yes" to God regardless how old you are!

God continued to pour out his mercy and blessing on our church community. Now that the church building was complete, our home was back to being somewhat normal. All the prayer meetings, visitation evenings, and Pete's study was moved to the church. I found a new joy in our marriage, in our home, in mothering and in our ministry. I was feeling well physically, and had a much deeper relationship with God than I had ever experienced before.

Once again I was singing about the goodness of God. God and I were at the top of the mountain. Our church leadership had decided to build a parsonage that would be very near the church. We would soon have a brand new home to live in. Our small little rental was really crowded and I was happily pregnant with our third child. A lot of joy and anticipation lay ahead of us, and just when things were settling down, the postman came…

Chapter Four

HOME ALONE

Kelowna, British Columbia, Canada

Briercrest Bible College, Caronport, Saskatchewan
1964-1969

My Child
Are you fashioning yourself a life of comfort, a place where you can
find success and contentment on your terms? Listen. Do you hear it?
Somewhere on the margins of your comfort zone there is a voice crying
out to you, a voice too persistent to ignore. "Follow me," it keeps saying.
"Follow me on my terms. Come away from the safe and the comfortable,
the predictable and the socially correct. Follow me into a life of risk and
challenge and high adventure, where the cost will be great but the rewards
will be greater.

"Follow me, and I will make your existence count for more than
comfort. I will lead you on narrow paths, up steep and rugged roads,
into dangerous terrains. But I will stay with you through the whole
journey and teach you things you would not otherwise learn." Trust me.
Come away and follow me!" Jesus. Anonymous

I had said a deep, honest, "Yes" to my God on a bed of sickness, and
that "yes" soul cry included everything. I was finished with fighting,
anger, bitterness, and wrestling with God. I would follow Him all
the way, whatever the cost. My resolve was sincere and complete. My
ability to carry out this new commitment, however, would be soon
tested. I found it easier to give God my verbal heartfelt commitment to
surrender to His leading than to actually follow that commitment with
the reality of life choices. Living a commitment is vastly different from
speaking a commitment. God was about to give me a chance to put my
words into action, and my heart into shoe leather and follow Him.

Shortly after my mysterious illness, we were delighted to know that
I was pregnant with our third child. I was feeling healthy by now and
during the pregnancy, was strong and full of energy. The church work
was going better than anyone could have imagined. Life was good. Our

marriage, our children, and our church was alive and growing. We were in a beautiful place of peace and blessing. As a new life began to grow within me, my joy knew no bounds.

Yes, it truly was so sweet to trust in Jesus, and then the letter arrived in the mail. The letter was from Briercrest Bible College, our alma mater where we learned, dated, and graduated together. They were now officially asking Pete if he would be open to being their full-time traveling evangelist. Their plan was to have a representative in Western Canada, and we would be that couple. We would live out west, but Pete would travel Canada and the United States, as the invitations came in. When Pete showed me the letter my joyful heart sank.

My first response was a sense of disbelief. I looked at Pete and said, "You aren't even going to pray about this are you?" His response was, "Well, what do you think?" I was quick, as usual, to be able to articulate what I thought. I said, "There's no way I would be willing to do this. We are in the best place with our church, that we have been in over three years. We are expecting our third child. I don't want you to be on the road most of the time, and me home alone with three preschoolers. I don't think I could do it. And besides, we are about ready to move into a brand new house, that the church has built for us. The timing is all wrong. No, I don't want to make this move!"

Pete was silent and supportive of my cautions, fears, and logic. He, too, thought it would be asking a lot of both of us and our young family. But he did say, "I think we should pray about it, and see what God would have us do." I wasn't willing to pray, think or consider doing such a sacrificial thing. Pete wisely gave me time. I was confused in my spirit. How was it that just a year earlier, when lying on a bed of mysterious illness that I had said an unconditional "Yes" to God and to His will in my life, and now I was saying an unconditional, "No?"

My problem was that I just couldn't imagine this to be God's will for us. I couldn't imagine Pete away from home eighty percent of the time. I struggled with even the thought of looking after three little preschoolers by myself. I knew about the terrifying nights when our second son was rushed to the hospital with croup. I knew how hard it was when we both were there to tend sick children during long feverish nights. How could I do this alone?

I have often said, if God would just float a paper from Heaven with His perfect will written on it, I would do it. My confusion was discerning what God's will, my will, or my husband's will was. And yet, how could I close the door on what might perhaps be God's call on our lives at this time? I wrestled and prayed and tossed and turned in my heart and in my mind. I knew I did not want to be out of the will of God. I knew the story of Jonah well. I didn't want to run from God's plan, no matter how hard it would be. I knew when God calls He equips and gives strength and joy. At this time I believe God gave me another life changing thought. The bottom line question was, "Who is in charge of my life? Is it me or is it God?" I knew I could say, "No" to the decision that lay ahead of us, but then the pressure would be on me for making that decision. I didn't want that pressure. I also realized I could be a widow, raising three preschoolers on my own. Life held no guarantees.

I knew that one of the best gifts I could give my husband was the freedom to follow his dreams and God's leading in his life. A man who is fenced into his wife's dictates was not the man I wanted to be married to. How could I shackle him and take away his freedom to follow the call of God? That would be too unwise and even scary for me. Only God saw the big picture. God was the Head of our home, I was not. With that image in mind, I told Pete, "If you believe this call to be the will of God for us, I am willing." Pete did feel this was the plan of God for us and so we began the painful process of telling our church and making plans for our move.

Telling our beloved church that we would be leaving, was one of the hardest things we had ever done. This church felt like our baby. We had been there when it was conceived, birthed, and now was fully grown. We had walked with our beloved people through conversion, baptism, dedication, involvement, and commitment. We had rejoiced with them over births, marriages, graduations. and promotions. We had wept with them in times of loss, death, and sorrow. In recent months they had built a beautiful parsonage for us. It was near the church. We moved into that new home and camped there until our third baby was born.

I had been asking God to give us a baby girl with this pregnancy. We had our two healthy growing boys and I so wanted a girl. Together,

Pete and I prayed for a healthy child, and also that God would grant us a girl. When our third baby arrived, it was a healthy, big boy. My reaction was a surprise to me. When we were told we had a boy, a thrill went through my whole body. I thought, "I am God's child, I have given my life to God. I have tried to be obedient to God at every turn in my life. God loves me. He loves to give good gifts to me. This little boy is God's choice for me."

The God, who loves me, said, "No" to my prayer because He had some unique purpose for this little boy, we called Kim Peter. As I clung to that realization from God, and as the years have unfolded, I have seen just how special and unique this little boy has been. He grew tall in body, reaching six foot four, and he grew tall in wisdom and favor with God and people.

So the baby was born, the boxes were packed, and our tearful good-byes were over. We did something at our farewell service that we will never do again. Pete and I often sang duets. On this night we sang a heartfelt song, "When you pray, will you pray for me?" We had the whole congregation in tears. We cried with them as we sang. We never sang that song again, although it is a very beautiful touching song.

Ahead of us lay the snow covered flat prairies in late March. Soon we were into the majestic mountains of British Columbia, on the road west and into our unknown future. Once again all our belongings were packed into a farm truck. The baby was just four weeks old. I had not yet recovered my strength, but God gave me His strength and I had a deep settled peace that we were walking in the steps of God's plan for us.

Our new home out west was wonderful. To our surprise, friends of our Bible college built us a brand new spacious home in Kelowna, BC, Canada. It was in the same city that we were married. I was literally going back to my home roots. My parents lived in this city, as did my sister. They would become a great source of help and comfort to me in the months that lay ahead.

Pete had time to unload the truck, hook up the appliances, and kiss me "good-bye". He was off to one of the most exciting times of his life, and I was off to one of the hardest times of my young life. I had a lot of unpacking to do while looking after a newborn, and two lively preschool boys. Pete's first series of meetings was thousands of miles away in Nebraska. I was literally, home alone with my three little boys. My family was wonderful, but they couldn't stay with me during the long nights and the early mornings, and the uncertain days. I didn't have a car. I didn't know any of the neighbors, and our new baby boy was sick most of the first year of his life. I spent many hours in the hospital and doctor's office with this baby. His resistance was so low that he got everything imaginable, even scarlet fever, spiking to 105 degree temperature. That was a fearful night for me with my husband far away. My neighbor came over and helped me get the baby's fever down, and the crisis was over. I felt bad for Pete, but there was a price for him as well.

Pete was often gone two weeks, three weeks, up to six weeks at a time. One time I counted, out of sixty-eight days, he was home eight days. I missed my husband terribly, and the raising of the boys by myself was daunting. Pete always drove the car to far off places. To fly was out of the question. During my 'home alone' days, God was with me in ways I didn't even realize at the time. I struggled with this call of God upon my life. I was willing to be a missionary, and a pastor's wife, but had never dreamed of being the wife of an evangelist home alone with three preschoolers. This did not seem like a high and holy calling.

Every day was filled with wiping dirty faces, seats, and noses. I couldn't get out much with three little ones in tow. To put it mildly, I was miserable. I also struggled greatly with insomnia. Once I got to sleep, the baby would wake me up. Once he was back to sleep, I couldn't fall asleep again. Then the two older boys would be up early and needy.

Pete knew I was not happy, even though I was trying. I had literally clenched my teeth, determined to get through this time, no matter what. At one point he said to me, "God does not want us to endure His will, He wants us to enjoy it."

Today my husband often laments the fact that he wasn't more sensitive to my needs but those were the days when one just sucked it up, didn't complain and put one step ahead of the other. There wasn't a lot of sympathy for weakness in Christian circles. After all, didn't I have God's Word and God's Spirit to lift me up? What more could I want? This was a very simplistic theology that we were taught.

God however, had put me in this place and it was once again my choice as to how miserable or victorious I would be. I was finally sick of my discontent, and once again cried out to the Lord for His mercy, forgiveness, and strength. I did ask God to give me a joy that would surpass my circumstances. I did not want to just endure His will. I claimed as a lifeline verse, Philippians 4:13, "I can do all things through Christ who gives me strength" (KJV). Could I look after my boys alone, in God's strength and find fulfillment there? Could God really give me His strength and His joy in this difficult place? I was to find out in time that He could, He would, and He did. I resolved to give it all to God, once again. Once again I realized that I had the freedom to choose my attitude. The choice had been made. It felt like I climbed up into the arms of my loving Heavenly Father and asked Him to love, carry and provide for me and for my precious boys.

Each morning when I woke up I would claim the strength of Christ. During the day I often retreated to my bedroom and, on my knees, I cried out to my God for strength and wisdom. Little by little God began to replace my discontent with peace and even a glimpse into the importance of what I was doing. I began to see that Satan had been speaking lies to my mind and heart, telling me that what I was doing was of little value, and what Pete was doing was of great importance. God's Word showed me that my calling as a mother was a high and holy calling, and I should not belittle it. I began to have a new outlook on the ministry of mothering. I was learning that raising children was the most important work that I would do. If this was my mission field, then I would do my best to represent Christ, first to my sons and then to those around me. When I opened my eyes I saw how eternally important it was to be laying a firm foundation in the lives of my sons. I believed that someday I would see the fruit of these years of pouring my heart into their lives.

I chose to step outside of my comfort zone and get to know my neighbors. They got together every morning with all their kids for a fun connecting time. I told them I couldn't come every morning but I would come when I could. I found them so friendly and welcoming. The problem was, when I got home I got sick. My heart was racing, I was shaking and drained. At first I thought that I was so void of being with strangers that I couldn't take it emotionally. I talked to my doctor about it. He asked me what I was drinking at these gathering. When I told him coffee, the lights went on. I was extremely allergic to coffee and haven't had a cup since. I never did like it, so that was no great loss. I continued visiting with my meighbors just finding something else to drink.

One neighbor had three children the same age as ours. They were often at our place to play. She was a nurse and helped me out so much with my sick baby. One day she asked me if I would look after her kids, while she went back to work for a short time. I considered it and said, "Yes." These kids were at our house almost all the time anyway, and made great playmates for our boys. Now I had six preschoolers to care for. But I loved it and I also made quite a bit of needed money, which was a good reward. I was running a small "daycare" without realizing it. I'm still friends with this lovely neighbor and her children.

I also began to see the mission field around me. We lived in a new subdivision where there were lots of young families and many young kids. Our place became a beehive of activity. I asked a friend to help me, as I dreamed about having a "Good News Club" for my boys and the neighbor kids. What a joy to have many children coming to hear about Jesus. I didn't have to go to New Guinea to find people who had never heard about having a personal relationship with God. I just needed to go across my street. I was fulfilling my desire as a teen to tell people who did not understand how to know God, to hear the good news. At times, in our basement, we had over thirty kids come every week. One day, one of my sons came to me after Good News Club and told me he would like to ask Jesus into his heart. Can there be any greater joy than giving birth physically to a child, and then helping that child in his spiritual birth? I think not!

The Bible college we represented had a policy that a male staff member could not travel with a girls' group, without the wife being along. One spring a phone call came from the college telling Pete that I would have to travel with a trio of girls, as they represented the college. I was shocked. How could I do that with three small boys, the youngest just thirteen months old? The consensus was that I could easily take them along. Well, these were our orders and we obeyed. For six weeks, we traveled with a wonderful trio of girls. We crammed the trio of girls, our trio of small boys and ourselves into our six-passenger car. We had meetings every night. When we arrived at our place of ministry, I would find some lady who would look after our youngest, while I played the piano for the trio. When my part was done I would go to the back and look after the boys while Pete preached. I'm sure we made quite a sight as we arrived at church after church for our evening meetings. I do remember how good the boys were, and how many great talks we had in the car with the girls trio. I could see that God was giving us strength and wisdom mile after long mile. The trio saw marriage and family life up close and personal. We had hours of discussions about dating, marriage, and child rearing. We are still in contact with those girls today. I know we had a greater ministry in the car those weeks than in any church service

During the summer months, the whole family traveled together to various camps across the country. There, Pete would be the camp speaker and the kids and I would enter into the wonders and fun of camp life. What a break for me, not having to make any meals for the whole summer! I was often the lifeguard at the waterfront. Pete was a gifted communicator with young people and we saw God greatly bless his ministry and many came to a place of personal salvation and greater growth in their Christian life. I knew that God was using Pete and I knew now that God was also using me, as I stood beside Pete, worked alongside of him when I could, and gave myself wholeheartedly to mothering.

Pete and I purchased a small fifteen-foot travel trailer that we used to travel across the country. It certainly wasn't a dull life for any of us. The kids loved the various camps and I had the challenge of adapting to each new situation as the summer rolled on. We've had the privilege of ministering in over sixty different camps throughout Canada, the USA and Europe. Not a dull life to be sure.

One summer we were to travel from the west coast to Ontario, speaking at camps along the way. It was a hot summer. We didn't have air conditioning. For five days of travel we hit the nation's highest temperature each day. We were often driving in 107 degree weather. We found out a way to create our own personal air conditioning. We all wet our bathing suits in the trailer sink and then put them on. We then wet big towels in similar fashion, draping them over our bodies, as we drove with the windows down. The air on the wet bathing suits and towels that covered our bodies cooled us down somewhat, until the towels got dry and we'd have to stop and wet them again. It worked, but it was a wild and wacky time.

Of course we knew nothing of disposable diapers. We washed out the diapers by hand and dried them on the park lawns where we stopped to make our meals in the trailer. I'm sure we were a point of interest to many who passed by. To eat in a restaurant never entered our minds. To begin with, we could not afford it, and there were no fast food restaurants in those days. To say the least, our life was full of variety. We survived this busy demanding schedule in the strength and mercy of God. I know God used our family as we traveled and preached and lived and shared. I do believe there will be people in Heaven because of our gospel witness during those years.

Soon the older boys were in school and the baby was a healthy toddler. We were settling into the routine of Pete being away so much. I can't say that I ceased finding this lifestyle hard, but I was getting to know my God better, and experiencing how His strength was made perfect in my weakness. I had a sense that this time was a character building time for me. I had a pretty soft upbringing. I hadn't faced a lot of trials and hardships. God was doing a work of molding and enlarging my capacity to face life's challenges. Of course, I had no idea of what lay ahead of me, but God knew and He was preparing me.

When Pete was home, he was all there. He was a wonderful husband and father. The best month for us was December, when there was little call for evangelistic services or camp responsibilities across our land. There was time for Pete to deeply enter into family life, to use his skill at building creative things for the boys for Christmas and a time to relax in our busy life.

Once again, just as I was settling into our present life, a call came from our Bible college, asking Pete if he would consider moving to the campus of the Bible college to teach full time and travel only on weekends and in the summer months. For once, this was not a hard decision for me. Even though I had made peace with this calling, I had longed to have the many weeks and days of separation behind us. As the boys grew older I could see they needed their dad more. The move would take us from one of Canada's most beautiful vacationing spots year round, to one of the most desolate areas of our country. But I didn't care. I was delighted with the thought that our family would be together more, and my husband would be home each night of the week. Once again we moved our family halfway across our country, from the mild balmy winters of southern British Columbia, to the wind swept, flat prairies of southern Saskatchewan.

Pete went back to Jamestown, North Dakota for the summer of our move, to continue working on his Bachelor's degree. The boys and I found ways to make our lives interesting as we bunked into a small trailer for two months. I decided this would be a good time to get my certificate as a registered lifeguard. I had been a lifeguard for so many years without any certification, now was my chance to make this right. When I took my lessons at the city pool, my three boys sat on the bleachers and watched me learn how to save a person's life. This added some diversions to our lives.

Our move back to Briercrest Bible College campus was a delight. We knew a lot of the staff and had a sense of coming home with this move. The weather was harsh, with high heat and mosquito- infested summers, to freezing cold, forty below zero winters, and always, the wind. But I didn't mind that hardship. My husband was home. His schedule at the college was unbelievable. He taught nineteen hours each week in the classroom. He was also in charge of all the Christian service that each student was required to do every week. He was also responsible for the large youth weekend that happened once a year called, Youth Quake. At this event, thousands of young people would come from all over the continent. It was a huge undertaking for him. On top of this, he often traveled weekends to speak at neighboring churches. We also continued doing camp work in the summer months.

Pete didn't walk in those days; he would often run. He often said that he was only ten minutes ahead of the class, from preparation to teaching. The young people loved him. He spent many hours talking and counseling with his students. I enjoyed having students over to our home, making their lonely days away from their own homes a little more bearable. I became a leader of Pioneer Girls and went back to teaching piano, a forever love of my heart. The President of the college, Dr. Henry Hildebrand and his wife Inger, were of great encouragement to us and our small family. What a joy to exchange meals and evenings in each other's homes. Little did we know that many years down the road, Pete would be this precious couple's pastor?

To our great surprise we learned the happy news that we were going to have another baby. In my mind I imagined the joy of being settled with this new baby and raising our family in a safe and secure environment.

And then we got a phone call…the church calling us was a leading church in the denomination that Pete had grown up in. This church was in the State of Oregon, forty-five minutes from the beautiful Pacific Ocean and all the Oregon Coast attractions. The church was willing to wait until the baby was born. It was all very appealing to Pete. He had felt over his head with the Bible college opportunities and demands. Through all the years of traveling as an evangelist and teaching at the college, Pete had greatly missed pastoring. He began to know, without a doubt, that he did have a pastor's heart and he wanted to be back shepherding a flock. Pete had previously held evangelistic meetings in this church. They fell in love with him at that time and now wanted him to be their pastor.

As we talked and prayed, we began to know this was God's plan for us, even though my heart longed to stay in the safe and comfortable nest we had made in this place of peace. We accepted the call and prepared our hearts for a new baby and another move across the nation. It seemed that we were always moving when I was in the last months of pregnancy or with a new baby in my arms. I knew God was going before us, and with us, and would give us all that we needed through Jesus, our Savior and Lord.

Chapter Five

A NEW BABY...A NEW CHURCH

Evangelical Mennonite Brethren Church, Dallas, Oregon 1969-1977

"God is too good to be unkind, too wise to be mistaken; and when you cannot trace His hand, you can trust His heart." Charles Spurgeon

It's a girl! Those words sent a thrill through me. My joy was so overwhelming, that I began praising and thanking God out loud as I relaxed on the delivery table. Kathleen Ann has been a constant joy to my heart from her birth to this day. After three boys, I was well prepared for another boy. In fact we had told people it didn't matter to us, as long as the baby was healthy. That was true in the big picture, but to have a healthy little girl was beyond the scope of my imagination. This baby was healthy. I was healthy. As I packed up our household things and cared for my new baby girl, my heart sang. This time it was a furniture truck that came to move all our belongings, and yes the eighteen dollar couch had been replaced.

In Oregon we were so warmly welcomed. Our boys were ten, nine, and five. Our baby girl was just six weeks old. We were a young, impressionable family. How these new friends loved us and our kids. Many were so happy to hold our baby and help us in any way. We were safely deposited in the parsonage that was on the same lot as the church. The church was an L-shape and the parsonage fit snugly in the center of that L. We did not have a backyard, nor a front yard, no basement and really no space for the kids to play outside, except the church parking lot. But nobody seemed to mind.

The boys were off to school while I had more time to devote to our baby girl. She loved to snuggle, to be rocked and sung to. Her favorite thing was for me to sing her stories I would make up about our day or a recent venture and sing them to her. I loved to listen to her pray. Her innocence, honesty, and purity was so heart touching.

The parsonage was a very old house needing lots of repairs, but the trustees told us they weren't going to fix it up anymore, as it wasn't worth it. In fact, they jokingly said, "If it catches on fire get the kids out and then let it go." That was not very comforting to a young mom who was ready to once again build yet another new nest. We fixed up this little home and made it work. We spent over eight years growing our family, our church and our character in this little home. We continued to enjoy having people over. Our living room was very small but that seemed to make the fellowship that much closer. Our hospitality was simple, but our home was friendly and people felt welcomed and cared for. Sometimes we were invited out on Sunday nights after church. Other times we enjoyed going to the local Dairy Queen for a treat. Doing something fun after the service each Sunday night got to be such a habit that if we didn't have anything planned, our kids made sure something fun would happen. We became addicted to "fun nights" on Sunday nights!

Pete loved the people of this new church. The people loved him. It would end up being the most peaceful and encouraging church of our sixty years of ministry. There was great unity among the leadership. In all our years there we only saw one couple leave the church because they wanted to attend a new church that was nearer to them. We also didn't have one couple move away or get a divorce. Those were stable, healthy years. There was growth in the church and in many people's lives. Pete has always loved to be with people, so he often called on the homes of our church families in the afternoons and evenings. I didn't complain. He was home every day for meals and the night.

We had lots of fun as a family. It was during these years that we decided to set aside one day a week, as our day off. The kids looked forward to this fun day. As they got older, we let them take turns planning what the event of that day would be. We would drive up to the snow line on the nearby mountains and have a wiener roast there. We would go to beautiful Mount Hood and try a little skiing, and then enjoy their spacious hot tub outside. Then there was a new fast food restaurant called McDonalds, where we could get a hamburger for eighteen cents. Now, that was a treat.

The kids loved to build forts in the living room. There was really no space else to build them. They would set up chairs, blankets and books in all sorts of intricate arrangements. When it was bedtime they would beg me to let their fort remain so they could play with it the next day. I relented, realizing I wanted to raise happy kids more than I wanted a spotless house. More than once, parishioners would come to the front door, which opened into a complete view of the living room, and they would stand aghast at the mess in front of them. When I saw their shocked look I would explain by saying, "Isn't it wonderful when kids have so much fun building forts out of such common, everyday things? They just got it built so I have let them leave it up for a few days." I felt like I had a chance to preach a sermon in what was really important in raising kids. Let home be a place where they can relax, play games, make a mess, and clean up later, I had heard this saying, "If people want to come and see your home have them make an appointment. If they want to come and see you, they are welcome anytime. You have to decide whether you are going to grow grass or children." Well, if someone had arranged to come and see me I would like our home to be tidied up as much as possible. I guess we made the decision to grow kids in various ways.

In those years, all the kids of our small city, harvested the crops that grew in that area. Bus loads of kids, as young as ten years old, would harvest in the fields all day. Our kids did not enjoy this opportunity to earn money to say the least. One son would weep at the bus stop so early in the morning, not wanting to pick berries all day. I thought it was a great character building opportunity for them to learn to work hard even when they didn't like it. There always seemed to be something to pick, from strawberries, to beans, to cherries, cucumbers, plums, and gooseberries. Most of their friends were out picking too. It did hurt me to see the boys leave home crying like this. But I thought toughness would help them grow up strong and independent. I think it did, but it still hurts my heart to think of them at the bus stop weeping.

One son constantly surprised us at how little he could earn during the whole day of picking strawberries. Pete decided to pick with him one day to teach him how to hustle and earn something. Half way through the day this son said, "Dad, I would much rather travel and see things than pick berries." Pete told him only those who worked hard could afford to travel and see things. Well, he never earned a lot picking berries, but today he is doing a lot of traveling and is seeing a lot of things, and sharing hope in Jesus wherever he goes.

These were our biggest canning and freezing years. With four kids to help, we worked as a family and canned over 500 quarts of fruit and vegetables each year. We also froze quite a lot of available food. This was a land of plenty and we took advantage of every offer. I grew up with the mindset that nothing should be left to waste. What a help that was to our grocery bill.

We were experiencing God's favor and mercy in our marriage, our family, and our church. We were a blessed couple. God was allowing us to realize many dreams and desires...and then an uninvited, unexpected crisis, called CANCER knocked at our door.

It was 1971. Our daughter, Kathy, was just one year old. Pete and I sat across from the top oncologist in all the Northwest United States. We had been rushed to Portland, Oregon by our doctor and two specialists in Salem, Oregon. Dr. Fletcher looked at me and said these words, "Mrs. Unrau, you have the fastest and deadliest of all cancer, black melanoma. I don't know if there is anything I can do. I don't know if I can save your life. I will do my best. This is Tuesday, I want you in the hospital on Thursday. Friday morning I will do massive surgery. It may take more than six hours. I don't know what the result will be. I will do all I can for you."

With that, Pete and I were left with the most devastating news we had ever heard up to this time in our lives. We had four small and growing kids. I was only thirty-four. What were we to do? All we could do was to trust in God and give Him our lives and my body. 1 had learned by now that I could trust the heart of God even when I couldn't understand the ways of God. Now we had the opportunity to see if our faith was only a fair weather faith, or if the God we preached was truly able to sustain us and give us peace in the midst of this uncertain storm.

By now I had walked with my God for a much longer time. I had proven that He was faithful. I must tell you, this time, to the glory of God there was no anger, no fighting, no demands. There was sweet rest in the pillow of God's love that can never be explained in human words. We had one full day between this doctor's announcement and the surgery. We decided to take the kids out of school and head for the

Oregon Coast. This place had always been a wonderful escape for our family. We loved to run in the surf, dam up the little streams and play in the sand. That day was so special to all of us. It was a good memory to feast on during the dark days that lay ahead.

January 15, 1971 was the surgery date. God blessed me with the joy of His presence and the comfort of His Word. I Corinthians 6:19-20 became a special lifeline to me. "Do you not you know that your body is the temple of the Holy Spirit, who is in you, whom you have received from God. You are not your own; you were bought at a price. Therefore honor God with your body." What a comfort. What peace when I realized I was God's property, created, bought and redeemed by Him. I was not my own, I was His. I would trust my God to look after His property. My heart rested in His sovereign plan and purpose.

Many, many people were praying for me. It's amazing when you are going through a trial how good it is to hear the words, "I'll be praying for you." Some would say, "I'll be thinking of you," but that meant nothing compared to: "I'll be praying for you." Never had I felt the power of prayer so evident in my life. God gave both Pete and me that "peace that passes understanding." Philippians 4:7 This time there was no bitter spirit writhing within me. There was no arguing or wrestling with God. I felt completely safe and secure in the arms of Jesus.

The surgery was long and extensive. It did take six-and-one-half hours. During the surgery, the cancerous growth that was in the calf of my leg, and a large area around the growth, was removed. To cover this hole, that was about the size of a saucer, they took skin off the thigh of my other leg. This skin graft proved to be the most painful part of the surgery. I know something of what a third degree burn feels like. The skin graft did take beautifully. Next, they made a large incision in the lower groin, only to find that the malignancy had spread to that area into the lymph glands. This was the bad news. This spelled real trouble. They removed all my lymph glands, some of which were already malignant. Then they went to the upper groin to find good news. There the glands were free of any malignancy. They also removed the lymph glands from this area, leaving me without any lymph glands in this groin area.

During the surgery, Dr. Fletcher did his famous, but controversial procedure, of isolating my right leg in order to pump anticancer fluids through it for one hour of the operation. The incisions for this procedure were very painful for many days after the surgery. This did take the place of having chemo and radiation treatment.

I didn't know until months later that, for ten days, it was feared my leg would have to be amputated. The doctor told Pete infection had set in and it didn't look good. I knew infection had set in, because of all the pain and treatment on that area. Long after the possibility was over, Pete told me how close I came to losing my leg. The doctor thought I would never be able to walk on my heel again, because so much of the nerve and muscle tissue was cut out of my leg in that area. At first I had to walk with a walker, then on my tiptoes, and little by little I was able to use my heel. Today I feel no pain when I walk. In fact walking is very good for me and I greatly enjoy it.

I had lots of visitors. Some would ask the strangest questions. One lady from the church sat beside my bed and said to me, in hushed tones, "How long does your doctor give you?" I was a little shocked at her question. Then I thought, nobody knows the answer to that question. I said, "He hasn't said. How long has your doctor given you?" She said, "You're right. None of us knows."

I was in the hospital for twenty-three days. Pete came to visit me every day but one, driving the distance of one hour each way. It was hard for him with the four kids at home. He did a masterful job of caring for me and for the kids and for the church family. Many people came to help. They brought food. They looked after Kathy, day after day. They came and cleaned the house. It was an amazing time to see how the body of Christ works together. I could sit back and literally see all the gifts of the Spirit and also all the fruits of the Spirit being so evidently showered upon me and my family.

It has been said, "There is nothing like the local church when the local church does it right." During all this time our church prayed for us and ministered to us in wonderful and unique ways. How blessed we were to have had such an amazing family of God to travel with us in love and integrity during this difficult time. We will forever be thankful to this church body who did it right!

My doctor often found me reading my Bible. The Living Bible had just come out in hardcover, not looking at all like a Bible. One day he said, "Aren't you finished reading that book yet?" I told him I would never be finished reading this book. I told him what the book was and what it meant to me. I had opportunities often to witness to my doctor, but I could tell he endured these times. His heart was not hungry or thirsting after God. He often traveled around the world teaching on his new procedure for the cure for cancer, like he had used on me. Only fifteen percent of his time was used in working with patients. The rest of the time was in research, teaching, and traveling. I marvel that God so ordained it that I was allowed to be one of his patients and to receive this special treatment that for me was life itself. Could that be one of the many reasons God had led us from a remote area of Canada to Oregon and this world famous doctor? We never know what God is up to, but looking back we can sometimes see His hand in the decisions we have made. Hindsight gives us more faith to trust God.

One time Dr. Fletcher asked me if I would visit one of his other patients who had the identical surgery to mine. He said, "She is not doing well. Somehow she does not have the same positive peace that you have." On one occasion this doctor told my husband that my positive attitude did more for my healing than anything he had done. That was God. I knew it right away. Only He could have given me such amazing rest and peace for all those days of pain, uncertainty, and recuperation.

I had many opportunities to tell the story of Jesus and His love to hospital staff and visitors. Even the nun who sat on my bed asked me, "What does it really mean to be born again?" I wrote a letter at one time to friends and family about how thankful I was to be able to share Jesus with many during my hospital stay.

I got many responses to my letter but one person gave me a hard message. This person said, "If you and Pete were not so proud, you would call in the faith healers and you would be healed. Then you would have a really good story to tell". This note upset me and challenged me. I ended up writing this person a fifteen-page letter. However, I had no peace in sending it. I knew God had lessons to teach me. I began to read through my Bible and took notes on every time God's Word mentioned suffering and sickness. I made a list of these verses and what God's purpose has in allowing pain, illness and suffering. I came up with twenty one reasons. I titled my paper: "Why God Allows Suffering."

Many people are puzzling over the "whys" of their own suffering and how to respond to it. By suffering we include physical, relational, emotional, mental, family, marital and vocational trials. We need a Biblical perspective as to the reasons for suffering. We can never know all the answers but we can know some.

As I searched the Scriptures, these are some of the reasons God allows us to suffer:

1. So that we can comfort others. II Cor. 1:4 It sensitizes us to be able to identify and relate to people.

2. So that we won't rely and trust in ourselves. 11 Cor. 1:9 Trials knock us off our proud pedestals and get us relying on God.

3. So that we may give thanks in everything. 11 Cor. 1:11, 1 Thes. 5:18, Eph. 5:20 Problems give us a chance to praise God even when it is hard.

4. It produces more fruit. John 15:2 The soil of my life is more prepared to grow the fruit of the Spirit.

5. It proves the reality of our faith. Job 2:10, 11 Cor. 12:10 Believing is different than understanding, we need a faith that afflictions can't shake.

6. It matures our faith. Job 40:3-5, James 1: 2-4, Job 42:1-3. Insisting on answers from God asks God to be accountable to me.

7. It disciplines and educates us. Heb. 5:8, 12:7, 1 Cor. 11:29-30, Ps. 119:67 Trials are often God's rod of correction.

8. It humbles us. 11 Cor, 12:7 God uses weak people. Trials show us how weak we are.

9. It shows the sufficiency of God's grace. 11 Cor. 12:9, 11 Tim. 4:20 Jesus said, "Trust Me Paul, I will meet your all needs". Phil 4:19, "My grace is sufficient." Phil 4:13

10. It purifies us. 1 Peter 4:1-3, Job 23:10 Trials give us a gauge to

measure the depth or shallowness of our commitment.

11. It brings glory to God. John 11:3-6, 9;1-3, Job 13:15

12. It drives us to the Word of God. Psalm 119:71, Isaiah 45:3, Col. 3:16 It forces us to read God's word more often and to pay more attention.

13. It causes us to grow spiritually. Rom. 5:3-5 All sunshine would make us a desert of a person.

14. It is the will of God. 1 Peter 4:19, Acts 9:16, John 16:33, 11 Cor. 12:8-9 God is in control; His ways are different and higher. Isaiah 55:8-9, 30:20

15. It makes us more like Jesus. Rom. 8:28-29 The great Sculptor takes in hand the hammer of suffering and chisels away at my character to shape it like Christ. He is the master Potter!!

16. It puts us on stage. Jobs life, Paul's life, Christ's life. Heb. 12:3-4, 1 Tim 5:23 Gives me an audience I otherwise would not have. Presents me with unique opportunities to share Jesus.

17. It's a testimony to angels and demons. Luke 15.10, Eph. 3:10

18. It drives men to God. 11 Cor. 7:8-11 (C.S. Lewis) "God whispers to us in our pleasures, speaks to us in our consciences, but He shouts to us in our pains."

19. It marks my ownership. - 1 Cor. 6-19-20, I'm God's property.

20. It puts my thoughts on Heaven. Rom. 8:22-23

21. It prepares me for Heaven. 11 Cor. 4:17, Heb. 11:32-40 It helps me fix my eyes more on Jesus.

I have often looked at this list, taught from this list and encouraged others who are suffering to use verses on this list. God used that letter to stir my heart to search the Bible for my answers to life's most confusing questions. To this day I have no answers as to why God allowed me to live, when others with more faith and greater abilities, did not make it through what I had experienced.

It was finally time to go home from the hospital. We had to secure a nurse to visit me daily, change the bandages, and make sure all was well. I gradually improved. At first, my visits back to Dr. Fletcher were weekly, then every third week, every six weeks and later, every three months. Every week was a call for celebration, but Dr. Fletcher never gave me words of hope. He didn't know what lay ahead any more than we did. I was able to do more and more of the housework and taking care of the children. They were really so very good during this whole time. Soon our life was back to normal or to a new normal with a leg that would take tender care and attention for the rest of my life.

The town we lived in was small, around 7000, but the church was big. Our kids benefited from great kids and youth programs as they grew up. The school system was also excellent. There for a while, we had four kids in four different schools. The boys all took piano lessons, and all three played the trumpet and were in school bands and choirs. For a while they played an amazing trumpet trio. We were often running back and forth to such events, giving our kids support and cheers from the side. It was a perfect environment to raise our kids. The boys also had paper routes, often having to get up early in the morning to deliver papers. Those were safe peaceful times in a safe small town. During these busy days of child raising and pastoring a growing church, Pete was also continuing his education, seeking first to get his Bachelor's and then his Master's degree. He accomplished both while we lived in Oregon. It was a proud day when he walked the aisle to get his Master's Degree. He often said he crammed four years into fifteen to get his education. For several of the Oregon years, Pete was president of our denomination. This meant regular trips to executive meetings and annual conferences. He always enjoyed this diversion. He was also granted several weeks a year in which to hold evangelistic meetings and Bible conferences.

As the kids got older, I became very involved in working with the women of the church. I was asked to speak at many different functions and to teach various Bible classes. I also led the Pioneer Girls program and played the piano when needed. I was asked to speak at Christian Women's Clubs throughout Oregon. I so thoroughly enjoyed these times. It was a constant amazement to me that such a simple testimony could touch people so profoundly, encouraging them to become followers of Jesus. Here is my simple yet profound testimony of the work of God in my life.

I was born and raised in a small logging community in the Rocky Mountains of British Columbia, Canada. When I was thirteen, I came down with the dread disease of polio. During the weeks and months of my recovery I began asking: "If I die, will I go to heaven?" No one could answer my question. When well enough, I was back at Sunday school. I asked my teacher, "Do you know if I die will I go to heaven?" Her answer was, "Oh Shirley, you are a good girl, just keep doing the best you can and God will take you into heaven." I knew in my heart that was not the right answer. A year later on vacation, our family was invited to a Youth for Christ Rally in Vancouver, BC. There I heard the words of Jesus. He had died on the cross to pay the penalty for my sin. Salvation was a gift, but I must receive it. That night I confessed my sins to Jesus and invited Him into my heart and life to be my Lord and Savior. This major decision changed my whole life. I had thirsted for a personal relationship with God. From then on I would never have to wonder where I would go if I died. I knew my place in eternity was settled at the cross and my acceptance of the price Jesus paid for my redemption sealed my longing to be God's child. Now I could share this wonderful story with so many others. There is no greater joy!! Once again, I was seeing the realization of my desire to tell people how to become a child of God.

This church body was really becoming "family" to us. We lived far from our parents and siblings. Pete's four brothers were all pastors or missionaries; his two sisters were married to missionaries. My brother and my sister were both missionaries. That meant we rarely saw our own families, except on special occasions.

I liked to do unique things with a few women of the church. Pete and I were planning a vacation to Europe and Israel. I made all new clothes for this trip, with everything matching, making it possible to mix up outfits to suit the occasion. I decided it would be fun to have some women over and show them what I had made. I put on each outfit and mixed and matched the ensemble. I went into the bedroom, changed and "came down the runway", with my new personal line of modern fashion. It was just a lot of fun and laughter. Some of those women still talk of that time, and laugh about my "fashion show" forty years ago. I think they remembered that a lot more than some of the Bible Studies I gave. Sometimes it is living life and connecting with each other in honest and real ways that leaves the biggest impact.

Pete and I did take our wonderful trip to Europe and Israel, just fifteen months after my major cancer surgery. We were gone for six weeks. My parents came and looked after the kids. It was such an adventure for us and the best time for our marriage. We visited eight countries in Europe and spent a week on our own in Israel. We spent quality time with Pete's twin brother who was a missionary in Germany. Together we travelled to Italy to spend time with my brother, who had married Pete's sister. Pete spoke often in the churches that our siblings were ministering in. What a joy to see the work God had called our loved ones to. We saw so many new sights and had so many new experiences. What fun and unique adventures we had; a celebration of life and health.

Another crazy, fun idea I had was to get help with our concord grape harvest. It made the best grape juice, so I canned one hundred quarts a year. Picking the grapes off the stem was a tedious, boring job. So instead of having a quilting bee, I planned to have a grape party. What fun phoning up my friends and inviting them to my "Grape Party." We women sat in a circle and picked the grapes off the stems and talked and shared, laughed and prayed. What a great way to get a group of women connecting.

In those days Pete had to be prepared to preach three sermons a week, one for Sunday morning, another for Sunday night, and one more for Wednesday night prayer meeting. This was all we knew, so it was not a burden to us. We had purchased a small television. It was hard on the kids, when the Walt Disney program came on right when the evening service began. There were no video recording machines at that time that we knew of.

Bevan had a very sharp inquisitive mind. Pete would often say, Bevan could tie him into an intellectual pretzel so quickly. He wasn't going to believe anything that he hadn't worked out for himself. His teen years were troubling years for him. We would often sit on his bed at night and listen to his doubts and his questions. We would say, "Son, you are going to get through this difficult time and you will be the wiser and better for it." We said this by faith. We claimed as our parenting verse, James 1:5, "If any of you lacks wisdom, you should ask God, who gives generously to all without finding fault, and it will be given to you." We were often lost as to know how to parent four very different kids. Day by day, decision by decision, as we asked of God, He provided us with His wisdom, just when we needed it.

At one particular time, I felt Bevan's questions and turmoil were reaching a decision making point. I told Pete, "I think we should phone a few of the leaders of the church and ask them to pray with us for Bevan." Pete said, "But what will the church people say?" I replied, "I don't care what they say. Bevan needs prayer right now." Pete did ask a few leaders to pray and to keep this request to themselves. The next day a friend of Bevan's said to him: "Hey Bevan, your parents phoned my parents and asked if they would pray for you." Bevan came home and said: "Mom, did you ask some people to pray for me?" I answered, "Yes, we did. We know this isn't an easy time for you." Thankfully, Bevan wasn't upset about this. I think it made him see how much we really cared for him and were willing to humble ourselves and ask for prayer.

Living in a home that constantly needed fixing up, caused me to appeal to my husband to do some repairs. I knew he could fix many things because he was a carpenter before he became a pastor. I would tell him of my need, he would listen, and do nothing. I began to observe, when anyone from the congregation called upon him, for anything, he was promptly there to help them. I started to get resentful over this and thought to myself, "He has time for everyone else, but no time for me."

At this time I had a desire to grow in my commitment to Jesus Christ. I realized that most of my concerns, problems and needs were small, but were important to me. I had heard that if Jesus isn't Lord of the small areas of my life, then he isn't Lord of about ninety five percent of my life. I decided to do what the Bible says when it challenges us to test our God, and to prove that He is Mighty. I claimed two lifeline verses that I now call my domestic verses. They are Philippians 4:19, "But my God shall supply all of your needs" (KJV). I thought about that. It says GOD will look after all of my needs, not my wonderful carpenter husband. The other verse that I held onto says, "My soul, wait thou only upon God, for my expectations comes from him" (Psalm 62:5 KJV). I had thought how often my expectations were in my husband and not in my God. I armed myself with these two verses, and began to give my small and large problems to God. It was and is a wonderful release to put my needs into God's hands and then to see how he was going to meet them.

I must add that sometimes God does not meet our needs even when we trust Him totally. Sometimes he leaves our needs as part of our lives, so that we will grow in character and in our trust in God. Paul had his thorn in the flesh and God did not answer his prayers to meet his need of healing. Instead God left the thorn there so that Paul would learn that God's grace would be sufficient for Him, even in his weakness. (11 Corinthians 12:8-9)

We made a decision during these years that we would save up and spend a little more on memorable vacations. This was a hard thing to do, because at that time we had just enough money to get us through each month. But with frugal living, we were able to build some amazing memories that remain in our kids' hearts to this day. We saved up for a special vacation to Hawaii. Our oldest son was graduating from high school and we thought this would be a good time to build some memories with everyone still at home.

One lady told me she didn't think that was a good example for the pastor's family to spend so much on a vacation. I told her, "Give ten people one thousand dollars each and they will spend it ten different ways. We have saved up for a long time and this is the way we are choosing to spend some of our money, investing in our kids and the bonding of our family." She had no answer. We have never missed the money spent, and the great fun and memories linger today. When we were on vacation, I would often just want to collapse and crawl into a quiet place and read. But no, my husband insisted, that we needed to make this a fun time for the kids. Now, I am so thankful he thought that way. Even though Pete was a busy, often-away pastor, the kids never seemed to feel that, because of our great days off and memorable vacations.

Seven years after my cancer surgery, a growth was discovered on my thyroid. Dr. Fletcher said we would have to watch that carefully, as often the kind of cancer I had travels to the thyroid. The next year gave us this news: "The growth is getting bigger. We will have to do surgery. There are five alternatives as to the outcome of the surgery and four are malignant."

Once again we fixed our eyes on Jesus, knowing that He was a God of Love, and had the best in mind for us. We had taken a Bible seminar earlier. Upon completion we were given a plaque that says: "God is the Blessed Controller of All Things." 1 Timothy 6:15 (paraphrase) That plaque has stayed on our bedroom wall, and has been a constant source of grounding and security for us. We believe this truth with all our hearts. Our God is Sovereign. He is in control of all things and he is a good, good Father. The surgery was done immediately. Coming out of the anaesthetic I was informed, "Honey, It was not malignant." Oh, what beautiful words. It was a very diseased thyroid. Ninety nine percent of it had to be removed, but no cancer was found.

During this time there was another battle going on that few knew about. Pete was wondering if he had taken this church as far as he could. He, himself, was feeling restless and hungry for a new challenge. After my thyroid surgery, we took a trip to Michigan, to check out a much larger church in answer to their call for him to come to be their Senior Pastor. As usual, I was feeling settled and so happy. My nesting instinct was once again tested. I had made great friends and was loathe to leave this wonderful body of believers. I considered how they had walked with us so beautifully through physical pain and months of uncertainty. How they loved us, prayed for us, and had truly become family. The church was growing in numbers, but more importantly, people were growing in their walks with God and each other.

Bevan had just graduated from high school. Brent was going into his final year of high school. I reasoned with Pete that this would just not be a good time to move for Brent's sake. Kim was going into Junior High, and Kathy was going into grade three. Was it fair to these kids to move them across the nation at this time? I asked Pete if we could wait a year, before another move, until Brent was able to graduate with all his many friends. No sooner had I said that, than I thought, "One year out of God's perfect will for our family could be dangerous. It could be a year that I would not want to experience." As we talked to the kids they too became more willing to move. I reasoned, that even though I had questioned the timing of moves before, God knew the bigger picture and had worked all things out for the best. I chose to trust Him again. I would trust Him again, as I looked at the plaque on our bedroom wall.

Saying farewell to our Oregon Church was so difficult. These people had loved and cared for us so well. They didn't want us to go. There were a lot of tears and well wishes. There is a unique bond that develops between pastor and people. About fifty people came to the Portland airport to say "Goodbye." Someone has said, "There is nothing fair about saying farewell and there is nothing good about saying goodbye." It was hard to see our tall sons with tears in their eyes at the airport. We took one step after another, trusting this was God's path for us. Soon we were on the plane, destined for Detroit, Michigan.

Chapter Six

A WHOLE NEW WORLD!

Michigan 1977-1983

"I could not comprehend God's plan; my understanding was not essential, my obedience was." Max Lucado:

Candidating is highly overrated and flawed! What does one know in two weekends of dating a church body? How can you really assess whether there is a true fit for the pastor and for the people. From the west coast to the east. From a small close knit community of 7,000 to Warren, Michigan, the largest white city in America on the outskirts of Detroit. It seemed that we had gone from logger boots to three piece suits. The cultures of Oregon to Detroit were so different.

The church building was large and very beautiful. It looked more like a cathedral with stained glass windows decorating the front. Never have we seen such a stunning church structure. It had a luxurious red velvet carpeted sanctuary, seating twelve hundred.. The church was adorned by a tall tower which rang bells at designated times. It was impressive. As an aside, it took one of our sons a couple of weeks to realize that these chimes came from the church tower not from an ice cream truck down the street. I think he would have preferred the ice cream truck.

This church had only one senior pastor in its twenty-four year history, except for the first couple of years. The pastor was a man of the Word who had worked out firm boundaries for his life. He always wore a black suit. He had strict rules about Sunday, as to what his church could and could not do on the Lord's Day. The large pulpit was bolted down and could not be moved. That was a sign to all that God's Word was central in this church. The communion table could have nothing on it but the Bible. We however, were told none of this before we came to pastor and we hadn't thought to ask. I don't know what made us think we could follow a pastor who had been in this church for so long and not run into problems. We were told that the church wanted a change and we believed them.

While there candidating, we were truly wined and dined; everyone put their best foot forward. We were shown the sights and ate at the best restaurants. Pete preached his heart out and the people loved him. I couldn't believe he was so relaxed. I sure wasn't. They were amazed at Pete's ease with people and his love of being with them. They also were drawn to his Biblical but practical, honest preaching. I wondered if it was wise that Pete wore his blue leisure suit and his white shoes the Sunday he preached, while candidating. Shouldn't he try and fit into the mold a little more? When I questioned Pete about that, he said, "We need to be ourselves. What they see is what they'll get." When the church body voted on giving us a call the vote came in at ninety eight percent. We were amazed as were the church people. There was great rejoicing.

The church leaders decided to have someone drive our two cars across the nation allowing our family to fly to Michigan. That would allow us to arrive refreshed, not weary. For the first time we had professional movers. What a gift that was. Until, upon arrival it was discovered that they had lost one box that contained my beautiful wedding dress, veil and all. It was never found.

Soon we were on board the 747 airplane. This special plane had the bubble with extra seats where you could sit on top. Our kids loved this additional attraction. The pilots were so good to our kids letting them in the cockpit and giving them special treats. Before we could catch our breath we were landing at the Detroit airport to the cheers of 150 new faces from our new church. They were cheering, waving flowers and banners, and welcoming us with hugs and good words. These people had never welcomed a pastor before like this.

Wow, how do we switch our emotions that fast? Maybe driving across the country would have been good for us to debrief, meditate, and prepare ourselves for this whole new journey. Never have we felt like such celebrities. A receiving line was formed. Everyone came by to shake our hands and welcome us. One couple on the plane had no idea who we were but thought we were certainly someone important. They got in line to shake our hands and decided that they would find out later what celebrities these people were. Everyone was in a festive mood, except our older two sons. I can still picture them out of the corner of my eye, standing off to one side, alone, in shock and looking at this sight they had never seen or imagined.

Arriving at the newly decorated parsonage, we found our things had been lovingly unpacked for us and put in place, as they thought we would like. We were presented with a lovely decorated cake that was in the shape of an open Bible. On one side it said, "Welcome Unraus". On the other side was this Bible verse "God has given us our heart's desire" (Psalm 21:2). We felt blessed, tired, and mostly overwhelmed. We had arrived at our new ministry to serve God and the people of this body of Christ.

For the first twenty years of ministry we would have to say that they were years of going from glory to glory. There was much affirmation, growth and blessing beyond our wildest dreams. And yet, in a lot of ways these were years of innocence. I had had my struggles personally and physically, but our ministry experience had been unusually blessed. We had not considered the warning of Jesus in Luke 6:26, "Woe to you when all men speak well of you" (KJV).

We arrived near the end of August. The first detail on our plate was for Pete to get settled into his lovely church office that even had its own private bathroom. On the home front we were hurrying to get Bevan ready for attending Grand Rapids Baptist College. Quite a few of the church young people went to this college and we were encouraged to have Bevan look into going there himself. It was about a three hour drive from our home to the college. He would be taking a business major but had to take one Bible course. God had great things in store for our son.

Before he left for college the family was around the supper table, when Pete spoke up and said, "Does anyone know what today is?" We all looked at him and said, "No, what is it?" He said, "It's my birthday." You could have knocked me over with a feather. Birthdays were greatly celebrated in our family, but in the midst of all the low and high emotions of moving, getting settled and college prep we all had forgotten. Pete well understood as we sang our sorry Happy Birthday to him.

We hadn't yet settled in before some problems also greeted my husband. A leader's wife had been suspected of stealing money from women's purses during choir practice and at ladies meetings. This had been going on for some time. The former pastor had not dealt with it, but now it must be looked after. The wife was found guilty, but denied it. Hard feelings arose and they left the church. Our welcome had been marred.

On the home front, our son Kim was having terrible difficulties at school. He was the one child who showed great enthusiasm in moving to Michigan. He has always embraced new and different challenges. Pete had just preached a powerful sermon called, "You are either a mission field or a mission force." Kim decided when he went to his new school that he would be a mission force and let his new friends know about his Jesus. He was going into grade eight. The school was made up almost entirely of Polish and Italian kids. Our area, to our surprise, was the home of numerous large Catholic churches.

The kids at Kim's school didn't want him to be there and they certainly didn't want to hear about his Jesus. There was a gang of dangerous, mean spirited boys that began roughing Kim up. They had chains and knives and were ready to do battle. Kim was still small in stature. He wouldn't get his growth spurt until Grade 11 and then he grew quickly to 6 feet 6 inches. But in junior high with his small frame and no friends, he was caught. It was really a very dangerous, difficult time. It was our first time of knowing what it meant to have one of our kids to be bullied and threatened. We didn't know what to do. If we went to the teachers and complained it might make it worse for Kim. We prayed for him and with him, asking God to protect him. We clung to this verse with all our hearts. "Let us then approach God's throne of grace with confidence, so that we may receive mercy and find grace to help us in our time of need " (Hebrews 4:16). God met both Kim and us, as parents, in our need for protection and wisdom.

Kim had saved up the money he had earned back in Dallas from his early morning paper route. With a little help from us he bought himself a small motorcycle. Between that bike and his dog he would take out his frustrations riding the motorcycle around the large, paved church parking lot and into the adjacent empty field everyday after school. Our dog, Willie sat on the front gas tank as they rode mile after mile. Kim put four thousand miles on that bike on the church parking lot. He eventually went to the Christian school, but found the strict rules almost unbearable. For his senior year he went back to the public school. A girl asked him, "Why did you come back?" Kim's answer was,"I came back to glorify God." She asked him what that meant and he was able to share Jesus with her.

Brent found going into his senior year stressful. He didn't know anyone. His first day at school he met a girl who asked him, "Where did you come from?" When Brent told her, Oregon, she asked him what he had to pay for marijuana back there. Brent said he didn't know, as he had never tried it. Her response was, "You will, everyone does." Brent said, "No, I won't. I know where I have come from and I know where I am going and I don't need marijuana." Then he added "And I am going to marry a virgin." Her response was, "There aren't any left." Brent came home, walked in the door and said, "Mom are there any virgins left?" I said, "Yes, there are. Keep your standards high and God will bless you with the wife He has chosen for you."

It wasn't long before Brent told us that since moving to Michigan his priorities had changed. We asked him to explain himself to us. He said, "In Oregon my priorities were tennis, girls, and God. Now my priorities are God, girls, and tennis." He was finished school at Christmas time and then went on to work and he took some classes at the local college. Graduation was a sad time for him as he graduated with a class of strangers. We put on a big party for him with his friends from the church. There really was a lovely group of young people at this church. Those friends helped filled the vacuum of the lack of friends at school.

Kathy had found a sweet girl her age that she could walk to school with and be friends with. This was a great gift for her at this time. Our kids also enjoyed the programs at the church that were geared to their age. They made lasting friends there.

Bevan was totally surprised at how much he was enjoying college. For the first time in his life his theology professor was going toe to toe with him intellectually. This became his favorite class of the week. He would phone us up and tell us the wonderful things he was learning in this theology class. We were thrilled. He also began to have great relationships with his three roommates. Their lives challenged him. They accepted him and became good friends. The four years at Grand Rapids became critical years for Bevan as he, step by step began to nail down his faith and trust in God. These decisions changed the trajectory of his life forever. I didn't know all the reasons God had brought us to Michigan, but I could see that our move had truly changed his life for good and for God. It was a reaffirmation to me that God goes before us.

Christmas was upon us, and with Christmas came many challenges. We soon began to realize that divisions in churches often are centered around petty things, not just theological issues. A gifted, artistic lady told Pete that she had been in charge of putting up Christmas decorations. She asked if it was okay for her to continue doing this? Pete was happy to give his approval. When she asked where she should put the Christmas tree, Pete said: "At the front of the church would be lovely." No one had told us that the previous pastor would not allow Christmas trees in the sanctuary. The tree was erected and tastefully and beautifully decorated. Then there was this lovely godly couple that came early each Sunday morning for prayer at the front of the sanctuary. Pete and a few other deacons always joined them as they knelt and prayed for God's anointing and blessing on the Sunday services. When they arrived this Sunday, to their horror, they saw the Christmas tree at the front of the sanctuary. It was wisely situated so it wasn't overbearing but it was there. This couple was not pleased and spoke to Pete about how Christmas trees were not acceptable as they were used in the Old Testament to worship false gods. This was news to Pete. He tried to reason with them but they remained unhappy.

During the next week a couple from the church came to Pete and said that they would like to gift the church with a nativity set they had made. They had also made a little barn to go with the ceramic figures. Pete graciously accepted the gift. When the couple asked where they should put the nativity set, Pete said that the communion table would be a perfect place. This was not unusual in our background or in past churches. The nativity set was discreetly set up on the communion table on one side, the Bible remaining on the other side. The next Sunday when our devoted couple came to pray at the front of the church all hell broke loose. They began yelling at Pete, accusing him of leading this church into idol worship. Pete tried to reason with them but they were resolute. They continued their yelling at Pete through the foyer and into Pete's office.

Pete found me in the Sunday school class, asked me to come with him, and told me the story. He asked me to find the couple who had gifted the church with this nativity set and remove it from the communion table and from the church before the morning service started. God bless this gracious couple. They could have easily been hurt. They took down their display and later gave it all to us as a Christmas gift. We put it up in our home that Christmas, but were never able to put it up again because it had too much pain attached to it. It was interesting to us to see how many families took pictures in front of the Christmas tree at the church. Many mentioned how lovely it was. The angry couple left the church that day, never to return. That hurt a lot. We can see now that we should have asked more questions and been more concerned with what the true DNA of this church really was. It made us realize that one negative voice in a church can linger on over time.

We hadn't been there three months and had already managed to gain a few enemies. This very wife was the one who had shopped with me for curtain and drape material for the parsonage. When I went for the cheaper material she would lecture me on choosing the best and to remember how beautifully the temple was decorated by God's instructions. I was confused as to how to marry all the love and outward signs of affection she gave me while making our parsonage curtains with the harsh words of judgment and condemnation given Pete at the altar, just weeks later. I never could make sense of it all. How could people kneel at the altar with you one day and the next, shout uncontrollably at you, shaking their finger in your face while they walked out of church and out of your life, never to be willing to talk or reconcile with you for the rest of their lives. Where was forgiveness and grace? We were left puzzled. The pain of having our first real enemies shocked us. Our Savior knew what it meant to have people either hating or loving him. He endured betrayal, false accusations, beating, and trial. It comforted us that Jesus knowingly walked with us through these trials.

We carried on into the New Year to smoother seas and steadier sailing. The people of the church truly did grow in their walk with God and in their love for their new pastor. Many found great blessing under Pete's leadership, example, and preaching. God was also increasing my personal ministry. I began a Ladies Bible Study at our church. In no time I had over one hundred ladies attending my weekly Bible study. Many were blessed and received God's Word humbly but honestly, spoken from my heart. I even taught them one year how to make simple quilts.

I also had an ever expanding opportunity to speak at Christian Women's Clubs throughout the greater Detroit area. Because I didn't want to drive on the busy freeways, my friend Barb, offered to drive me wherever I wanted to go. She became my dearest friend. What a gift. Once again I saw God use my simple testimony touch deeply the hearts of the women that attended these luncheons. These opportunities were God's gift to my soul, during some rocky times at our church.

At the same time I began to get invitations from other churches in the area to teach their women's Bible studies. God was enlarging my ministry and I was richly blessed to see my life being used by God in the growth and encouragement of other women's lives. Pete was totally behind me in the opportunities that I was taking. In fact, he prayed for me, encouraged me, and rejoiced with me. He never held me back in what I felt God wanted me to do.

Soon after our arrival in Michigan, Pete became aware of a problem on the seminary level of our denomination. There was a growing weakness on the part of the seminary president and some staff to hold the Bible up as the complete, inspired Word of God. They were doubting some passages and choosing other ones. Pete talked with fellow pastors in our area and said, "We have to do something about this. We can't let this go unchallenged." The other pastors said it would cause too great an upheaval on the denominational level, but if Pete would take the leadership they would back him. So Pete took the leadership in challenging the president and the dean of the seminary. There were a lot of meetings and discussions. The stand of the president and the dean became more alarming.

That summer was the triennial conference in Bismarck, North Dakota. This included all the churches in both the United States and Canada. Pete was asked to be one of the keynote speakers at this convention. As always, he preached with passion, compassion, and biblical foundation. It is interesting to us to know that sitting in that audience that day was a young seminary student who felt the call of God to preach. When he heard Pete preach he said to himself, "I want to preach like that someday." How wonderful to now sit under that godly man's preaching Sunday after Sunday in our home church in our days of retirement. Each Sunday we hear him preach, we get to pray for him, encourage him and hear wonderful solid Biblical preaching founded on the inspired Word of God. To God be the Glory!

At this convention there was a motion to establish a Baptist doctrinal revue committee to help clarify where we really stood on the inerrancy of the Holy Scriptures. Was the whole Bible inspired by God or was just some of it inspired? The motion was overwhelmingly approved. Each regional association was to appoint two representatives from their region. Pete was privileged to represent the Michigan Association. We were given three years before the next tri-annual Convention, which was scheduled to be held in Niagara Falls. The denominational leadership expressed a real fear that this issue would prove to be painfully divisive. We had no intention to make this into a witch hunt. When one of the key Sioux Falls Seminary professors found out that our statement in regards to the Bible would include the words: "without error", he phoned Pete with this statement: "I used to believe that, but for intellectual honesty reasons, I can't accept that anymore. So where does that leave me?" Pete's answer was: "If this is the statement that the denomination accepts you will need to decide what to do. We can't have the tail wagging the dog." To the surprise of the denominational leadership, the delegate body at the Niagara Falls Tri-Annual Conference, they voted overwhelmingly in favour of the Baptist doctrinal revue recommendation, with only four negative votes. With tears of gratitude they came to Pete and thanked him for his leadership in this whole process. Both the seminary dean and president resigned and new, thoroughly evangelical leaders were hired. We have heard since that time that to have a seminary change its stand on such an important and strongly held doctrine of the church is very rare. I have often wondered if this amazing result that would affect this denomination for years to come, was one of the reasons God brought us to Michigan, for such a time as this? Did God gift Pete with the passion and the connections to lead this major charge?

The people of the church were so gracious in blessing us in many ways. Some of them had cottages by a lake in upper Michigan. We were often invited to spend our vacation time at their cottages. One of the couples loved to have our whole family come with them for Thanksgiving, or during hunting season. They had motorbikes and other activities that our kids loved. They had a son the age of Bevan. They had lost their oldest son in an industrial accident. One day, our son and their son were playing tetherball. Pete noticed the dad weeping. When he asked him what was wrong, he said, "I was just thinking, that could be my two boys playing together." How they missed their older son. Wil and Barb became our dearest friends and are that to this day.

Back at the church, Pete was facing a myriad of pressures. He was pressured by some in leadership to have more public invitations. Once every Sunday was not enough. The former pastor had invitations on Sunday morning and on Sunday evening and at the Wednesday night prayer meeting. If people came forward in droves, they were happy. If few people came to the altar for prayer, it was not a good Sunday. All this kind of emphasis was new to us. In former churches this was never the focal point.

Attendance was taken and retaken, dissected and weighed out. This also was seen as a huge indicator as to whether God was blessing or not. Someone has well said, "It doesn't matter how many people come to church. What matters is, "do they leave with changed lives and new resolve to follow in Jesus' steps?" That was our heart's concern and we were seeing it happen. I would often see a few of the strong leaders gather around Pete after a Sunday morning service and my first thought was: "I wonder what Pete did wrong today?" That was the atmosphere that was developing as the years rolled on. It felt like they were trying to put Saul's armor on David, my Pete. It didn't fit and the changes they had said they wanted, they really didn't want. Some leaders really did want change. Others had unending energy to be in opposition to any change. There was lots of encouragement from the greatest majority of the people of the church but little encouragement came from a few leaders that were very powerful and very opinionated.

Pete began to get pressure to raise the standard of dress code. Jeans were not accepted. Three-piece suits were the only appropriate Sunday attire for men. Slacks for women were not allowed. It had to be dresses or skirts. The right length was smiled upon. After all, were we not coming into God's house and entering into the presence of the King of Kings?

When we arrived at the church we inherited the staff that remained after the long-term pastor had left. In some cases that was a great blessing but in other cases it was a challenge to develop a good fit.

We had the most wonderful music director. He was a gifted man of God and an exceptional tenor soloist. We had a choir of fifty to sixty people. We also had a wonderful sweet Spirit-filled "paid" organist. This was the first and only time I sang in the church choir and I loved it with all my heart. It was also a great blessing to have our three tall sons in the choir with me, when they were home. For some years, the choir sang the Messiah as a gift to our community at Christmas time. We had to rent tuxedos for the boys for this occasion. We had packed out concerts night after night. It was one of the most wonderful times of blessing and joy in our journey with this church.

As wonderful as the music minister was, there were rumblings about the songs the young people of the church wanted. Some of our youth were bringing in guitars and asking about drums and the synthesizer. Pete was caught between wanting to keep peace with a few of the strong leaders and wanting to keep our youth involved in church and continuing to come. He leaned toward the youth, including our own kids, and lost the respect of these leaders. Kim and his best friend Doug sang so beautifully together. They often had their guitars and would sing Spirit-filled, ballad-style songs. The guitars were soft and the music touched many people's hearts. Those songs these friends sang still ring in my soul today.

Such minor problems became our focus. Satan was having a hay day distracting this body of believers. We were troubled and confused. We had been in three different churches before this and had never come into contact with this mindset, on any of these issues. Where had we been? Was the west so different from the east? We began to realize that the glove of this church did not fit our personal hand. We were not a match. All the cheers at the airport faded. All the gifts given had a twist to them. We began to feel we were trying to be bought by a few people. When we would not go their way, the price was unimaginable.

Two couples in particular turned their backs on us completely. A judgment call had to be made regarding a new church organist. These two men, who were CEOs in their worlds, could not believe in the end that Pete went against their recommendation. Pete knew their information was faulty and biased. In the end Pete was proven right but that didn't remove any of the sting of the impasse with these leaders. The more they talked the farther apart they got. Eventually a chasm formed between them and us that could never again be bridged.

Now for the first time in our life we had true live enemies who disliked us with all their power. They were powerful. For two years they would not look at us or acknowledge our presence or shake our extended hands. How could it be that these were the very hands that invited us, welcomed us so warmly, and now, in protest, would not stop to shake our hands? They moved from sitting at the front of the church to the back pew and began their silent campaign of dissent against us. To be consistently ignored felt like the deepest punishment they could give us. Pete pled with these men to reconcile. When they would not, he invited them to find another church. They would not do that either. One said, "I was here before you came and I will be here after you leave."

I knew we couldn't stay here long. Pete told me at one time, "The blessings of the ministry are still here, but the joy is gone." I wondered if these leaders had ever read the words in Hebrews 13:17,

"Have confidence in your leaders and submit to their authority, because they keep watch over you as those who must give an account. Do this so that their work will be a joy not a burden."

I felt the burden too. I would wake up on a Sunday morning with such a sense of inner dread and fear, I would feel nauseated. "This is Sunday", I would think. "We have to go and face these silent enemies once again. We have to pretend everything is wonderful when it is not."

This was completely against our heart commitment of "No Pretending", but to live a life of honesty and integrity. We wrongly put on our masks, smiled and sought with all our hearts to trust Jesus in the storm. We believed: "God is faithful; he will not let you be tempted beyond what you can bear. But when you are tempted, He will also provide a way out so that you can endure it". I Corinthians 10;13 (KJV)

How often we sang comfort into our hearts with this amazing hymn. "Jesus, Savior, pilot me, Over life's tempestuous sea; Unknown waves before me roll, Hiding rock and treacherous shoal; Chart and compass come from Thee: Jesus, Savior, pilot me." Edward Hopper, had put our confused thoughts into life giving words in the year 1871.

"The Lord is my light and my salvation, whom shall I fear. The Lord is the stronghold of my life of whom shall I be afraid" (Psalm 27:1).

This verse had been put to music. My heart sang these songs over and over again as I battled with fear and my wish to hide. Isaiah 41:10, "So do not fear for I am with you; do not be dismayed, for I am your God. I will strengthen you and help you; I will uphold you with my righteous right hand." What precious promises from God. I would ask myself. "Who can we talk to? Who would understand our confusion, our pain and our turmoil?" I didn't know. If we talked to our close friends we would have to tell them about the treatment of a few in leadership, thus poisoning their minds towards the people who they would continue going to church with. So we talked to no one. Pete shared some with the young leadership deacons, but they were inexperienced and too afraid to take a stand against these powerful older leaders. What a lonely, isolated time for us.

During this violent storm, I memorized Bible verses and hymns, copied them out and put them on the doors of my kitchen cupboard. "God is my refuge and strength, a very present help in trouble. Therefore I will not fear, though the earth give way and the mountains fall into the heart of the sea" (Psalm 46:1.2). This became one of my all time favorite "lifeline" verses. God was walking with us. We were trusting Him step by step. He had called us here. He would not allow anything to touch us that He couldn't turn into good. We believed that by faith not by feeling. It felt like we were on the potter's wheel and

God was working on molding our character, making us more into the image of Jesus Christ.

I also memorized, wrote out and copied songs of faith and trust in God. Music has always been a predominant language of my soul. One of my favorite songs at this time was:

Be Still My Soul

Be still, my soul; the Lord is on thy side.

Bear patiently the cross of grief or pain. Leave to thy God to order and provide;

In every change, He faithful will remain.

Be still, my soul; thy best, thy heav'nly Friend

Through thorny ways leads to a joyful end."

Katharina von Schlege, 1697

Another favorite song when going through trials was:

Guide Me Oh Thou Great Jehovah.

Guide me oh thou Great Jehovah.

Pilgrim in this barren land.

I am weak but Thou art mighty.

Hold me with thy powerful hand."

William Williams, 1745

It truly did feel like we were pilgrims in a barren land, traveling through uncharted pathways, over rocky steep terrain. We knew we were in over our heads and we had no one to stand with us in mentoring us through this wilderness time.

During this time Bevan had graduated from college and was feeling God's call upon his life to become a missionary. He attended Missionary Internship, an organization that prepared people for foreign missions. This mission was located in our area of Detroit. He also was an intern pastor at our church for a year. How wonderful it was to have our son on staff with us. He did a good job but when he was finished he said: "If I ever pastor a church, it would have to be different than this one." We totally understood where he was coming from. He moved to Texas to attend a church that did things very differently. That pastor and that church would become the lifeline in his life up until this very day.

Perhaps if Pete had taken a few of the younger leaders aside and poured his life and soul into them we would have had a group of men that would hold Pete's arms up during this difficult battle. We could have done things better we know now. I think we were just working hard to trust God, minister to the majority of people who loved us and were receiving God's Word through Pete's ministry. We had many encouragements.

However, the negative voices often shouted louder in our hearts than the positive ones did. We felt all alone in this battle. We had never been mentored or even knew about that possibility. It was like we had been put on a high pedestal that would make us an easy target to put us off balance.

It was Christmas time again. The Christmas tree was safely tucked in its proper place in the foyer. Our kids came home from college and Texas. We were looking forward to spending quality time with our family. We had talked about resigning that next summer, once Kathy was finished her school year, but we never had the chance.

I've often been troubled by the timing of God in our lives. Our son, Brent, had been engaged since the summer. We invited our soon-to-be daughter-in-law, Denise, and her whole family to join us for Christmas. It was going to be such a glorious time of celebration and getting acquainted. This family was from a small farming community in central Canada. We were excited to show them the sights of the big city and get to know them.

One day, all the ladies went shopping for the wedding dress for Denise. What a glorious morning we had. Can there be anything sweeter and more enjoyable than to begin to get to know your first daughter-in-law, who was so pure and lovely in every way? Now I was being invited to look at wedding dresses and watch her try them on. What a morning of joy and celebration we had.

When I got home there was a call from my Pete, asking me to

come to the office. This was unusual. The parsonage was just across the parking lot from the church, so I immediately left all the family and guests and ran over to the office.

There I found Pete in such a state of shock and despair. He told me a group of three men had come into his office to lay down their charges against him that should result in his resignation. One of these men said that what he was doing was for the sake and good of the church. He told Pete, "Where there's smoke there's fire," and he began to carry out his plan to be the savior of the church.

The accusations made against Pete were shocking and totally false. In time, each one was dealt with and Pete was proven to be without blame. That however, didn't make any difference to his accusers. I wondered where Matthew 18:15-17 came into play in this scenario. Does it not say, "If your brother sins against you go and show him his fault, just between the two of you. If he listens to you, you have won your brother over. But if he will not listen, take one or two others along, so that every matter may be established by the testimony of two or three witnesses"? Psalm 41:9, "Even my close friend, someone I trusted…has turned against me." Psalm 55: 12-14, "If an enemy were insulting me, I could endure it… But it is you, a man like myself, my companion, my close friend, with whom I once enjoyed sweet fellowship at the house of God as we walked about among the worshipers."

There were other small issues, that when cleared up, didn't seem to matter. There seemed to be a total blockage on the path to reconciliation, understanding or restoration. One man told Pete, he would forgive him all his past faults, but could not allow one more mistake. Pete told him he was expecting perfection and that was realized only in heaven. That didn't change this man's heart. There was no possibility of change in the hearts of any of these few brothers in leadership.

The pain of betrayal and false accusations hit us in the stomach like a sledgehammer. Pete and I talked and prayed and cried and then I walked home alone, across that long parking lot, to face our happy company. Wretched timing, I thought! As I was making supper, I was shedding tears of unbelievable sorrow. I couldn't understand how such a thing could happen. What makes a person honour, love and respect you one day, and turn on you in complete resolve and coldness the next day with no chance of dialogue, explanation or empathy.

We couldn't keep our pain hidden from our kids or our guests. At the supper table, after the meal, we told them of our great sadness and our dilemma to know what to do. We had also booked and bought tickets to the Nutcracker Ballet in downtown Detroit for all of us to attend that very night. How could we go to such a wonderful celebratory event with our hearts and souls in such turmoil? We all went with heavy hearts and tried to enjoy the beautiful Nutcracker.

Later we heard from one of our accusers that he was extremely disappointed in us; that on a day such as this we would do such a frivolous thing. Well, we couldn't win whatever we did. So we took one unsure step after another, knowing that Jesus has promised to be with us in the storms of life. The next day our guests left for their home in Canada. It was a sad parting. Denise called us that evening to see how everything was going and we told her that we had made the decision to resign. She told us she understood and would be praying for us all.

We met on that Saturday night to talk with the deacon board. We wondered if anyone would speak up and stand up for the truth. All was silent. I had hope that Pete would speak up and name the false accusation and set things clear, once and for all. He remained silent, so I knew I couldn't speak. Pete always has said, "He who defends himself has a lousy lawyer." We knew we were in God's hands. Jesus understood, for all men forsook him in his hour of greatest need. We clung to His nail-pierced hands and asked Him to carry us through the next difficult uncertain days.

Pete's life's verse was Philippians 3:10 "Oh, that I may know Him, and the power of his resurrection, and the fellowship of His sufferings, being made conformable unto his death" (KJV). Yes, we did want to know Jesus more and more, and how we longed for the power of his resurrection to be part of our lives, but did we want to follow so close that we would have to share in His sufferings even to the death?

It did feel like we were dealing with a death, a death of a dream; death to our reputation and death to wanting to finish well at this beautiful church, with so many wonderful Godly people who loved us still. We didn't want to see them hurt, but we couldn't protect them. I wanted Pete to speak up and expose the false accusations and give our defense to them all. Pete was too beaten up to do this and I wondered if it would make any difference, if he did. He had shared his defense with his accusers and things just got worse.

At this time I told one of the leaders that this pain of betrayal and false accusations was more painful that my six-and-a-half hours of cancer surgery. He was very upset with me and said he could not believe that what I said was the truth. I stand by this statement to this day. There is little that can be compared to the confusion and the pain of unresolved relationships, false accusations, and betrayal in the church.

Pete read his resignation letter that Sunday, effective immediately. The shock that went throughout the church is hard to explain. So many who loved us so much put on their suits of armor and went to battle for us. They were sure that they could win the war and have us rescind our resignation and stay on. The battle was fierce.

Many meetings of loyal supporters were held. They hoped things could be worked out so we would be able to stay on. We knew differently. The die had been cast and the powerful leaders had won, or so they thought. People who loved us began to show that love in creative ways. One couple cleared out their basement, put up tables, and had a packed out party they called: "I Love You". Words were spoken and we were gifted and loved beyond measure. Others invited us out to a fancy dinner at an expensive restaurant. There they gave us a wonderful gift we treasure to this day. Others found beautiful ways to express love.

Our friend Wil, was chairman of the trustee board, at the time of our resignation. We were not given a severance package and had no place to live. Wil fought for us to be able to stay in the parsonage rent-free until we left Michigan. What a gift that was. Wil later told us that all that went on at the church hurt them more than losing their 16-year-old son in an industrial accident. We couldn't believe this could be so, but he stands by that statement to this day. This gave us a glimpse into the deep pain and hurt a church body goes through when there is division. We tried to go back to the church after our resignation but it was too hard on us and too hard on the people. I could only sit and sob uncontrollably.

Pete took a trip to Texas to see our son Bevan and to talk with his wise pastor. He talked to Pastor Lutzer of Moody Church in Chicago as well. He and Pete had taught together at Briercrest Bible College. They listened, cared and prayed for us but what could they really do? I stayed home with Kathy and Brent who was working at a local bank. Kim was attending Moody Bible Institute in Chicago.

During these days I would wake up with such a dread and overwhelming sense of loss, confusion, and turmoil. I didn't know what to do with myself. I felt I could talk to no one because that would be gossip and poison their minds against the people who had betrayed and offended us. I would often think, "I can get up and read God's Word, pray and journal." So that is what I did. I immersed myself in God's Word. God brought peace and life back into my soul as I read His promises, worshiped Him in prayer and in song, and journaled pages upon pages the cry of my heart.

Journaling is such a therapeutic way to write out your confused thoughts to God. My thoughts were disentangled as I journaled my heart to God, who was always listening, always loving, and always kind. In the thirty-five years since we have left this church I have never once wanted to read this journal or felt it would uplift my soul. I believe it was a sacred time between God and me for that season only. It was healing and precious.

One set of verses that ministered to my soul was Psalm 66:10-12, "For you, O God, tested us, you refined us like silver…You laid burdens on our back. You let people ride over our heads. We went through fire and water, but you brought us to a place of abundance." How clearly this verse mirrored my heart. It truly did feel like men had ridden over our heads. I wondered if there would be a place of abundance for us. We felt so beaten down. Who would ever trust us again?

Romans 12:18-19 became the foundation for our relationship with our enemies. "Do not repay anyone evil for evil. Be careful to do what is right in the eyes of everybody. If it is possible, as far as it depends on you, live at peace with everyone. Do not take revenge…but leave room for God's wrath, for it is written, 'It is mine to avenge; I will repay,' says the Lord."

We had to make the decision to forgive or to let bitterness grow in our hearts. We chose to forgive in the strength of the Lord and leave our reputation and the church in God's hands. We felt we had done our best for six long years. We also knew that we could have done better. We should have asked more questions, taken a few leaders aside and poured our lives into them, thus having leadership support surrounding us in the battle. As we put all into the hands of our God, who is all knowledge, all love and sovereign over all we could leave with settled hearts.

Pete and I didn't share our feelings very deeply with each other. I figured he was hurting so deeply I didn't want to burden him any further. This was a mistake that I would pay for later. I did ask Pete if it could be possible that he could go back to carpentry, the job he loved before he became a pastor. Pete said to me, "No, we couldn't do that. God has called us to ministry. He would make a way." I told him that I didn't think I could be a pastor's wife again. I couldn't give my heart so completely to people with the chance that I would once again be betrayed, ignored, falsely accused, and discarded. I decided that from now on my heart would be more guarded. I would distance myself from people and let Pete be the pastor. This was my pain speaking to my heart but for me it was very real.

We were six months without a salary. Pete did a lot of preaching in nearby churches but the honorariums were small. That we didn't have to pay to rent the parsonage was a huge help to us.

Brent was leaving in February to live near his fiancé, as they planned their wedding back in Canada. Many people put on the biggest wedding shower for Brent in yet another loving couple's basement. Brent said afterwards, "I think we got such lovely gifts because you were so loved and this was one way they could show it."

The church did their best to put on a beautiful farewell for us. It was hard coming back to the church to let them say "farewell." We were severely wounded and knew the church was too. I remember someone pinning a beautiful corsage on my garment. I said to her, "I'm not sure I can do this." She said, "Oh sure you can. You will be just fine." Well, I wasn't just fine and remember little of that farewell. I know we spoke and I know we hinted at Jesus being with us during the storms of life. We thanked the people for their love and prayer and encouragements over and over again and we meant it and so did they. They took up a gracious love offering that helped us with the expenses for our long-planned Orient Mission's trip and our move to come.

During our time in Michigan, Pete had been in association with a wonderful mission called Send International. It has hundreds of missionaries all over the world. Years earlier Pete was asked to be the head of the Personnel Department of this Mission, that would begin the process of screening new potential missionaries. He loved this diversion and opportunity. This was a voluntary position with no remuneration involved.

We had been invited by Send International to go to their mission fields in the Orient, to speak at their conferences in various places, and as well to encourage and bless the missionaries. This was such a delightful anticipation. When the leaders of our denomination heard about our trip they asked if we could minister to their missionaries in the Orient while we were over there.

This was all worked out beautifully. We were to spend six weeks ministering to two groups of missionaries in the Orient. We were concerned for Kathy. Bevan was in Texas, Brent in Manitoba, Canada, and Kim was at Moody Bible Institute for his first year. We wondered if we should take Kathy with us. We talked it over with her principal at her school. He said, "By all means take her. What an opportunity for gaining knowledge this trip would be." Then he added, "If she doesn't want to go, I will be glad to accompany you."

In the end we didn't have peace to take Kathy. There would certainly be many interesting things to see and do, but there would be boring long air flights and endless meetings, conferences and hearing her Dad preach daily. We had a beautiful couple in the church, who weren't able to have children who had become Christians under Pete's ministry. They would be happy to look after Kathy. She was quite game that we go. Soon her big six foot six inch brother Kim would be home and they were the best of friends.

Our trip to the Orient was truly a dream come true. It was our first international ministry trip and we loved it. What open arms and open hearts received us and our ministry. Our first stop was the Philippines. The people were so warm hearted and so was the weather.

The temperature hit record highs. We would take many showers a day just to cool off. Occasionally we had air conditioning in the bedroom but there were many times we experienced "brownouts", and without electricity we had no fan or air conditioning.

We actually had a call to be the pastor of an English speaking church in Manila. Pete was very attracted but when he saw how my body responded to the heat he knew I couldn't take this extreme heat. After my major cancer surgery it was discovered that my body thermostat had been affected. For the past forty-seven years I have dealt with heat and cold issues constantly. I am forever putting on or taking off clothes, coats and blankets. When I talked to my oncologist about it he said, "Considering what you have been through, consider yourself fortunate." I do consider myself fortunate, but it honestly has been a long journey of adjustment to extreme temperatures wherever we go.

We went on to Japan. What a beautiful country with such gracious people. It was, however, a very difficult place to preach Jesus. The missionaries there worked so hard and saw such little fruit.

Next was our time in Korea. What a difference in spiritual climate. When we got on the bus early Sunday morning, we saw everyone on the bus carrying their own personal well worn Bibles. Here we attended the biggest church in the world. They had thirteen services each Sunday with 13,000 at each service. Worshipping with these Korean believers was an experience we will never forget. It was truly a taste of Heaven itself. We even borrowed a car and drove up to the DMZ border between South and North Korea. We had some amazing highlight days in Korea.

We stopped in for a few days at Hong Kong and bought all the kids amazing gifts that lived short lives. Our last place of ministry was Taiwan. Here we fell in love with the missionaries and the people they were seeking to share Jesus with. We experienced many unforgettable sights, sounds and smells.

Oh how sweet this trip was. What healing came to our souls. And yet the unresolved relationships back in Michigan were ever with us. Over the next year we would try many times to initiate conversations and correspondence that would lead to reconciliation; all to no avail.

We came home to Michigan to a surprise 25th Anniversary Party put on by those who loved us so dearly. Our friends were told they couldn't hold this party in the church, so they rented a school gym. The gym was packed out, standing room only. People spoke of their love and their changed lives under our ministry. What heartwarming testimonies these people gave. We were presented with a lovely 25th anniversary cake. There was another gift these people had worked very hard at. They had heard that one of the men who was instrumental in pressuring us out had told Pete, "You are the third pastor that I have been responsible for his removal from ministering at my church." He added, "If you get a call from another church I will make sure that they will hear from me and you will never pastor a church again."

When our supporters heard this they individually wrote letters of recommendation regarding Pete's character, Biblical preaching, and Christ-like living. We were so very grateful, but never had to use the letters in that book. This reception of love and blessing would be the last time we met with many of these dear beloved people of God. We gave them and ourselves into the care of God.

Chapter Seven

A PLACE OF ABUNDANCE

Campbell River, BC 1983-1991

" He brought me out into a spacious space." Psalm 18:19

Now it was time to pack the overflowing U-Haul and start our long journey west. The U-Haul had "Adventure In Moving" boldly written on it. A few days into our trip we didn't think that was truthful advertising. We had gotten their biggest truck but it was a lemon, finally needing all new tires. Kim and Kathy pulled the car behind the U-Haul and made up a fun song that rings in our minds today, "We love you U-Haul man, Oh yes we do.." They made lemonade out of the lemon. What a blessing these kids were to our hurting hearts. They could laugh again. Maybe someday we could too.

Our first stop was at Brent's soon to be in-laws. They lived and worked on a farm in Manitoba, Canada, that had been in the family for over 100 years. Everything was meticulous. I had never seen such a beautiful, weed-free garden. The whole place spoke to me of peace, order and stability. And here we were with our overloaded U-Haul van and car, crammed full with "stuff." We had brought some things for Brent, so a lot of the back end of the U-Haul had to be unloaded to get Brent's things out.

Denise's Mom stood with me as we watched from their front door, all the goings on of unloading, sorting, and getting everything back into place. As I looked over our situation I felt very disorganized, unsettled, and embarrassed. I looked at Denise's mom and said, "Sometimes, I long for a life like yours that is so stable and so organized, with your family all around you."

She replied, "That's strange. I was just thinking what an exciting and adventuresome life you have. I kind of envy that today." I then realized that God has different paths for each of us and to be an excellent farmer is God's call just as much as it is to be an excellent preacher.

All during this trip we grieved, we prayed, we cried, and we chose to let God do His work. Now we must cling to some of our favourite lifeline verses of comfort and blessing. "Trust in the Lord with all your heart and lean not on your own understanding. In all your ways acknowledge Him and He will make your paths straight" (Proverbs 3:5-6). "Be still and know that I am God" (Psalm 46:10).

We travelled on through the many miles of flat prairie land, through the city where our daughter Kathy was born, past our college, where we both graduated and were on staff for six years. Finally we were bathed in the splendor of the majestic Rocky Mountains of British Columbia. I was born and raised in these mountains. How good it felt to be coming Home. We stopped in to see our parents and then kept driving west to our new place of calling.

Soon we could see the glorious Pacific Ocean. We would travel by ferry for almost two hours across the Strait of Georgia, arriving on Vancouver Island.

God was speaking to my heart, "Remember, I promised you I would bring you into a place of abundance" (Psalm 66:12) I have good things in store for you because you are my child, my Beloved whom I love! We were nearing our "place of abundance" that God had promised us while in the battle.

It had been a long road to travel. We travelled two hours north on Vancouver Island, along the winding highway that followed the sea. We were awe struck with the beauty all around us. We grew up in British Columbia, but had never taken this trip before. We rounded a corner and before us lay the loveliest sight. In the distance, bathed in light was the city of Campbell River, situated on the terraced bank along the ocean's edge. Could God have brought us to any place on earth that would be more different than Detroit with its miles of freeways and buildings? It felt like we had arrived at the other side of the moon.

While staying at the head of the search committee chairman's home. I noticed in our bedroom was a scripture verse framed and hanging on the wall. The words I read solidified in my heart that this was God's place for us. It said, "Though you go down to the sea, I will be with you there."

I believed God had chosen this place of ministry for us. There was no fanfare at our arrival. We settled into a rented home. There was no parsonage, so nearing the age of fifty, we dreamed of the possibility of owning our own home. People came around with baking, wood for the fireplace, and welcoming hugs. There was a lovely, low key reception at the church to welcome us. I loved the level plane we felt we were on with these people. We were following a beloved pastor, who was very much like us in personality and in preaching style. There was no hidden list of expectations. The atmosphere was relaxed, friendly, and accepting.

The main economic base of this city was tourism, fishing, mining, and logging, which included the big pulp and paper mill. We had rugged loggers and seasoned fishermen, who were in leadership at this church. They were down to earth, friendly, godly people. The church building couldn't have been any different than the Michigan church was. It was flat roofed, with the main entrance at street level. It was built on the ridge so the back entrance brought you into two stories of Sunday school rooms. There was no choir for most of the years we were there. The music was not the finest but we grew to love the people who gave God their best as they worshipped and served Him.

We were barely settled into our rented home and church when it was time to make the long journey back to Manitoba for our son Brent's wedding. This would be our first child to get married. It was such a delightful time, as we watched these two young people so in love, make their vows before God and man. Our whole family was there as were quite a number of good friends from Michigan. Denise's family treated us royally. The whole experience was so lovely, pure, uplifting, and God honoring.

We were nearing the date of our twenty-fifth Anniversary. Our kids took this opportunity, the day after the wedding, and after the gift opening, to have a small celebration for us. They had worked together to honor us with a plaque of blessing. To this day this plaque hangs in our living room and is one of our most treasured possessions. Here are their words of blessing:

Dear Dad and Mom,

Each of us has been marked by seeing and following the example of your lives. Most important, each of us has been brought into relationship with our creator through your influence:

Thank you for,

> Loving God in a way we could see.
>
> Crying, praying and fasting on our behalf.
>
> Providing for our physical needs.
>
> Being humble enough to apologize to us.
>
> Listening to us when we were frustrated and confused.
>
> Teaching us to work hard.
>
> Treating us as unique individuals.
>
> Encouraging us in spite of our failures,
>
> And disciplining our sins.

This world may not give out awards for parenting, but we would like to recognize you and express our thanks for your faithfulness to us, your children.

May we bring honor to you, and most of all to God by our lives,

> *Bevan, Brent, Kim and Kathy*

There is no amount of money that could compare with this loving gift to our hearts, and at such a time as this. We have marvelled with all that we and our kids went through in Michigan, that not one of them turned their back on God or the church. Many were praying for them and God heard their prayers.

It was a wonderful feeling when we drove back into Campbell River, feeling like we were home. We were told that the next week the church was putting on a skit night and we were expected to be there. I thought it was a nice change to have such a fun evening as a skit night. However, there was a conflict in my mind. The very time of the skit night was the time we were expecting Brent and Denise to come and visit us at the completion of their honeymoon on the Oregon coast. I wanted to be like my mother always was, ready and sitting at the window, waiting for their arrival. I told everyone I wouldn't be able to come to this skit night.

The pressure for me to attend was greater and greater as the day arrived. Kim and Kathy were urging me to go, Pete thought he should, but I could stay home to welcome the newlyweds. In the end, a deacon's wife phoned me and said, "Shirley you must come to the skit night. If you don't you may upset some people and disappoint others." At the last moment when they said: "We are coming to pick you up," I relented and went with them. I didn't want to start our ministry with offending and hurting people. They brought us in the back way, as we were a little late. When they opened the door, we were amazed to see the whole fellowship hall full of people shouting: "SURPRISE." Well, you could have knocked us over with a feather. Such elaborate decorations, with a banner beautifully painted with these words, "Welcome to our beloved Pastor Pete and his gracious wife Shirley." What a thoughtful, loving congregation these new people were to us. When things settled down they said there were a few guests they wanted to introduce. The first people who came out were my Mom and my Dad (who had been sick for months), my sister, and my aunt. Next to be introduced were Pete's twin and his wife, then his sister and her two daughters, and lastly, out ran Brent and Denise. Oh my, what an awesome surprise. We hugged and laughed and cried our tears of joy.

Then they did have two skits of our dating years, worked out to be exactly as it had been. They had been in touch with our family and gotten all the details to put these skits together. They gave us a beautiful silver candlestick holder and silver mounted bowl. They rejoiced with us, prayed for us, and celebrated our twenty-five years of marriage. This touched our hearts in ways we couldn't express.

Our son Kim was Kathy's best friend. When she was little, he spent hours making her laugh and played with her. As they grew up he became a companion and a great brother. Before we moved, Kim told us, "I'm moving with you. My plan is to drop out of college for one year and just be there for Kathy. I don't want to see her moving all by herself." We could hardly believe the soft caring heart of this tall son of ours, for his younger sister. What a difference he made in her life. As we settled in and Kim got to know the college age young people, they would call and invite him to some activity. Kim's answer always was, "I will come, only if I can bring my sister." Kim took some studies at the North Island College in Campbell River and found various jobs. He would often come home from work and say, "Well, I know I don't want to do that job for the rest of my life."

We had always lived in parsonages, so were unable to gain any equity for ourselves. In Oregon, in the 70s, the chairman of the board was a wise and good friend. He suggested to Pete that we buy a little cheap house and begin to accumulate some savings. He said that you will need some money to help your kids through college and then there is retirement to think of. He even lent Pete the fifteen hundred dollars down payment on that little house. It wasn't much but it was a start. The total cost of the house was seventy five hundred dollars. We owned that house for over twenty years. It helped us out with a little extra income so many times.

Now we were looking for a home to purchase that would be our very own. We did not have a down payment but the church offered to give us ten thousand dollars interest free, for a down payment for a house. They would forgive this loan at one thousand dollars every year that we stayed as their pastor. What an awesome gift that was to us.

I grew up with a family that loved a beautiful view from our home. As a teen it was the lake and the glorious Rocky Mountains. Now I really wanted a house with a view. We looked everywhere but could not afford homes with a view. Pete heard about this new house, that hadn't passed final inspection yet. It sat empty and neglected for some time. We had a look at this house. I was captured by the most amazing view out of our living room window. Could it be possible that we could get this house? It was in a good, well looked after neighbourhood but stood uncared for, waiting for us. Pete checked on what would need to be done for this house to pass inspection and almost everything that needed attention, he could do himself. Before we knew it, the house was ours and we joyfully moved in.

Our view looked out over the amazing Discovery Passage of the Pacific Ocean. The ocean ran through a narrow passageway that would accommodate any size of water traffic. Oh, the hours we enjoyed watching the fishing vessels, the barges being towed to and from the mill, and then there were the cruise ships. We moved in during the summer months when all the cruise ships going to Alaska passed by our front door, or so it seemed to us. We never tired of this view and the soul-feasting effect it had on us. Whenever we saw a cruise ship coming we called out: "Cruise ship", and the rest of the family dropped what they were doing and ran to the window to enjoy the sight. It was also very wonderful to be on the shore when these big ships passed by. Even more exciting was when we were out fishing a few times, as a cruise ship came through the Narrows. We could almost touch this floating hotel. We would look at all this and say to God, "How blessed we are to live here. God you are so good to us when we, at times were disappointed in Your ways in the past. You truly have brought us into a place of abundance. Our hearts are full of thanksgiving to You."

We loved the church people and they were so blessed by Pete's Biblically-based, practical, sound preaching and his love of people. I could see the blessings of God all around me, but my wounded soul was still very raw from our experience in Michigan. For months I had stuffed and ignored my emotions and my pain. Life was busy with many changes.

I am a processor of the joys and the sorrows of my life. I had no one to talk to about our difficult journey in Michigan. I had tried to talk with Pete in Michigan, but for some reason, he was not able to engage in this topic of conversation. He was trying to put food on the table, find a new place to minister, pack us all up, and get us to our new place of ministry. One of our kids said, "I bet Dad hit the ground running in Campbell River." And that was the truth. There was a whole new congregation to get to know, to bless, to teach, to care for and encourage.

I was outwardly friendly to these wonderful people but inwardly guarded. I also was struggling with a measure of frustration with Pete, that he didn't stand up for himself in Michigan. Why didn't he fight back and tell the truth against these false accusations that were being spread. I basically am more of a person of justice and wanting to tell our side of the story. Pete is more forgiving, thinking the best of people and when hurt, he will not press into the issue.

Now I wanted to talk through our Michigan experience with Pete and he would have none of it. As time went on I began to share a little with Kim. I knew immediately that this was wrong. If Pete and I couldn't go below the surface and share the depth of our hearts, our marriage and ministry would be shallow, skimming over the surface of life. This would result in distance in our marriage which would be dangerous to us personally and thus to our ministry. God's call was to live lives of honesty and integrity with "No Pretending." Without permission my physical body and psychological being began to react to the unresolved pressures with which I was dealing. I began waking up in the morning with a sense of dread and overwhelming inadequacy. I couldn't face the day. I couldn't do what was required of me that day, I thought.

The first time we invited a group of people over I had a major panic attack. I told Pete I couldn't do it. "Can't do what?" he would ask. I couldn't put into words how I was feeling. Pete would tell me he would help and I knew he would. He was a great helper around the home and shared a lot of the home chores with me when needed. But that was not the issue. Emotionally I just couldn't handle it. What was this all about, we both wondered?

Pete's sister and husband came for a visit. I was anxious and unorganized in preparation for them. I was making a batch of buns and couldn't remember how to do it. That was something I had done regularly for twenty-five years. What was wrong with me? When the doorbell rang announcing their arrival I couldn't go and answer the door. I felt shame and fear and totally out of control of myself. I covered it up so the kids or the church wouldn't know, but I knew and Pete knew. I believe now I was very close to a nervous breakdown, as it was called in those days. We didn't go for help, not knowing who to go to.

Pete finally realized just how much I had needed him. He began to invite me to open up my heart to him. He wasn't judgemental, nor did he want to quickly fix me. He gave me what I so desperately needed. He gave me himself, who would love me through this time and listen to me. Just listen to me was my plea. Journey with me and with what I am struggling with. And he did.

In time the dialogue went both ways and I got to hear Pete's heart in a way I had never heard it before. We were giving each other the best gift a marriage could have. We were being honest, real, and mutually vulnerable with each other. If just one person is vulnerable there is not a deep relationship. It takes two people to be vulnerable, open, and transparent to have a deep growing relationship. We chose to go below the surface with each other. We chose to live with No Pretending. No more stuffing our pain and ignoring our emotions and the reality of what we had been through.

Looking back we now know that Satan was out to kill, steal, and destroy our very lives. We were, in fact, saving our marriage by being real and honest with each other and thus we were saving our ministry from destruction. "Greater is He that is within us than he that is in the world" (1 John 4:4 KJV).

We had trusted God through Michigan and we chose to trust God through this unexplainable psychological detour. God began a work in our relationship that we now call, "the choice to go below the surface." It takes hard work and difficult talks. We made the commitment to each other that we would work through any situation and would not be content with a shallow marriage that doesn't deal with the small stuff. If we push things under the carpet, afraid or unwilling to take the time to work through, stuff just keeps growing and the marriage keeps shrinking. We knew too many marriages where both husband and wife have given up, and were living lives of mediocrity. The depth, the passion, and the joy had gone from their marriage. We chose to "work through, not walk out," Walking out may, at the time, seem to be the easy way out. But the results are devastation and pain for the whole family for generations to come. God's way is never the easy way, but oh the blessings and depth of relationship we have gained for the last 35 years since this momentous time in our marriage.

We look back on this time now and thank God for bringing us through a very difficult time. I didn't get better right away. God and Pete and I gave me time. Today our marriage is so safe, so below the surface, so rich and so free. I can't thank Pete enough that he was man enough to journey with me into the depths of uncharted, fear-filled waters. We have realized over the many years of marriage that you never get to the place where you don't disappoint, hurt or respond selfishly to each other. It's the price of being human. Someone has said, "In order to have a good marriage you both have to be professional repenters and professional forgivers." We have to all learn how to say, "I was wrong. Will you forgive me?" That is God's way to humble and soften hearts. It paves the way for a growing marriage or any relationship that has less and less struggle and more and more safety, depth of love and joy.

We knew that Campbell River Baptist had begun its own Christian school. Kathy was going into grade nine. We felt it was important to be supportive of all aspects of our new church so we put Kathy in the Christian school. It was not a good fit for her. One awesome teacher saved the day for her.

We hired a young couple to be our youth pastor. Many new young people were attending Sunday evening services. Eventually our church was the happening place to be on a Sunday night. Looking back, Pete would have to say that under God's guidance, hiring this couple would be his best decision in hiring staff during his pastoral years. They were fun, energetic, and loved Jesus fully and contagiously. We were so happy Kathy had such great leaders who became lifelong friends with her and with us.

Kim transferred from Moody Bible Institute to Briercrest Bible College, our second year in Campbell River. He loved it there. Kathy came out for the weekend of the big Youth Quake. Everyone thought they were boyfriend and girlfriend. That was just the kind of relationship they had. Kathy will never forget the difference it made having Kim by her side during that first year in Campbell River. He was there for us too. He was God's gift to our wounded, healing souls.

Each of us has to be on guard and "Watch out that no bitterness takes root among you...hurting many in their spiritual lives." (Hebrews 12:15 TLB). We had to be on guard that we not let this root of bitterness grow up in our hearts. Only faith in God and His unchanging Word will keep out bitterness and revenge.

One day I asked Kathy why she wasn't bitter towards the people who had hurt her Daddy so terribly. She said, "I watched you and Dad and saw that you weren't bitter, so why should I be?" I was taken back. How much our attitude as parents is passed onto our ever watching children?

We eventually put Kathy in the public school. This was where she belonged, thrived, and blossomed. In Michigan cheerleading had been a big part of her life. There were no cheerleaders in her new large high school, so she decided to form a group of interested girls. Together they would learn different routines and cheer at the games. In this group were twin sisters from our church, Kathy's age. They became bosom friends. They had so much fun practicing and performing at the games. Sometimes they even went on road trips. We never worried about Kathy remaining committed to her faith. She enjoyed being a positive influence to her friends. Those were really great years for her and her friendships.

Our family was enjoying the beauty of our area more and more. There were the walks on the rocky beach, picnics beside the ocean, and long walks through aged forest to glorious waterfalls. I had been reluctant to get too involved with people, but once I was well again, and feeling the tug of God on my life I began to walk through doors God was opening for me. I taught the women's Bible class. I pulled all the women together during the Sunday school time and taught a large group Biblical and Personal Helps in Marriage, Raising Children and Being a Woman of God in the place He has put you. These lessons were taped and had a great growing and bonding effect on the women of our church. Pete and I team taught both men and women sessions on Biblical Marriage and Family Life. It was our first time to do this as a team, and we found it most delightful and bonding in our own marriage and growth. We were living out our marriage theme: "United to Serve." We were also once again having groups of people to our home for meals or after church on Sunday nights for coffee and goodies. The fellowship ran deep and rich.

We began to reach out to our neighbors in non-threatening ways. We invited them over for an evening of getting to know each other. Then the next time we got permission from the city to block off our street and played volleyball on the street before refreshments and sharing. We always were the ones to initiate, but others were so appreciative. One day I was calling on a new neighbor welcoming them to our neighborhood when she said, "Are you the Good News Ambassador of this neighborhood?" I said, "I don't think I would call myself that." She said, "Oh yes, you are. We heard about you and your open home before we even moved here." My heart was warmed and encouraged.

I began my most disciplined teaching course to a group of women called Navigator 2:7. I had always loved the emphases of the Navigator Mission, that placed a high value on reading God's Word and putting many Bible verses to memory. Navigator 2:7 is based on Colossians 2:7, "So then, just as you received Christ Jesus as Lord, continue in Him, rooted and built up in him, strengthened in the faith as you were taught, and overflowing with thankfulness."

There were three books that we went through over three years. We were encouraged to write down how God had spoken to us during our daily Bible reading. We each had a packet of 83 verses to memorize. At the end of the three-year course we were to say them all at one time, without a mistake. We were also asked to prepare and present our personal salvation testimony, that we would share in our group sessions. It sounds like a highly regimented course and it was. But each of the women knew what was expected of them and were anxious to strengthen their faith and be rooted and built up in Him. I can't think of any course I have led that gave me, personally, and the group I led, a deeper sense of a close and growing walk with God. This group met in our home faithfully for three years of study, memorizing, sharing and connecting with each other. What a precious time!

We were all building up our reservoirs of faith and trust in God. Many of these verses became lifeline verses for us. Pete and I also led a couples group that we found a little more difficult to keep on track. Any time spent in studying God's Word, memorizing it, and practicing the attitude of thanksgiving will always be a time well spent. Seeds sown during these three years bore fruit for eternity, in our lives and in the lives we touched.

Our son Bevan, found the love of his life. He and Rebecca were married in Fort Worth, Texas in 1985. We flew the whole family there for the wedding. What a God honoring, joyful celebration. How wonderful to see God leading our children to mates who also knew Jesus and wanted to follow and obey Him.

I wanted to do something special for Pete's fiftieth birthday. I talked to a bush and water taxi pilot, to see what would be the cost to take us into a hidden lake for the day. He got all excited and said, "I would love to do that. We will tie a canoe onto the plane and fly into Gold Lake. You can only get there by plane and it is wonderful. We could take six people on this flight." I decided that this would be a secret for Pete. I asked him to free up a given Saturday and invited the pilot's wife and another couple to join us on this trip.

God granted us a perfect blue sky day in August of 1986. Pete had no idea of what was in store, but he was so excited when we ended at the spit that moored the bush pilot's company float plane. Everyone was full of anticipation and joy. The women brought along picnic lunches, bathing suits and fishing gear. As we neared Gold Lake, in the middle of a dense forest, the beauty of it took our breath away. The pilot said this was going to be a hard landing since the lake was like a mirror. The landing was perfect, as was the picnic, the canoeing, the swimming, and the celebration of Pete's life. The other couple made Pete a wonderful scrapbook full of pictures and notes about this special day.

The church put on a surprise birthday party for Pete at a park, after a baptismal service, that was held at a beautiful ocean beach. There was a procession of trumpets blaring and people cheering as the cake was brought in. What a large cake with fifty candles. Oh my, what gracious people we were ministering to and who were ministering to us.

On Pete's actual birthday, life took us on another detour. I woke up in the morning with a large growth about the size of a small egg, that had popped up overnight, on my cancer leg, just above the original surgery. I had been cancer free for fifteen years. Soon we were on our way to see the cancer specialist in Campbell River.

Dr. Fletcher, who had done the original cancer surgery in 1971 in Portland, Oregon, had called me every year for fifteen years to see how I was doing. I was his success story. Now, I called him and through my tears told him what had happened. He said the doctor in our area could do as much for me as he could, but he would call him and they could talk things over.

I was booked for surgery immediately. We called for the elders of the church to come to the hospital to anoint me with oil and pray over me according to James 5:15. This is the first time we had done this. The sense of being obedient to God's Word and letting others inside our pain and hearing their prayers of faith, was a special sacred time. It gave me a peace that is beyond words or understanding.

After Pete left the hospital the night before my surgery, I had a deep longing to have my kids around me. I was missing them so much. I decided to write them a letter and share my heart at this time, the night before surgery. Here it is in edited form:

Facing and Fighting Cancer, August 27th, 1986.

> To my dear kids: (Since you can't be by my bedside in person, I need to share with you in this way.)

> My heart is full of praise to God that He gave you to me. How you all have enriched and blessed my life in so many, many ways.

> Now I sit alone in my hospital room. Dad has just left but his heart of love and total empathy has stayed here with me. Again how blessed I am. Tomorrow I once again face the surgeon's knife. Once again my future is uncertain. Will the growth be malignant? Has the cancer returned? No one knows. We pray for the best and prepare for the worst. As much as I'm loved, to some degree I must bear this burden alone. Dad's hand can hold mine only till the surgery doors swing open. Then he must leave me and I must go on alone. Which side of those doors is harder? I hardly know. I have only ever been on the inside. I often think the loved one standing by, has the harder trial. We both know that Jesus goes with us. He has promised to never leave us, to never forsake us (Hebrews 13:5). The blessing of all blessings is to know Him. To know Him is to trust Him and that, we do.

> How does one face an uncertainty like this? They are now preparing me for surgery. What have I done to prepare my heart? I want to share these things with you because that may be part of the "good" that God is going to work out through this trial (Romans 8:28). Maybe, in this area

102

too, you can learn with me.

The importance of a daily, growing walk with God, asking others to pray, aligning myself with Scripture, keeping a clear conscience, looking after my body well, keeping the path of fear closed with a No Trespassing sign, (2 Timothy 1:7), times of laughter, tears, and singing, presenting my body to God and trusting Him with the results.

I love you, my children - all of you, by birth or by marriage.

You are my special delight, God's love gifts to me.

Love, Your Mother

The next morning we prayed, and trusted God as I was rolled into surgery. As soon as I woke up after my surgery, I did the same thing that I had done fifteen years ago. I felt to see if I had two legs and I still did! The report came back that it was, indeed, the same type of cancer as my first major surgery, but it was encased and confined. The pathologist told Pete he had never seen such a healthy active immune system with the good cells fighting the bad cells. The cancer sack was removed, the flesh was stitched up and bandaged, and I was on my way home in a couple of days.

It wasn't long after my surgery that Pete asked me if he could share the letter with the church people. Eventually a number of magazines wanted to print my letter. I freely gave them permission. One magazine paid me one hundred dollars for the rights of this letter. When my letter was published they changed the title from "Facing and Fighting Cancer" to "Living with a Dying Mother." I was shocked at this change and the kids were very upset. We phoned the magazine to have it changed but it was too late. Then, I realized that I was a dying mother. No one has any idea just when that time will come. The fact that I am living today is only because of God's plan for my life, even before I was born. Psalm 139:16 puts it so plainly, "All the days ordained for me were written in your book before one of them came to be." I am invincible until my time comes and then I am ready and waiting to leave this earth to be with Jesus for all eternity. How interesting that this magazine no longer exists but I live on today. The church folks ministered to us in helpful and wonderful ways. Once again, we experienced a wonderful church doing it right as they ministered to us, prayed for us, and loved us. That was 32 years ago and to this day, I have had no more problems with cancer.

The year 1987 was a "shower of blessing" year for us. Kathy graduated from high school with a host of great friends. We had taken the whole family to Hawaii ten years earlier when our first child graduated from high school, now we wanted to take our whole family to Hawaii once again after our last child graduated. By this time, both Denise and Rebecca were expecting our first two grandchildren. Kim was engaged to Darlene, the lovely gal he fell for at first sight at Briercrest Bible College. We came from so many different places to board the plane in Vancouver. Kathy's graduation events took us pretty close to departure time for Hawaii. We left one event with Kathy, Kim and Darlene, and once again our bush pilot came to our rescue and flew us to the Vancouver airport. I said, "If we all get on the plane to Hawaii on time, I will stand and sing the Hallelujah Chorus," and I did! Words fail to express the joyous relational time we had as a growing family. What a great opportunity to get to know our three daughters-in-law better. We had great times of fun and bonding.

That fall, we all flew to Winnipeg for Kim and Darlene's beautiful, God-honouring wedding. Oh, what joy unspeakable and full of glory. My dad went home to be with Jesus, a few weeks after the wedding. This too was a gift from God. He had suffered for so many years. Now he was finally HOME! Soon after my father's death, the good news reached us that Brent and Denise had just had a baby girl, our first grandchild. They were pastoring two churches in rural Saskatchewan. We planned to visit them when baby Sara was three months old. Just before we left for this visit, the church planned another surprise shower for us. a grandparent's baby shower. Now, how cool and creative was that? I had never heard of a church blessing their pastor couple in such a lovely way. We were given the most beautiful assortment of baby clothes and accessories. What a fun, heart-warming event. We went for our visit with hearts of blessing and suitcases full of lovely gifts for Sara.

How can one explain the joy of holding your first grandchild?

Pete had many opportunities to assist on the governing board of our denomination. In time he became president of the B.C. Fellowship Baptist Conference. This gave him many open doors to share his passions, encourage pastors, and help the denomination to stay on track with God's Word and God's ways. Our conferences were often held out east, so we got to travel to places we had never gone. We had the joy of ministering to churches in Quebec.

In 1988, Pete had meetings out east so we combined that time with a visit to our friends in Michigan. They had invited us to come to a welcome reception they were planning to have for us. We flew from Vancouver to Toronto. Upon landing I told Pete: "That was the best flight. I was able to stretch across three seats and have a sleep." I felt fine upon landing. Brent, Denise, and baby Sara were now in Toronto, preparing to go to Italy as missionaries. They picked us up and we headed for our friend's home in Michigan. As we travelled in the car I began to feel my facial glands swelling up. I tried to ignore it, but the swelling continued. The conference was held in Windsor, Ontario, just across the bridge from Detroit. We arrived at our friends with my face now swelling up. In the morning my face was beet red, my nose had almost disappeared and my eyes were almost closed. In alarm we went back to the hospital in Windsor. All in all I met with seven different doctors and had been given seven different diagnoses. Little by little the swelling went down. I was able to make our welcome reception, barely pushing myself through. My face was still swollen and I was feeling uncertain and weak, but these people wrapped their arms around us, loved us, blessed us, and spoke words of encouragement to us. This did more for my body, soul and spirit than any medication could possibly do. Oh, the joy of friends who remain friends regardless of the circumstances.

We had accepted an invitation to go to Medellin, Colombia soon after the National Conference was over. We were praying often, if it was God's plan, that we could continue our planned trip to Colombia. We had been asked to minister in the churches and to speak at a missionary conference, as well as gatherings of missionaries. I was getting better day-by-day, so we decided to continue on with our plans, trusting God for continued healing.

On our way to Medellin, we had a one night stop over in Cartagena, Columbia, the famous sea port resort city on the Caribbean Sea. We got to our hotel at sunset. The hotel was right at the edge of the alluring famous beach. We asked at the desk if we could swim at this place? They said we could, but they wouldn't advise it as it was going to be dark soon. We rushed to our room to put our swimming suits on, and rushed to the beach. Oh, how wonderful it was. It was the warmest ocean we would ever swim in. We didn't linger long but got back to the hotel feeling young and adventuresome. We asked where would be a good and safe place to have dinner. They recommended a Brazilian restaurant down the street that served twelve different kinds of meat. We thought that would be a great new experience, so off we went. It was an amazing experience. We asked if their water was safe to drink and if we could safely eat their salad? They strongly assured us that there would be no problem. We went home very full and very happy.

At one a.m. in the night, I awoke with severe cramps and knew I was in for trouble. We had to catch the plane the next morning as our friends were waiting for us at the Medellin airport. I hardly left the bathroom until I boarded the plane. For some unknown reason we sat on the hot tarmac with no air conditioning for an hour before we took off. God answered the prayers of these unprepared naive travellers. We safely arrived into the arms of our missionaries. This was the delightful couple who had been the head of the search committee when we arrived in Campbell River. They eventually resigned from teaching public school and went to Colombia to be missionaries. We told them of our "adventures" in Cartagena. They were caring and so very helpful. How thankful we were that our bedroom at their home had a large bathroom attached right to it. Strange as it may sound, I was quite relieved when Pete came down with the same Montezuma Revenge as I had. In the past he was never sick and I was the one that came down with the strangest maladies and always felt weak and a bother. Pete never made me feel that way, but I did battle the thorns and major physical problems in my life. Now we were in it together and it felt good.

Our dear hosts loaded us down with Imodium, broth, crackers, and 7-Up for two weeks. We never missed an appointment, a speaking engagement or the conference sessions. We give thanks to God for answered prayer, for the care of our hosts, and the wonders of a little Imodium just before we spoke. The last few days we were well enough to see some sights and enjoyed a lovely Colombian dinner out, with an awesome Mariachi Band, at our request. God blessed us, spoke to us and through us in spite of our foolishness and weakness. "When we are weak, He is strong" (2 Corinthians 12:10b).

We were having many opportunities globally and across our nation, but I must say, one of my greatest thrills was to see God at work right in my own backyard. A hesitant woman by the name of Shirley came to an evening service. I befriended her, talked and lovingly welcomed her. She was back the next Sunday. Soon I invited her to my home. Then I heard her story of being on the streets since she was 12 and her trouble with addictions. Many roller coaster rides with Shirley were my new experience. She still had ups and downs but she knew Jesus. She left this world quickly with unexpected cancer. I know I will spend eternity with her in Heaven. No greater joy.

During the years in Campbell River I took classes at the community college and correspondence courses from two different colleges. Eventually after long hours of work, I gained my Bachelor Degree in Arts and Christian Education. It was my hope to go on to get my counseling degree but God had other plans. The church began talking about building a larger building. A lot was purchased and plans were being drawn up. It was an exciting time to see God at work in His body of believers. Experiencing the unity in the body of Christ was like salve to our souls.

In 1990 we had an invitation to go to Pakistan to teach and preach at a large interdenominational conference for missionaries. What an awesome opportunity. I kept an extensive journal of this entire trip. We read it now and are amazed that we could fit so much into one day. Our first stop was in Bangkok, Thailand. We saw the many wonders of this amazing city.

Traveling on to Pakistan, we had an overnight stop in Karachi, Pakistan. The plans made by the missionaries were not carried out. We had a difficult and somewhat scary night. The next day we flew on to Islamabad where we met our missionary hosts. With the hosts we started our road trip journey to Murree, situated in the mountains of Northern Pakistan. This is where the missionaries went during the hot summer months.

This road trip was the most terrifying travel experience we would ever have. The road was narrow, along the side of steep mountains. There were many busses and cars packed onto this road. The busses were a sight to be seen. They were so overcrowded with people hanging onto the sides with one hand. There were chickens in crates, people sitting on the top of the bus and crammed into whatever space they could find. They had great difficulty getting up the steep grade and were very skilled in their manoeuvres around the corners. Without signaling, a car or bus would speed by us on a corner and just hope for the best. The thinking was, "If Allah wills me to die, I will die." Well God willed us to live and we arrived safely.

We began to unpack our suitcases. The large suitcase had many things tightly packed as gifts for the missionaries or things they had requested. When we opened it, we were shocked to discover that the sealed chili powder had exploded in the suitcase and chili powder was ingrained into everything!! Oh, what a mess.

We were often in the homes of the missionaries for meals. We knew this food and this water would be safe. They told us to never drink water unless given to us by a missionary. They also said to never eat salads or fruits that could not be peeled. When they would take us out to eat, our choice of drink was always a Coke. We had learned our lesson in Columbia. From that time on we never had a problem when travelling abroad.

Pete spoke at a large interdenominational Missionary conference in this hill country. There were 400 missionaries gathered for the days of the conference. These missionaries were from many different denominations, but all loved Jesus and came together yearly for personal replenishment, biblical encouragement, and fellowship. It was a time of great opportunity and responsibility, with an awesome response, and blessing from God. Pete also spoke at a pastor's retreat and other meetings with the missionaries. I had the opportunity of speaking to all the ladies in different settings. At times I spoke to one or two, or fifty or one hundred. I was blessed to give my testimony. They gave me a lovely traditional Pakistani outfit that I wore with joy. We had other opportunities to minister and felt the beautiful power of God's hand upon us. What a gift from God that He would entrust to us the opportunity to bless, encourage and challenge missionaries in this difficult part of the world.

We spent a couple of days in Islamabad before heading home. It was so very hot and humid. This was the hottest, most humid experience of my life. It was 41 degrees Celsius which is around 106 degrees in Fahrenheit. I could hardly stand to be outside. In the evening I did get to see the world famous Faisal Mosque that could accommodate 300,000 people with the open sides. The main hall of prayer accommodated 10,000 people. It covered 46 acres. It was a gift from Saudi Arabia's King Faisal and named after him. What respect rose in our hearts for these missionaries and the difficult challenge they had in presenting Christ to these Muslim people. "Not by might, nor by power, but by my spirit, says the Lord Almighty" (Zechariah 4:6).

We arrived home after spending fifty hours in travel from bed in Pakistan to bed in BC. We were just in time to make it to our denominational conference in Victoria. Pete was the President so we had to be there. We were jet-lagged and filled up with the blessings of the Lord, and now trusting Him for strength and empowering one step at a time. Our next stop was HOME!!

Kathy was dating Bruce, a wonderful man of God, who had graduated from Briercrest Bible College. She attended two years at Briercrest and then transferred to Trinity Western University near Vancouver, BC. She was just a ferry ride and two-hour drive away from us.

A year later we would experience our only time to have a young man ask for our daughter's hand in marriage. We were overjoyed. We couldn't have chosen better. It was my first time to look for a bridal gown with my own daughter.

The whole family came for the June 8th wedding in 1991. By now we had five grandkids under three years of age. The two oldest granddaughters were the flower girls. Oh, what little sweethearts. What a joy to have the whole family there, helping out, laughing, sharing and in harmony with each other.

When the music began for the bride to enter, I turned to see one of the most beautiful sights of my life. This was our sweet baby girl that we had waited for so long. She was simply a delight to raise and eventually would be my dearest friend. She was just beautiful inside and outside.

Now God gave me one of the dreams of my life when Pete walked Kathy down that aisle to meet her beloved. Kathy couldn't have been more lovely, pure and sure of this step of commitment to leave father and mother and to cleave to Bruce for the rest of her life surrounded with God's presence and blessing. Tears come to my eyes again today as I write this. Pete then officiated at the wedding, as he had for all our kids' weddings. One of the sweetest parts of the wedding was when the bride and groom asked their immediate family to come and surround them and spontaneously pray for them. What a solid foundation to begin their married life on.

Before the wedding, our son Bevan, now pastoring in California, was taking pictures of our amazing view. He said, "Mom and Dad, if you ever move away from this place I am never coming home again!" We all laughed, but Pete and I knew there was a moving of God in our hearts that we could not escape.

We had received a phone call from a church in Abbotsford, BC, Pete's hometown, just one hour out of Vancouver. They were looking for a lead pastor and wondered if Pete would be interested. The first thing Pete told them was "If God is in this, I want you to know right away that I am a Shepherd Pastor. I love to be with the sheep and have a deep calling to relationship with the people of my church." They said, "That is exactly what we are looking for." The church had been through a troubled time and was looking for stability, solid preaching and, yes, a pastor with a shepherd's heart.

We met with the search committee before Kathy's wedding at the Vancouver Airport. They were thrilled with our commitment to God, our love of people, and our vision for the church. Growth in people's hearts and lives would be our major focus. We agreed that we would meet again after the wedding.

I pled with Pete not to tell any of the kids about this invitation until the wedding was over. I didn't want anything to take away from the focus on Kathy and Bruce's beautiful wedding. Our kids were shocked, as we were. We prayed much, sought guidance from God's Word and, for once, I was as ready to move as Pete was.

It would be another new denomination and a big challenge, but we felt the call of God. It would be far easier and safer just to say "no" to this large church and live out our pastoring days with this beautiful group of people in Campbell River. But if God was calling, how could we say "No"? God's call upon our lives was not to follow the easy road and stay in the safe green pastures but to say, "Here am I, send me Lord!" (Isaiah 6:8). Trust in God and obedience to His Word and to His will had always been the priorities of our hearts.

We told our church God was calling us elsewhere. There were many tears and sorrows. We shared those as well. A lovely farewell was held for us. We were packed up before we knew it and by September we were at our new place of God's appointment.

Campbell River had truly been a place of abundance. Our wounded souls were healing, and we could see that God had softened and humbled our hearts and grown our character through the suffering of Michigan and the healing oasis of Campbell River.

At this point in our life, our hardships, betrayals and pains had lessened but the joy of seeing people coming to know and follow Jesus for their whole lives right into eternity, had grown sweeter all the time.

Chapter Eight

GOD IS NOT FINISHED WITH ME YET

Abbotsford, BC 1991-1997

"The things we believe have broken us become the very things that mold us and make us into the likeness of Christ." Unknown

It was a quick emotional switch from our daughter's wedding to candidating for a senior pastor role in Abbotsford, BC. We were aware that this was a church that had gone through its own wounding and attempt to find healing. We were warned that this would not be an easy church but we couldn't shake the inner nudge of God. The people were so warm and friendly. The elder board treated us wonderfully, with unusual care and tenderness. The Sunday Pete spoke was a day of wonder in my eyes. He had so much passion in his preaching, so biblical, so relational with a great amount of liberty granted by the blessed Holy Spirit. This was the first church that asked me to speak and to give my testimony. I felt honored to share a bit of my heart with this congregation. Pete spoke both morning and evening and then we were taken to the home of the chairman of the pulpit committee and left there while the members of the church stayed to vote.

Never have we seen men and their wives more excited, when they arrived back at the home in which we were waiting. They came rejoicing and praising God, with hugs and laughter. This was really something to see, as the chairman of the board was such a soft spoken, reserved man, but not that night. And then they told us the good news that the vote had been 100% in favour of calling us. They said that had never happened in their church before and it had not ever happened to us either. They said as the vote was being counted, near the end they were holding their breath just praying there would be all "yes" votes. To everyone this was almost a miracle, that a congregation of around 1,400 people, would be of one mind and one vote. This was an indication to the leaders of the church that God was at work. The church had come together in unity once again. It gave us the message that God was truly in this move and we had the support and prayer of every person in the church. What an amazing Spirit-led beginning.

Of course we knew this job and opportunity was too big for us. We, however believed God had led us here and He would be our guide, our wisdom, and our strength. Pete was excited about this new wonderful body of Christ's church! To be their shepherd pastor was a great privilege and a great responsibility. We daily presented our bodies to Christ as living sacrifices (Romans 12:1). We knew there would be trials ahead because we would be working with humans who, like ourselves, were flawed.

We were excited to be living in Pete's teenage hometown. He comes from a family of eight children. All five boys were ordained ministers. Two sisters were married to missionaries. The oldest sister was salt and light in her home church and beyond. Five siblings were missionaries and two were pastors and evangelists. We were thrilled to spend more time with these siblings after being continents apart from each other. His brother Henry, who led him to Jesus, was now a member of our church along with his wife Jennie. Henry had actually given the pulpit committee Pete's name as a possible candidate for senior pastor. Another brother was also in our church. They were always sources of blessing and encouragement.

We bought our most beautiful house ever and, yes, it did have an amazing view, not of oceans and cruise ships, but a green park with beautiful Mount Baker in nearby Washington State, in full view. We were delighted. We dedicated this home to the Lord and purposed in our hearts that we would use it for His glory and to the encouragement of His church, our soon to be friends.

We began by inviting Sunday school classes over on Sunday nights after the evening service. We had a large and growing Sunday school. Our first class to be invited over numbered sixty people. We told them to bring a few plates of finger food and we would do the rest. We focused our entertainment on building relationships and connecting with the people. I think that was the largest group we ever had over at one time. We worked our way through each adult Sunday school class.

When we finished with the Sunday school classes, I put an

invitation sheet up on the information desk and we announced that the first thirty people to sign up would be invited to our home the next Sunday evening. I would make simple cookies or cake, coffee and tea, and that would be all. Sometimes, we would decide to just have a few people in and we would phone them and personally invite them. Many, many people told us they had never been in a pastor's home before. Their delight at being in our home made us realize we were meeting a need in their lives and that doubled our joy. Our conversations were not lengthy or intimate, but our desire to be part of their lives shone through. We also had the young people over from time to time. Our park was a perfect place for them to play volleyball. One time we had 100 young people in our home for a watermelon feed. We wanted them to know that we were there for them and were cheering them on in their walk with Jesus. We were used to doing something fun and relational on Sunday nights when the kids were all home. Now, we ourselves, also needed friends and fun times as well. I didn't know Pete was keeping track, but in the first four years we had close to one thousand people over to our home.

Pete also had a desire to get to know the men of the church. Most lunch breaks he would make appointments and have lunch with the men of the church. Sometimes he would go to their business or to their farm. Often they were nervous about having the pastor come to their place of work but after a few minutes they relaxed as Pete was so relational and personal. He wanted to learn about their business, their family, and how the church was meeting their need. Another idea Pete had, which in retrospect was perhaps a little over the top, was to phone every person on their birthday. People still tell him they miss his birthday calls.

We had a couple of staff who stayed on from the previous pastor. They were solid gold. We hired other staff. Our music director came from California. He was a gifted leader of music. The choir was large and the congregational singing was, to us, the most worshipful experience we had ever had. Our music leader somehow combined beautiful hymns with modern choruses that brought us right into the presence of God.

This church was was known for their annual singing Christmas tree. People came from many miles away to hear this wonderful choir singing from within the tree. Dedicated men spent a whole week putting this tree up. It rose so high, it nearly touched the ceiling. The choir, with lit candles, would walk in from the back of the church, up the aisle and circle around the tree until it was filled. A professional live orchestra was hired. It couldn't have been more beautiful. It was a magical, reverent, rejoicing time. We held six Christmas concerts annually without any cost to those who came. It was our gift to the community. The sanctuary held 1,200 people. It was packed out at almost every presentation.

At the close of each evening concert, Pete would warmly speak to the people of the Greatest Story Ever Told. The story of Christ's birth, life, death, resurrection, and coming again. He would then give those who did not know Jesus as their personal Savior an opportunity to follow him in a prayer of acceptance of Christ. This was a highlight time in the year for our church and God gave the fruit and the blessing. I thought back to our problems in Michigan, over one small tree at the front of the sanctuary and compared it to this huge tree that covered the complete stage of our present sanctuary. What differences we had been through.

At our new church, I was enjoying the ministry of hospitality and encouragement, it was a great way to get to know the people. Then I became involved in the women's ministry almost right away. At first I was asked to lead different parts of the women's ministry. I often spoke at various events. One of my favourite opportunities was to plan the women's spring event. This evening gathered in all the women from the church and was a wonderful time to uniquely focus on Jesus. I had a great committee and together we put on some fantastic, unforgettable evenings of testimony, song, unique themes, and messages.

We gave our all to the ministry at this church. We worked too many hours. We spread ourselves too thin and we didn't develop intimate friends that we could share our hearts with. Our vision was big and broad and we would later suffer for that. Occasionally I had the staff women over to our home for a luncheon and a time of sharing and fellowship. We visited the staff in their homes. Pete had weekly meetings with the staff and an open door policy that said, "If you need me for any reason, I am available." The staff also took three or four days away annually together for what they called PEP times. That involved, Prayer, Evaluation, and Planning. Pete would come home from these times with the staff so very encouraged. It was good to have iron sharpening iron. PEP days happened on a regular basis to keep the staff united, connected and focused. The staff of nine was working so well together. In retrospect, we should have done more with the staff, had them over more often, mentored them and invested deeper into their lives. As it was we were working overtime weekly.

We were well into our second year at this church when we got a letter from the Michigan church asking us to be their guests at the fiftieth anniversary of the church. We were unsure. Our dear friend and mentor, Dr. Hildebrand said to Pete, "Go! Remember you go from a place of strength not weakness." That settled it for us. We told our kids. Our son Kim and wife Darlene were pastoring in Niagara Falls. They wouldn't let us go unless they could come with us as our " bodyguards". Pete had a chance to speak for ten minutes. He used his time to share a nugget from God's Word and to encourage the pastor. We knew that since we had left this church they had been through much difficulty. Pete wanted to encourage and bless the present pastor and people.

Before a lovely banquet, there was a receiving line. People came by shaking our hands, hugging us and saying words of love and affirmation. One woman held onto my hand and said, "I need to ask your forgiveness for the terrible way I treated you when you were our pastor's wife. Will you forgive me?" With the lineup waiting I quickly said, "Yes, I will totally forgive you." We hugged and she moved on.

I had been doing a lot of pretending that weekend, hugging people and letting them speak words of love to me, when there were unresolved issues between us that we had tried to address many times. Now we just let it pass. The next morning I awoke with the resolve that I would not pretend anymore. I phoned the woman who had asked my forgiveness and said to her, "I appreciate you asking me to forgive you and I do, but can you help me out? I am wondering what I did that offended you so much?" Quickly she said, "Oh you didn't do anything wrong. I had lost my husband a few years ago and my church had become my safe place. Now it was going through difficulties and the only one I knew to get angry with was you. I am truly sorry." Wow, what a difference it makes when we can speak the truth in love and get to the root of the problem instead of this forever pretending.

That weekend didn't bring any healing to our hearts. We rejoiced to be with people who continued to love, connect, and support us. Our heart did go out to the present pastor who didn't last much longer. The church really never recovered from our wrongful dismissal.

Back in our home church one Mother's Day, Pete's sermon title was Help!, I'm a Mother. As he began preparing his sermon he thought, "Hey, I'm not a mother. Why don't I get Shirley to speak on this subject." I agreed to do that, giving handouts of my message notes at the end of the service. This was so well received that I spoke every mother's day from that time on. People received my teaching with such grace and I felt blessed to be able to share my heart with our congregation.

When everything at the church was going well, Pete and I would often pray together and tell God, "We are humbled at your mercy and grace. We know in ourselves there is no good thing. We are but clay. We place ourselves daily into your hands. Mold us and make us into what your desire is for us. Anything good that is happening is from your gracious and merciful hand."

We were also offered one seminar or Deeper Life Conference per year, that we could attend at church expense. We seldom took those times of refreshment, but others of the staff did. When an opportunity to take a week away at a Billy Graham School of Evangelism, held at Lake Louise in Alberta, Canada, we felt led to go. The more we looked into it, the more excited we got about it. There would be some excellent speakers and classes that would help us in our own walk with God and pastoring the church

Pete presented the idea to the board. He explained that the Billy Graham Association paid for our lodging at the spectacular historic Hotel Fairmont, overlooking beautiful Lake Louise. They also looked after the registration fees, as well as some travel costs. Pete figured that this wonderful opportunity would not cost the church very much. The board was in total agreement. We were excited to be heading to a place of beauty in the Rocky Mountains, where our souls would be fed from speakers from across North America. We were not disappointed. We took notes and drank deeply of God's Word, spoken through God's servants.

Pete was challenged by one workshop to be more open, honest, and vulnerable with his staff and board. He took this seriously. The speaker challenged the pastors to share their goals and their disciplines with those in leadership, thus giving a model and example of ways to grow in our walk with God. Pete worked out his goals for the next year. He presented them to his staff and the board. Among them were: 1. Regular, unhurried time in God's Word for personal growth and blessing. 2. Prayer time that wasn't rushed or mechanical but heart to heart with God. 3. Focused time with his wife and with his family. Letting them know that he was not married to the ministry. The church would not be his mistress. 4. He would be faithful in giving to the Lord's work. He figured out a percentage that he wanted to commit to giving to the church and to missions and Christian agencies that we were already supporting. Pete felt good about being honest, open, and vulnerable.

We have since learned that to have meaningful relationships, there needs to be openness, honesty, and vulnerability going both ways. If I am vulnerable with a woman and she never shares her heart with me, that is a sign that this relationship cannot go deep. To go any deeper has potential for me to share too much of my heart and, in the end, be hurt or betrayed.

We had five wonderful years in this church and then a change, unknown to us, was brewing under the surface. After prayer meeting one night Pete had the shock of his life. He was met in the foyer with anger, criticism, and faultfinding. To our surprise, there had been a restlessness among a very few people of the church. Now he was confronted, "Pete, you have to get this church to grow dynamically like our sister church down the road. You have three to six months to grow us explosively or you are out of here. We used to be the flagship church of this denomination. We have to get back to those days."

What could we possibly do with this complete blind side? We had been given an impossible task. We were disheartened and confused. Pete's answer to this criticism "We believe that Jesus is the Chief

Shepherd of the church. It is in His hands if we grew explosively or not. Did God's Word not say that Christ would build His church (Matthew 16:18)? Was it not the Holy Spirit who would convict, convince, and draw people to Jesus? Did not Jesus say that, "No one can come to me unless the Father who sent me draws them" (John 6:44)? We believed our call was to plant the seed of the gospel, to water the seed with prayer, counting on God to give the increase for that seed to bring forth fruit. We were also called as a pastor couple to feed the sheep, care for the hurting, rejoice with those that rejoice and weep with those that weep.

Our calling was made plain before we even accepted the idea of pastoring this church. Pete had told the search committee that he was a shepherd not a rancher! The search committee at that time had said that was exactly what they were looking for. A shepherd leads with love; a rancher drives by force. We felt we were doing the best we knew how to be the shepherds we were called to be. We had given our all to the work of this church.

Pete tried to reason about our call, our gifting given by God. No amount of dialogue, discussion or heart pleading would change the criticism and the ultimatum. The die had already been cast; the decision had already been made. This kind of agenda matched what Pete had read in an article by Richard Foster. He called it the curse of the modern day church culture, where everything is centered around the ABC's of Church Success: Attendance, Building, and Cash. In other words, if attendance is growing, buildings are being built and are bursting at the seams, and adequate and abundance of cash is flowing, then God is blessing.

When we heard of these ABC's from Richard Foster, it immediately triggered our minds. This is what we were battling against. This focus is not what we had given our lives to accomplish. Pete asked God, "What is your focus for our ABCs"? God gave him this answer. God's heart for us was for "Availability, Brokenness, and Connection; Connection with God first and then with people." We have henceforth, sought to live our lives with this foundational focus as our bedrock, out of which flows ministry.

Our hearts and minds were thrown into confusion. Everything had been going so very well for five years in the church. Our two Sunday morning services were identical. Our evening service was more relaxed with good fellowship and connection. Now it seemed that all that came to a screeching halt. We didn't know who to talk to or what to do with this agenda. Pete had heard Lyle Schaller, a respected authority on church leadership issues, say, "Most pastors who leave churches under pressure, do so because of two or three people, regardless of the size of the church." Pete thought he would never let that happen. Now this situation had the seed of doing just that. Of course we cried out to God, we prayed constantly, searched the scriptures and asked God to have mercy on us. Behind our backs, there began a campaign to discredit Pete's reputation, to slander, falsely accuse and betray. People told us later what they knew far before we knew it. So much was going on that we were not even aware of. We found ourselves surprised, shocked, and blind-sided.

Campus Crusade had asked us months before this, if we would lead a group of about fifty Canadians on a Jesus Film Outreach to Mexico. They wanted us to be their teachers, their pastor couple, and to also experience a Jesus Film Outreach for ourselves. We left on that trip with heavy hearts because of the church situation. We were confused, hurt beyond belief, and felt the deep pain of betrayal. All we knew was to take one step at a time, trusting Jesus and asking Him to guide our lives and to look after our beloved church people and use us in Mexico.

Well, Mexico was like a fresh new opportunity. Pete taught the group every morning on subjects that would deepen their walk with Jesus. We prayed with them, listened to their life concerns, and counseled them. It was a rich time of blessing and sharing. We joined a small team that would go each night into a different neighbourhood to share the message of Jesus' love through the Story of Jesus, beautifully told on film.

We grew to love our Mexican driver. He came every afternoon to take us to our new place to show the Jesus Film. One night he asked us if we would come to his home and have supper with his family. We gladly accepted this opportunity. I couldn't get over how small and primitive the home was and how many children they had. They were so happy to share what they had with us. We asked God to protect our physical system as we ate their food. Oh, how we sought to love these people to Jesus. They slept in hammocks at night. There was lots of laughter as Pete and I tried to get into the double hammock. We finally made it. Pete spoke every Sunday in churches, at a pastor's conference, and at their prayer meetings. We saw God open spiritual eyes and people responding so beautifully with the simple gospel of Jesus Christ. Our hearts were overflowing. We faxed a couple of messages home to our church to tell them of God's answer to their prayers for us.

Soon it was time to leave these wonderful new friends in Mexico and face the situation of a church in crisis. The first thing we heard was that there had been false accusations about us going to Mexico. The rumor was that we had gone to the World Figure Skating Championships in Edmonton instead and just pretended that we went to Mexico. Our faxed messages were all lies we made up. We couldn't believe how ridiculous this was. We had our airline tickets; the people who had taken us to the airport were friends from the church. Plus we had been with a group of fifty people, who could all testify that we had indeed been in Mexico and our faxed messages were the truth of God's hand of blessing. We had to just trust God with this rumor. These were the kinds of false accusations we were going to be facing.

There was a devastating letter that was circulated among an ever-increasing number of people in the church and eventually to people from other churches. I never saw the letter. However, the accusations of lying, stealing, giving false reports were all in there. The claim was, that Pete was not a man of integrity. Oh, how that stung our hearts. Pete had built his life on the principles of honesty and truth telling. Those who were part of this letter belonged to a small group that was committed to ending our ministry at Central Heights.

We could have written David's words in Psalm 56:1-6, "Be merciful to me, O God, for men hotly pursue me; all day long they press their attack. When I am afraid, I will trust in you. In God, whose word I praise; I will not be afraid. What can mortal man do to me?"

During all this confusion at the church our extended family was going through a crisis. Pete's brother Henry's wife, had just died. Pete, as her pastor took the funeral. What an honour to hear her six kids give such loving tributes to their mother. Six months later, Henry died of a sudden heart attack. Pete had lost his oldest brother, the one who led him to Jesus. Henry was Pete's best friend and mentor. And now, in the heat of the church crisis he was asked to officiate at Henry's funeral. Pete preached every Sunday during the church problems, and now, while grieving the loss of his beloved brother. The Sunday before Henry's funeral, Pete was going up the steps into his office, when a dissenting member caught up to Pete and said, "You lied to the elder board." Pete was shocked. Pete asked in what way had he lied? The answer was, "When you gave your report after the Billy Graham School of Evangelism, you gave us your yearly goals. You told us how much you planned to give to the church that year. I have checked the records and you have not kept your promise." Pete said, "I said what I was trusting God to give to His work, which includes our church, plus a number of missionaries we personally support. And, if you will look back to last year, I gave a large amount for the Thanksgiving offering, which I was planning to do again this year." None of Pete's explanation made any difference to our accusers. The rumor continued that Pete was not a man of integrity. Here Pete stood grieving his dear brother's sudden death and having to preach in the midst of his sorrow and now, instead of sympathy, there were more accusations.

Oh how deep the betrayal went. What gave this person the right to go into the financial files and find out what Pete's giving was? Why would such a former friend be so full of bitterness, anger, and false accusation?

At this time someone gave us this article called The Pain of Betrayal.

"Betrayed!" "Father, forgive them, for they know not what they do." If there were ever a binding contract to sign before entering the ministry, the fine point would include: "The undersigned acknowledges that the pastoral ministry may be hazardous and subject the undersigned to expressions of animosity, including slander, misrepresentation, and betrayal.

Being betrayed is so profoundly painful. Few pastors can talk about it, yet if they do open up they can't stop talking about what happened to them. Let's admit what most seminary classes and church leadership seminars skip over, being betrayed is fairly common for godly leaders. David had his Absalom, Paul had his Demas and Alexander the coppersmith, Jesus had his Judas.

What makes each case of betrayal so painful, is that someone who knows your heart – who knows your longings and character – turns from that and chooses to believe that you are really dangerous. The mind freezes as it tries to grasp how a friend, someone who knows you deeply, intimately, could turn on you and attack you. Michael Card wrote and sang: "Only a friend can betray a friend, a stranger has nothing to gain. Only a friend comes close enough to ever cause so much pain." by Kevin Miller

This article gave us insight into what we were facing and the comfort to know that others had been betrayed and understood what we were going through. God was bringing us into the dark night of the soul, into wilderness wandering, sleepless nights, pain filled days of choosing to trust God rather than to fear. Our pain could not be described, only lived out one step at a time, letting Jesus lead the way.

There was a Christian Retreat Center on the Island of Bermuda. Pete had been asked to be their Prophet in Residence for one week. He would teach at the morning chapels and then be open to people's need for counsel, prayer or encouragement during the retreat. Pete had been given full approval to take a Sunday off and spend this glorious week in Bermuda. When those in opposition to Pete heard about this opportunity they told Pete he could not go and if he did there would be serious consequences. Pete caved in and sent me on ahead. I had to find my way from the airport to the retreat center. Nothing had been arranged (a story in itself). I had to take the first chapel and felt totally out of my area of gifting. I was so glad to see Pete arrive. We did have a wonderful time at this retreat center. God blessed in spite of our churning hearts. We swam in the deep turquoise ocean and soaked in the magnificent beauty of this British Island. When it came right down to it, it wouldn't have made any difference if we had stayed away for a month. The lies and false accusations were like feathers thrown to the wind. They could never be gathered back. People in the community knew more about what was going on at our church than we did.

We talked to our kids on the phone by the hour. They had all lived the life of a pastor. They were not only caring listeners; they had helpful advice for us. They were safe, loved us unconditionally, knew of the pressures of being a pastor, and would listen to our broken hearts.

We noticed the silence and distancing of some people who clearly were our supporters. I told Pete at one time that their silence was deafening. No one on the elder board was brave enough to speak up and say, "This is wrong. We are letting the pastor that we voted for 100% to be our shepherd leader, be crucified for small offences that he had totally cleared up. I, for one, will not let this unbelievable charade continue under my watch." No one spoke those words. Silence and protection of their own reputation was what predominated. We remembered Martin Luther King's statement, "In the end I was hurt more by the silence of my friends than by the words of my enemies." In many ways it seemed to me that this whole problem started as a small snowball at the top of a hill. Gradually that snowball started rolling down the hill, gathering speed and more snow. It felt like we were close to having a huge avalanche wipe us out. And there seemed to be nothing we could do to stop it.

I did have a faithful friend with whom I could trust my heart. I shared with her deeply. She didn't have simple answers or give me a Bible verse that would solve everything. She walked with me in integrity and wisdom. Today, Susan is still my dear friend. We still deeply share hearts about the trials and the blessings of our lives. Finally, the leaders of the denomination stepped in and held a church-wide meeting.

The date for the church meeting was set. Neither Pete nor I felt good about this meeting, but we couldn't go over the heads of the denominational leaders to cancel it. The Thursday before this Sunday night church-wide meeting was to be held, the phone rang. It was our son Kim calling from Toronto, where he was pastoring. He said, "Mom, are you and Dad busy Saturday night?" I said, "No, what do you have in mind?" Then Kim said, "Could you pick me up at the Vancouver airport? I'm coming to be with you and support you for that church wide meeting?" Pete cried that whole day for this unexpected, expensive, unconditional love of our son. Kim came to church with us Sunday morning wearing a suit. Suits were not worn in his church in Toronto. He didn't want to be a stumbling block in any way so brought his suit along. He was our tall son. I stood in his shadow as he put his arm around me during the morning service. After the sermon, he walked with Pete and me to the foyer as we always did at the end of every service. Kim stood with us as our literal bodyguard. We felt his love and protection in a profound way. Our daughter and husband and baby boy also came from Kelowna, BC (a four- hour ride) for this meeting. Bruce tended the baby at the back while our two kids sat with us in the front row, guarding us. Words cannot express what the love of our beloved kids meant to us. They knew us better than anyone. They knew their dad was a man of integrity, honesty, and truth speaking. They were bleeding with us.

Eight hundred people turned out for that meeting that would determine our future. Forty four people spoke that night. Some of the first to speak were very strongly against us and had their case clearly defined. They went beyond the given parameters and were asked to sit down and stop talking. They wouldn't, and no one made them. Some we thought would clearly support us, but were weak in their presentation and in the end they guarded their reputation instead of speaking up. Some of our strongest supporters were just silent.

There was one dear soft-spoken professional man, who went to the microphone and gave the most profound speech in our defence. He pointed out the wrong that had been done to us; the false accusations, the wrongness of the anonymous letter and the seriousness of touching God's servant. Finally, I thought, someone has spoken some words of truth and dared to do it in a public setting. To this day we honour this dear man for his boldness, which had consequences for him as well. God gave us these friends, who walked with us through all the crisis, who stepped up to speak their mind to our hearts, to pray for us and to be safe, tested friends that we could share our hearts with. They shone like bright stars in a very dark night. Oh, how wonderfully God used them in our lives then and now as best friends. We ask God to reward them, as there is no way we can thank them enough.

The meeting didn't accomplish anything but more confusion and more pain. Some people came to us after and asked our forgiveness; saying they hadn't spoken the truth that was in their heart. Others said when they got up to speak they couldn't say what was on their mind, or that they were going to speak up but just didn't. This situation is best summed up in the words of, Edmund Burke, who many years ago said, "The only thing necessary for the triumph of evil is for good men to do nothing."

After the meeting was over we got in our car. Our family, present with us at that meeting, traveled with us until 2:00 a.m. to get to our daughter's home in Kelowna. We talked, cried, and debriefed the whole way. What therapy for us. Can you imagine how hard it would have been to have gone home alone and to sit in our living room speechless in each other's arms? What a Godsend these kids of ours were. Eventually there was some laughter and some wise words spoken. And we began to feel like we just might live through all of this.

That night, Pete and I prayed together before we went to sleep. We never failed to close a day praying in each other arms. That night Pete started to pray. He said, "God, tonight I have a problem with you. I don't understand your will in this whole mess." I was proud of Pete that he could be that honest with God. The next morning we went for a walk in the beautiful orchard. Pete began praying again. He said, "Dear God, I'm back to trusting you." "Lord, to whom shall we go? You have the words of eternal life" (John 6:68). You said: "I am the way, the truth and the life" (John 14:6).

Back home there were many, many long board meetings. It seemed like everyone was lost and confused. I identified with Jesus' words on the cross when he prayed, "Father, forgive them for they do not know what they are doing" (Luke 23:34). I really think the existing leaders of the church were in confusion and indecision. They were in way over their heads and did not know what to do! No one was brave enough to stand up and say, "This is wrong. We must speak up and do what is honest and right." By now, different close friends began to write letters to the board, pleading with them to look at the big picture to see the man of God and the preacher of the Word Pete really was. Others prepared their requests and went in person to meet with the board. It seemed it was to no avail.

We had heard the following message from Charles Swindoll. He talks about Paul being falsely accused and criticized in 2 Corinthians 10-13. The accusations were: 1. Paul wasn't a good preacher. 2. He was a hypocrite. 3. He was an incapable leader. Swindoll then goes on to give advice on how to act when falsely criticized: 1. Readily admit when you know you are wrong. 2. Humbly stand firm where you know you are right. 3. Calmly rest your case with God.

Pete and I had been leading a care group that was made up of broken, needy people from the church. We loved them, prayed with them, and shared the Word with them. They, in turn, ministered to us. They knew a few details about the crisis we were in and lifted up our arms. Diane, a part of this group was a twice widowed lady. She became another dear friend who carried my heart with love and tenderness throughout our trials and to this day.

One day Pete had a troubling, disappointing phone call. Because of that call, we were late for the care group meeting and he was too upset to face the group. He said, "You go in. I can't go in. I'm going for a walk." My heart bled for him. There was so little I could do to really help him. I told the group about the phone call and Pete just feeling like he couldn't face anyone. They gathered around me as we all poured out our hearts in prayer for Pete. It was cold outside, so he came in shortly. Once again the group gathered around him and prayed for him. This group stood firm throughout the whole crisis. They were one of the groups who wrote letters and met with the elder board.

It was suggested that Pete and one of the dissenters meet with a reconciling mediator to see if they could come to some understanding, forgiveness, and reconciliation. We prayed much if this would be God's will for us to do. There was willingness and desire on Pete's part to do almost anything for understanding and reconciliation to happen. Our dear friend and former boss, Dr. Hildebrand, was chosen by others to be that mediator. The member in opposition to Pete asked if he was willing to have Dr. Hildebrand hear some negative things about me? Pete said, "I want the truth to come out. If I'm blind to something I want to be shown my faults and be willing to repent of them."

These meetings went on for many weeks. Finally, Dr. Hildebrand said, "I think it is time we meet together. I think we are ready for reconciliation." Pete was overjoyed as he left for that meeting. But it turned out to be a complete disaster. More anger, more false accusations, more bitterness was levied at Pete. Dr. Hildebrand was shocked at what was happening and closed the meeting down. Pete came home very disappointed. That night the phone rang with Dr. Hildebrand on the line. He said, as he wept, "I'm so sorry Pastor Pete; I thought he was ready to reconcile. You came with a broken, soft heart. He, on the other hand, was on a warpath". He then added, "If I could state one fault of yours, it would be that you trust people too much." Then he quickly added: "I'd rather see you err on the side of trust."

Another friend said, "All the false accusations were never proven to be right and didn't hold to the truth. Just think, you came though all those attacks with a clean record." We knew this was true but we were also willing to be found guilty if we truly were in the wrong and needed to make things right. A friend told us, "You both were like Shadrach, Meshach and Abednego in Nebuchadnezzar's fiery furnace. You came through the fire without getting burned and there is not a smell of smoke on you (Daniel 3: 1-27)." That rang a bell with us. During the fire Jesus stood with us and protected us and we came through the fire broken but alive.

People were closely watching us as to how we would react. We didn't know it but our lives, our humility, and our responses were preaching a living sermon. Many couldn't get over how solidly Pete preached all during this crisis time and never used the pulpit to get even with people. God was with us even when we felt everything was falling apart.

We were asked to be the speakers at the Campus Crusade Annual Conference in Whistler, BC. We were totally honoured but felt so inadequate. We spoke to the whole group of around 400 missionaries with Campus Crusade from all across Canada. We were then asked to break out into sessions where I would speak to the men and Pete to the women on "Loving your Spouse." I had already written a paper for my married boys on "How to Love your Wife." I took that material and reworked it and presented it to the men. I had no idea the high calibre of spiritual leaders that I was speaking to. God gave liberty and I shared my heart with these teachable men. I gave each a copy of the letter I had written to my boys. One city leader and member of the board tells me that he still has the booklet and reads it over every so often. God used us in our brokenness and in our willingness to share our hearts with this fine group of people who had given their lives to follow and serve Jesus.

During this time, a singing group called the Continentals, came to our church to present a concert. Our daughter and husband and their young son were staying with us and I felt they would appreciate an evening alone, so I decided to go. I sat up in the balcony and was being quite anonymous. God gave me a special gift that night. In the midst of all the upbeat happy songs they gently sang this song:

HEAL MY HEART

Words have been spoken,

Vows have been broken

Promises made are yet to be kept

A family divided,

love seems one sided.

Night after night, alone I have wept.

(Chorus)

Heal my heart.

Take away my pain.

As I choose to forgive and I learn how to live

With the hurt that has wounded my soul.

Heal my heart, heal my heart.

Friends have rejected, other expected

More than I'm able to give but I've tried.

My heart is dismayed.

Trust is betrayed.

Night after night I ask myself why?

Down on my knees, I am asking You please.

Whatever you do Lord, do this for me. Heal my heart.

This song spoke to my heart so deeply. I sobbed and sobbed as they so beautifully sang it. God touched my wounded heart. I went to the group and asked them if there was any way I could get a copy of this song. I told them how deeply it touched my heart. They could see my pain. The young man at the control booth said, "Here, take this copy. It is our gift to you." I took it home and played it over and over again. How could one song so completely express what was going on in my heart? When Pete would be in a long board meeting, I would put this song on, get on my knees and let this song sooth my soul and direct my thoughts. I loved the part about "choosing to forgive and learning to live with the pain that had wounded my soul." Yes, those choices were what I was seeking to do. Forgive and live wounded. Another part of the song, put it in words I hadn't been able to: "Friends have rejected, others expected more than I am able to give, but I've tried." This song would have a much larger impact in our lives than we could ever imagine.

During our crisis, our son Brent and family were living in Milan, Italy. They were also going through very difficult times. I felt like I needed to go to them, love them and hear their hearts if they wanted to share. I had one request. I wanted Brent to take me to Venice. During that long train ride to Venice, Brent poured out his heart to me. So much brokenness. So much disappointment and confusion.

When I got back home, I found Pete in a terrible state. While I was away, the elder board met on their own, to discuss what should be done with their pastor. Pete was told he would be phoned when the meeting was over. It was a night of torture for Pete. Why were these men doing what God's Word plainly says not to do? " If you have ought with your brother, you go to him." (Matt 18) You don't meet behind closed doors to discuss his faults.

Pete waited and waited but the phone didn't ring. The minutes passed by so slowly and I wasn't there to hold up his arms in this difficult battle. Finally after the meeting had gone on for five hours, the phone did ring. The results of the meeting would be shared with him in a meeting the next morning. When he asked for a hint of what to expect the elder said he was too tired to talk now but Pete didn't have to worry. With that, the conversation ended and a long sleepless night followed for Pete.

The next day Pete did meet with the members of the elder executive. These men plainly did not know how to pull things back together to save the church from disaster. Pete decided after talking with the elder executive that morning that we needed to resign. This time he had worked hard to reconcile and bring healing to broken relationships. I now knew that staying and trying to work things through was worse than resigning quickly. It was a long slow death. We had worked ten months to resolve these problems and we were getting nowhere. Pete was wearing out. The approaching avalanche was about to sweep us off our feet and bury us. His preaching was still strong, and most of the people of the church didn't know there was a problem. Some did. We could not go on like this. If the leaders of the church would not stand with us and support us, we were done!

During this time we began to hear some of our supporters telling us that a disturbing statement was going around the church and around town. It was a lethal, underground statement that went like this: "If you heard the other side of the story you would not support Pete either." We asked what the other side of the story was and no one would or could tell us anything further. This kind of statement is so devastating. It encourages people's minds to go in many different directions, wondering where Pete had failed. He finally went to one of the leading elders and asked him, "Is there another side to the story? I want to hear it. If there is something I have done wrong I want to make it right." The elder said, "I know of no other side of the story. I don't know what these people are talking about." Pete then told him: "You have a responsibility at the business meeting tonight to put a stop to this kind of statement. You need to make a plea to the people to stop this kind of communication." But he didn't. In reality, the only audience we needed to please was God Himself. Somehow we felt His "well done" even in the fire and in the darkness.

In mid December Pete read our resignation letter. He told the church that we would be joining Campus Crusade for Christ with the job description of Director of Pastoral Care and Church Relationships. The Canadian headquarters would be about thirty minutes from the new house we were building. Pete said our resignation would take effect in three months. His whole hearted desire was to help the church through this transition time. He was so committed to the church, the body of Jesus Christ, His Bride, and he didn't want to see it split in two. His prayer was for reconciliation, healing, and the mending of brokenness. We didn't see that happen, but we did feel that people got to see us trusting God in the storm. How to respond to the difficulties of life is often more powerful than any spoken words. People were stunned, shocked, and very upset. A few vocal men had won and we were leaving. We were in shock but we kept getting up each day, reaffirming the fact that we would trust in God, though He slay us. The Sunday that Pete read his resignation letter was a sad Sunday for us and for the church. There were many, many tears, but the end had come. We tried to comfort others and ourselves. But the painful reality was there. Eventually pain gets stamped into your passport. We were finished trying to resolve and work through the issues.

The day after Pete read his resignation letter, our house sold. It had been on the market for quite some time. The new owners wanted possession in two weeks. Oh no! This couldn't be happening. We were worn out and bleeding from the intense spiritual and relational battle. We didn't have the strength to pack up our home in two weeks It was December and we had no place to go.

Dear friends were leaving for Arizona for three months and gave us their house in which to stay. It was a frantic two weeks of packing up our four bedroom home, putting what we wanted into storage, and keeping out what we would need while staying in our friend's home for three months. We quickly chose a good builder to build our new house. We had purchased the lot and were ready in January to begin our retirement home, we thought. We would have never done this if we had known what would happen at the church. But God has shown us His ways are best.

Pete met with the Campus Crusade leaders, and there was a definite excitement about the assurance that we would join their staff. He had spoken at their conference and a number of other opportunities. They were looking for a couple just like us. At this point we were amazed that anyone would want us.

After our move, we experienced our last ever Christmas Eve

presentation. We had done our Original Christmas Eve for thirty seven years. When it was over we got in our car and headed south to spend Christmas with our oldest son and family in California. What a soothing balm of love and acceptance these loved ones were. We did fun things with them and caught ourselves laughing once again. We then drove on to Arizona to stay with dear friends from our church. We drove with them to the Grand Canyon to view it during the winter season. There was snow on the ground, everything was closed down, but I wanted to walk to the curio shop to see if the Bible verse was still near the entrance. I thought by now someone would have objected to it being there and it would have been taken down. But it was there! Oh how my soul rejoiced. I love the verse carved into a plaque on a stone that protrudes and looks over the Grand Canyon. "Sing to God, Sing praises to His name: Lift up a song to Him who rides upon the clouds; His name is the Lord, Exult before Him" (Psalm 68:4). My heart sang with prayer, "Thank you God that you reign supreme. You are in control." When we got back to our friend's home they told us right away that they wanted to support us financially when we began our ministry with Campus Crusade. We were so surprised. We hadn't even begun to think about the need for us to raise our own support. What a new chapter we were embarking on.

Our time away was so delicious but things at the church had not changed upon our return. We did our best to seek to bring healing and hope to the church body. Our last three months as pastor of this church were filled with many failed attempts, on the part of many well meaning members of the church to try to get the board of elders to ask us to stay on as pastor. We did not encourage any of that at all. It is rarely wise for a pastor to rescind his resignation. We continued to perform our pastoral duties with diligence and passion, even though we felt deeply hurt by the betrayal that we had experienced.

The new elder executive and the board tried hard to deal rightly with some of the key perpetrators of the false accusations and rumors. Some were threatened to be removed from church membership if they did not ask forgiveness for their wrongs towards Pete. Rarely do forced apologies produce lasting positive results, because they lack the heart attitude of genuine repentance.

During our last full month of ministry at the church, we had booked Dr. James Cook from Colorado to be our main speaker at our missions conference. He knew nothing about the turmoil going on in our lives and the church. He had been through a very painful time in his last large Baptist Church in California, before he retired from pastoral ministry. When he first met me in Pete's office, before the Sunday morning service, he looked at me and in his gentle way he took my head in his big hands and said, "Oh sweetie. You are a hurting woman." I just melted into tears at his truthful words. Pete had told him just a little about our resignation and the reasons for it before the service. The church was filled that morning. Sitting beside Pete on the platform, he leaned over to him and whispered these words: "Just look at all these people. You're not a failure. They are here because of your God-blessed ministry. Don't ever forget it." He proved to be a real God send to us for those few days. When we took him to see our new home under construction, he stood there with us on the main floor of our unfinished house. He spread out his big hands, one on top of the other, and said to us, "Pete and Shirley, remember that everything in life is Father-filtered." We will never forget that. Later that day we took him to the Campus Crusade headquarters in Langley to show him this new building and Pete's new office. On our way out of the building he said, "Remember, Pete, at your church you were the big fish in a little pond; here you will be a little fish in a big pond. That will be a big change for you." And it was.

Pete found great release and joy in helping build our new home. His love of framing houses had never left him. Our contractor was very willing to let him work when he was able to. He wanted him to keep track of his hours. and he would subtract that off the cost of the house. How refreshing for him to be at the end of a hammer, seeing progress, nails being pounded in, and work accomplished. God has unexpected ways of bringing release to our life's pressures. We were building a ranch style home with everything on one floor, our retirement home we thought. Our kids were far from us. Bevan and Rebecca were pastoring in California; Brent and Denise were missionaries in Italy; Kim and Darlene were pastoring in Toronto; and Bruce and Kathy lived in Winnipeg, Manitoba, where they had moved with their band to be salt and light to the arts community there. We thought that we would eventually retire in Abbotsford and let our kids come to us.

Soon our three months had come to a close and it was time to say our farewell. This was a very difficult time for us and for most of the church people, who still loved us so much. We in turn had poured our hearts into their lives. The church had a beautiful farewell service for us. We both spoke. Pete's message was one of healing. Mine was perhaps too honest as I told of the pain, betrayal, and false accusations we had endured. I also added that I, too, believed God would restore this church and healing would come. After the service, a luncheon was planned in the fellowship hall, with a chance for an open mic time, when people could bless and encourage us. We were shocked at how crowded the fellowship hall was. People were standing all around the walls as the seats were full. Person after person approached the mic and told of the blessing our ministry had been to them. How Pete had married them, led them to Jesus, officiated at their father's funeral, counseled them, helped to save their marriage, and on and on it went. Why this huge outpouring of love when the leaders could not support us? What would happen to this beloved church?

My thought was, "Some people love us too much. We are not that good. Other people hate us too much. We are not that bad." We were humans, with clay feet, who were trying with all our heart, soul, mind, and strength to serve and please God. After all He is the audience of one whom we seek to honor and hear His "Well done." We have and will make mistakes but our daily choice has been to be true to God's Word and His call upon our lives. We had sought with all our hearts to live out the high ideals of Romans 12:18-19, "If it is possible as far as it depends on you, live at peace with everyone. Do not take revenge my friends, but leave room for God's wrath, for it is written; It is mine to avenge; I will repay says the Lord." With that declaration, we found peace and rest.

We got many cards of love and farewell. This card kind of sums up what a lot of people were writing and saying, "Dear Pastor Pete, You have journeyed through a battleground and are on the victory side! We are SO glad!! Yet, each day is still a day of healing and struggle. We pray for continual restoration and rejuvenation for you. Thank you for being a great example of faithfulness and courage in the face of adversity. You truly are a pastor to us! In the gratitude journal of my heart, your name comes up again and again."

As we drove home that night, we were thankful for such an outpouring of love, but in shock as to what was really happening. I told Pete, "That felt like we just attended our own funeral. The only things missing were our caskets."

Chapter Nine

WRESTLING IN THE DARK

Abbotsford BC 1997-98

"Faith does not always come by quiet contemplation. It is sometimes born among the raging of questions that have no answers." Reny Benkin.

When all was said and done and the dust had settled, I felt an overwhelming sense of shock. I was shocked at what Christians had said and done. I was shocked and disappointed at what my God had not done. I was sure in the end there would be victory for the church and for us. Never had we prayed and fasted, relied upon Scripture, and searched our hearts as much as we had done throughout this whole crisis. We totally put our trust in God and were confident the victory would be His. I claimed Psalm 34:7, "The angel of the Lord encamps around those who fear him, and he delivers them." I was waiting and expecting the deliverance but it never came. In my short sightedness, God did not keep His word.

Pete had more problems forgiving people. My problem was with my God. I had never before had this kind of reaction toward God. I knew God could have delivered us. It felt like God was silent, distant, and uncaring. It felt like I was plunged into a dark pit of emotional, spiritual, psychological, and physical darkness. I was living in a world of shock that was continually before me. The crashing disappointment was at the forefront of all my thoughts which turned to horror and unbelief. I would replay times of betrayal, false accusations and slander, and shuddered to think of what we had just gone through.

I found myself wrestling with my God in this dark uncertain time. I knew my Bible well. I had a deep relationship with God. I had trusted Him and found Him faithful through many trials of life, but at the age of sixty-one something snapped. It seemed to me that I was out of control. I tried to read my Bible and it actually made my condition worse. All God's promises seemed to cause me to feel angry toward God. Once again I was dealing with how different God's ways are than my ways. During the crises at the church I claimed God's promises, but I felt so lonely, isolated, and abandoned in the battle. My soul did not respond to the promises of God. They seemed to mock me and my faith. It just didn't work for me, at this time.

My core value has always been deep integrity, truth speaking, and honesty. If family or friends would ask how I was doing, I would have to say that I was struggling. To only a few could I share how deep my struggle really was. Pete stood tall and faithful to God and to me through the whole crisis.

Unlike Michigan, all through this church crisis, I was not disappointed with Pete. I honored and blessed and walked side-by-side with him. Now when it was all over, I could share anything with him, no matter how dark and unreasonable it was, and he would not put me down or give me a quick fix. We had learned how to go below the surface with each other and how to feel safe regardless of the situation. Oh, what a blessing it was to have a beautiful, mutually vulnerable marriage that could stand the most difficult of times.

Pete didn't understand my wrestling with God and neither did I, but I could not deny that it was there. It seemed no amount of knowledge could change my feelings. I did take comfort with Job as he sat on his ash heap, totally shocked with God's actions, and totally confused with the ways of God.

Wrestling with God is not a new response to the ways of God. Abraham wrestled with God over Sodom and Gomorrah (Gen.18:16-23). Jacob wrestled with God (Genesis 32). Moses often wrestled with God, and even persisted until God changed His mind and gave Moses his request (Exodus 33). Jesus agonized over God's plan in Gethsemane, asking God three times if the cup of sorrow and death could be removed from Him. Each time He quickly added, "Nevertheless, not my will but Thine be done" (Matthew 26:36-46).

Pete and I were talking with our Godly mentor one day. Pete said, "I am having more trouble with forgiving humans. Shirley is having more trouble with being angry with God." His response took me back when he said, "I'm glad that Shirley is angry with God instead of Pete, because He can handle her anger much better than you could, Pete." That he wasn't shocked and he didn't give me a quick Bible verse to end my wrestling, made me want to hug him.

I cried buckets of tears. I could not stop crying. I wondered as God gathered my tears in His bottle; did He have to get a few extra bottles to hold all my tears. "You keep track of all my sorrows. You have collected all my tears in your bottle. You have recorded each one in your book" Psalm 56:8 (TLB). God was so totally aware of my sorrow. He cared about each teardrop I shed.

Tears are God's release valve for our emotions. Tears are a gift. We need to take time to taste our tears and know they are a language God understands. How much healthier it is to cry than to hold everything in until it explodes in an unhealthy way. Of course, I wasn't thinking these thoughts at this time. I quite plainly was crying out of my pain and loss. Charles Dickens said, "Crying opens the lungs, washes the countenance, exercises the eyes, and softens the temper. So cry away!" I liked that quote. Someone understood and valued my tears. "My tears have been my food day and night" (Psalm 42:3). King David experienced what I was going through. I could relate to many Psalms. I was so thankful for David's honest Psalms of lament, which comprise more than half of the Psalms he wrote.

I couldn't pray. I tried, but I was prayed out. I had said everything I knew what to say to God. I had poured out my soul to God for months and months. Now I was struck dumb. I did keep my promise to God to pray for my children and grandchildren daily but that was it.

A tremendous comfort to me was how Pete took me in his arms every night and he prayed for me. He was in deep pain as well, but he could pray, and was so sensitive to my soul's unexplainable needs. I was thankful that the night of our wedding day, we knelt by our bed and prayed. And we have never stopped praying together for all our married lives. Sometimes we needed to resolve a disagreement between us before we prayed, but we always prayed. This habit of nightly prayer was to be one anchor for me during this time. This was a great gift to me from my husband, my best friend. Deep inside and underneath my wrestling, this discipline alone did give me hope.

Nights were so hard for me. My insomnia went into overdrive and my overactive mind could not turn off the replay button, no matter what I tried. One morning when I woke up I thought of the Footprints poem. It is a story of a person who could see Jesus' footprints right beside him as he journeys through his life. And then he experiences a very difficult, dark time in his life and is surprised to see that there is only one set of Footprints. He asked Jesus why there was only one set of Footprints when he was walking through the darkest part of his journey. He assumed Jesus had stopped walking with him. Jesus' answer was, "It was then that I carried you." My heart leapt at that thought and I began to pray, "Jesus, carry me", over and over again.

It seemed to me that prayer was enough. Every morning and throughout the day I would stop and pray, "Jesus carry me." As I write this, the tears are rolling down my face. What a beautiful Savior I have who understands when I am sick emotionally, spiritually, psychologically, and physically and who does carry me when I don't deserve it. I was doing nothing that in my mind would be pleasing to God, but He loved me anyway. God is Love. Period. There was nothing I could do to stop Him from loving me. He loved me as much in my pit of darkness and confusion as He did when I was sharing my salvation testimony with someone. When I was well again, I would look back in amazement, thinking and feeling that this dark time was the time I experienced the unconditional, undeserved love of God more than any other time in my life.

My thoughts were also drawn to the verses in Romans 8:26-27, "the Spirit helps us in our weakness. We do not know what we ought to pray for, but the Spirit himself intercedes for us with groans that words cannot express." Oh, how I embraced those words. I would ask the Holy Spirit to pray for me, because I didn't have the words to pray. Then I found in the same chapter, Romans 8:34, "Christ Jesus...is at the right hand of God and is also interceding for us." Oh what comfort, what release to not have to force myself to have long labored prayer times, but to simply ask the Holy Spirit and Jesus to intercede for me the words I could not utter. And I rested in that.

I would often debate with God, that His ways were not good. He was not a fair God. I had many "why" questions. My wrestling with God was something I could not stop. I had to communicate with my God how I felt and why I was angry with Him. I did not feel God's anger toward me because I was being a naughty child. I felt He understood my wrestling. None of all this made any sense to me, but I was to find out later that this time of loss, anger, and disappointment with God was necessary for my spiritual and emotional wellbeing. If I had buried all these feelings and questions I may not have come through this time whole and healthy.

We did make ourselves venture out to our local theatre to go to the live performance of *Shadowlands*, the life story of C.S. Lewis, and his devastating loss of his beloved wife, Joy. His honesty with God, his agony and his wrestling were so powerful. It matched our emotions so much that Pete and I sobbed our way through that whole presentation. We were a mess and we could not hide it. Lewis shares his experiences that mirrored our own. Heaven was silent, God was distant, and no amount of begging would get God to listen and respond.

God is a relational God. He made Adam and Eve so that He could have a beautiful relationship with them. I can just imagine the joy of their evening strolls through the beautiful, uncursed Garden of Eden. After sin entered the world, God still sought out people that He could have a relationship with, people who would love Him, trust Him, and obey Him. Somewhere I heard that God would rather have me be angry with Him, even to fight with Him, than to be silent and lethargic. Relationship is not always smooth. But if it is real and growing it has to be honest and open, with God and with humans. God doesn't like plastic saints, those who wear masks and sanitize their grief before sharing it.

I know sometimes people just give up on God and give Him the silent treatment. That is the most deadly tool in building a viable growing relationship. My anger and wrestling with God later made me realize that I was engaging God as I poured out my confusions and frustrations to the God of the universe. To turn silent and unengaged would spell disaster in relationship building. We have found that to be true in our marriage as well. A few times when I have been angry with Pete or he with me, we would grow silent toward each other. We found out how deadly that can be. We decided not to use that kind of response with each other or with any other relationship. If there is a problem, Matthew 18 is clear that we must go to that person to seek to work out the problem.

Another thing I could not do was journal. How could that be? In the last church crisis in Michigan, journaling God's Word and prayer were my lifeline. What had gone so terribly wrong within my being that none of these timeless helps were of any use to me at this time? I honestly could not journal because I had no words to say. My mind was too conflicted. My heart was too wounded. My thoughts, for now could not be untangled.

I had nobody with whom I could share my confusing thoughts. I am a processor. I need to work things through in my heart and mind in community. I need to talk to people and receive their care, support, and wisdom. God gave me a few special people with whom I could be real. My friend, Susan, who went through the church crisis with us and knew more about what was going on than we knew, was so open and caring to hear my wounded heart. Sometimes I said things to her that actually scared me. How could I be so beaten down and off the rails? I would talk to process my feelings and weep while I was talking. A friend who understands your tears is much more valuable than a lot of friends who know your smile.

At one point in my confused and traumatized mind, I thought of all the different ways we had lost out. Our losses were ever before me. I finally decided to write out my losses just to clear my mind of this constant obsessive thinking. Maybe once they were written down I could empty my tangled thoughts and eventually come to accept them. The losses I experienced shook my life to its very foundations:

Losses

1. Loss of meaningful, structured ministry. The church has always been the tracks on which we have managed our ministry. It now feels like we are like an unruly train crashing through the bush, trying hard to find our tracks and stay on course.

2. Loss of a place of worship. Little did we know how much worshipping with the same church family meant to us, until it was gone.

3. Loss of significant involvement in people's lives. As pastor to people, we have always been deeply involved in their lives in

times of rejoicing and in times of trial and loss.

4. Loss of connectedness with people we loved and had come to know was a big loss. Where do I go for my laughter, my hugs, my sharing of joys and sorrows? God made us for community and tells us, "Let us consider how we may spur one another on toward love and good deeds. Let us not give up meeting together...but let us encourage one another" (Hebrews 10:24-25). He knew that we would need the church for mutual blessing and encouragement. This opportunity had been taken from me.

5. I lost my song. Music has been a large part of my life for as long as I can remember. I took classical piano as a child into my teens, then switched to playing hymns and choruses with variation and feeling. I was our church pianist while still in high school; at college I was the pianist for chapel and many travelling singing groups. When our crisis at the church began I lost my song. I didn't do it on purpose. It just wasn't there. That was a great loss for me.

6. We had lost the daily routine of life. For forty years, we knew what we were doing each day, each month and each year. We scheduled our plans over a year in advance to coincide with the other staff vacations, speaking assignments, and seminars. Now, we were faced with an ever-changing schedule, often with little notice. We constantly had to be ready to preach, pray or die!

7. Loss of understandable ministry. Now everyone wanted to know what we were doing, and where we had been. Were we keeping busy, was the most often asked question?

8. We had lost our place of prominence. We must face it. Being the pastor and wife of a large, healthy church was a position to be looked up to. Wherever we went we were well recognized, given places of honor and introduced at functions. Now, we often entered a church, and unless Pete was preaching, we were unknown and unengaged with the people there. It was very different coming in the church from the back door rather

than through the front door. Now we knew how hard it was to choose a church and become a connected part of that church. Now we knew how hard it was to be behind the curtain, not front and center of the stage.

9. Loss of reputation. Now people looked on us and wondered, "What really happened at that church"? We had no chance to explain or defend ourselves. We had to let the scattered feathers blow where they may and rest our reputation with God. In writing this I thought of Jesus who came to this earth to be our Savior, Lord and Master. Philippians 2:7 says, "But (He) made himself of no reputation, and took upon him the form of a servant, and was made in the likeness of man" (KJV). I grieved the loss of my reputation while Jesus gave up His reputation. How far off the track I was.

10. Loss of our chance to finish well. We didn't see the minefields up ahead and got blown out of the water just before the finish line, without any warning. I could not conceive of the fact that God's finish line might be different than the one I had envisioned.

11. Loss of my closeness to God. This was my most devastating loss. God felt distant and unloving. How could a God of love let all these terrible things happen to us, at age sixty? What an age old question this was, but at this time this was my journey, my reality. We had heard a grief counselor on television say that healing from any crisis in life takes three steps that all begin with the letter T. We need: 1. Talk 2. Tears 3. Time. There were not any quick fixes for my wounded soul. I was learning valuable lessons while wrestling in the dark. Of course I would not be able to see that until much later.

People were concerned for us, of course. Often women would call me to show their love, prayers, and care for me. I did appreciate each call, but what they said often left me empty or upset. One lady said, "God has taken you out of this church because He has a much greater calling for you." I could not believe this could be true. Pete and I often said to each other that this church was the best of times and the worst of times in our life. We had hearts called to pastor and nothing could be a more beautiful fulfilling call than that. Pastoring was a huge part of who we were. It was our public identity. A huge sense of loss and isolation came over us. We felt shame but didn't know why. We felt abandoned but wondered why.

Well meaning people would give me Bible verses that were meant to settle everything. Just cling to this verse and you will be okay. People were trying to help me feel different than I was feeling. They didn't like it that I was in turmoil of soul. An obligation to feel a certain way can freeze our ability to be honest and real. These people had no idea of the darkness I was walking in. In many cases people were wanting me to put a Band-Aid on my wounds and a smile on my face. I could not in all honesty do that. My heart of commitment to No Pretending couldn't fake victory. I couldn't and wouldn't wear a mask, pretending to be something I was not.

At this time someone gave me a book that changed my life during the darkest days of my wrestling with God. It is called A Grace Disguised by Jerry Sittser. I read and reread this book many times. It felt like for the first time, someone was speaking to me in a language that I could understand and spoke of some of the feelings of horror, loss, and mystery that I was feeling. Jerry had lost three family members in a horrific car crash when a drunk driver crossed the median and hit his van. His wife, young daughter, and mother were all killed. He was left with three traumatized young children. In his book he writes with No Pretending, the struggle he had with God and His ways. His honest sharing deeply touched me and made me feel like I was not alone in the struggles of my life even though my losses were very different than his were.

I had never written an author before and didn't even know if I could. I got the address of Jerry's publisher and wrote out my heart to him. I really never expected to hear back from him but it wasn't long before this letter came in the mail.

17 July 1999
Dear Mrs. Unrau,

I am deeply grateful that you would take the time to

write me about my book, A Grace Disguised. Your story was very moving to me, as well as troubling. It reminded me once again why I wrote a book about loss, not death. Your loss is incomprehensible to me. I lost three loved ones, surely a severe loss. But I have enjoyed professional success my entire adult life. My work as pastor and professor is part of who I am. I cannot imagine facing such betrayal.

That you are continuing in ministry, though along very different lines, is a testimony to God's grace working in you. Your ministry will have authority to it because it has been born out of suffering. I hope that you will continue to find grace and that your story over time will show clear evidence of God's redemptive purposes. That your kids are walking with Christ and doing some kind of ministry demonstrates that God has shown you favor.

I agree with you that most pastors are very lonely and isolated, afraid to share themselves with their congregations, too threatened and protective to share themselves with colleagues in ministry. I wish you well as you continue in this ministry.

God bless you. Sincerely, Jerry Sittser

What a balm to my soul this letter was. I read and reread it. Here was someone who had gone through such great loss and was validating my loss as important and terrible. He understood that our work in the ministry of pastor and wife is part of who we are and that it is lonely and threatening at times. He gave us hope for the future as he shares his belief that our future ministry will have authority because it has been born out of suffering. What a beautiful mantle of blessing and hope Jerry placed over our lives.

I lifted out a few of my favourite quotes from the book "A Grace Disguised":

"A devastating loss never leaves you, but it will lessen in its ability to level you."

" It is not the experience of loss that becomes the defining moment of our lives, for that is as inevitable as death, which is the last loss awaiting us all. It is how we respond to loss that matters. That response will largely determine the quality, the direction, and the impact of our lives." (p. 9)

"Catastrophic loss wreaks destruction like a massive flood. It leaves the landscape of one's life forever changed." (p. 16)

"I wanted to pray but had no idea what to say, as if struck dumb by my own pain." (p. 34)

"All I could do was let God love me, even though I hardly believed that he loved anyone, least of all me. I had no idea how I could really believe or whether I even wanted to. I had no will or desire for it. But somehow I believed that not even my weakness of faith bothered God much. God loved me in my misery. God loved me because I was miserable. I learned through that experience that nothing can separate us from his love - not even our inability to love him in return!" (p. 92)

"Joseph's life does not consist of a succession of isolated events randomly strung together but rather a story with a purpose that he does not see and will never entirely understand. I have often imagined my own story fitting into some greater scheme, the half of which I may never fathom. I simply do not see the bigger picture, but I choose to believe that there is a bigger picture and that my loss is part of some wonderful story authored by God himself. The Joseph story helps us to see that our own tragedies can be a very bad chapter in a very good book." (p. 104)

"Unforgiveness does not stop the pain. It spreads it. The process of forgiveness begins when victims realize that nothing – not justice or revenge or anything else can reverse the wrong done." (p.125)

I will forever thank Jesus and Jerry for this book and how God used his story to help me in the struggle of my story. God gave me clear evidence that He was at work and my response to all we had suffered was to simply choose to trust Him and let God work out His redemptive purpose.

This book, written on suffering and loss, was like a lifeline to me for many years. I continued to read it and find understanding, identification, some answers to my raging "why" questions, and eventually hope for the future. I felt and knew the love and care of my God, that would give me such a gift in my state of wrestling, anger, and lostness.

People were hurting at the church and they were hurting for us. What could they do to help us? I didn't know. I didn't know how to help myself. Some friends often had us over to their home to play games and have dessert. Two couples continued to do this. They wouldn't ask how we were doing. They wouldn't talk about the church although all of us were stunned, confused, and deeply hurting. We played our favorite game. We laughed, which God says is like medicine to our souls. (Proverbs 17:2) We shared about our lives and we went home feeling like we were healthy and normal enough to do that, and it was good.

Creation Calls. In my crisis time, God in His mercies opened my eyes and my heart to the glorious "Works of God." God began to speak to my heart as I went for nature walks, camera in hand. The beauty of His creation began to call my heart back to the heart of God. Abraham Lincoln said, "Never lose an opportunity of seeing something beautiful, for beauty is God's handwriting." I love photography and everywhere we went my heart was touched by the "Works of God." There are so many scriptures that speak of the greatness of God's creation.

Psalm 19:1-4 "The heavens declare the glory of God; the skies proclaim the work of His hands. Day after day they pour forth speech; night after night they display knowledge. There is no speech or language where their voice is not heard; Their voice goes out into all the earth, their words to the ends of the world."

Psalm 145:10-11, "All that you have made will praise you, O Lord; your saints will extol you."

Psalm 8:3-4, "When I consider your heavens, the work of your fingers, the moon and the stars, which you have set in place, what is mankind that you are mindful of him?"

Nehemiah 9:6, "You alone are the Lord. You made the heavens, even the highest heavens, and all their starry host, the earth and all that is on it, the seas and all that is in them. You give life to everything, and the multitudes of heaven worship you."

Isaiah 6:3, Holy, Holy, Holy, is the LORD of hosts, The whole earth is full of His glory."

On a plaque overlooking the Grand Canyon is this verse and then a poem,

"O Lord, how manifold are thy works! In wisdom Thou hast made them all; the earth is full of thy riches." Psalm 104:24

Father Almighty, wonderful Lord. Wondrous Creator, be ever adored; Wonders of nature, Sing praises to You, Wonders of wonders- I may praise too!

In honor and praise to the God who made this beautiful creation to speak to us of the glory of God and the works of His hands, I made a collection of my best pictures of God's "works" in nature. I called my book, My Best Shots. My picture of the verse over the Grand Canyon is the first page of my book. I gave this coffee table hardbound book to all my kids, to my mother and sister, and kept one for ourselves. I put this quote in the flyleaf of the book, "Great writing makes you think and then feel. Great photography makes you feel and then think." (Rich Boychuk in Through the Lens, Canadian Geographic, 1999)

Today it sits on our coffee table as a reminder of the wonderful works and ways of my God. He was continuing to carry me. God in His gracious love and tender mercies once again brought beauty out of my wrestling in bringing His amazing handiwork out of this dark time of my soul. " Unless a kernel of wheat is planted in the soil and dies it remains alone" (John 12:24, TLB). Darkness brings life! After a time, my wrestling eased. I knew who would win and I wanted God to win. I just didn't know how to get back on track with Him. I was out of ICU, but I was still in the recovery room, and would be there for much longer than I would have imagined.

Our children were solid rocks that I could depend on all during the crisis and after. Most of them were in ministry themselves at this time. They had never been through these kind of church problems but somehow they were able to journey with us. One son said, "Mom and Dad, 'GO FOR THE GOLD!' God wouldn't give you this much pain unless He had a good reason for it." I thought of the Olympics and how coveted the gold was. How could we ever find gold through all this mess? Or was God putting us through the refiner's fire to bring forth the gold, and mold us more into the image and character of Jesus?

Another son said, "Mom and Dad, all your lives you have been at the center of the stage. You have held places of prominence and importance. You have been highly valued. Now are you willing to let God put you behind the curtain for a time? Are you willing to be unknown for Jesus' sake?" Our daughter said, "I treasure moments when I'm allowed to be around brokenness on its way to healing." Another son said, "God is a wild God, you will not understand Him, but the kind of worship God treasures most is the worship of lament – the praises to God, out of a broken, confused heart." Wow, what insight. How convicting and 'right on' these kids were in many ways.

In a strange way, in the midst of my confusions and wrestling with God, I knew God had given us a situation we were to steward carefully for Him. I knew God was up to something in our lives but I certainly did not know what. My calling for now was to steward my raging, terrifying emotions well. To be honest, real, and open first with God, then my family and a few trusted others. Would I allow myself time, tears and talk? We eventually had to let it all go. That was a long and a bit-by-bit process. We had to gradually rest our case with God. We chose to believe in the sovereignty of God, even though we may never understand why.

Helen Roseveare, a great missionary doctor, spoke at Central Heights and told us her story. She gave her life for the people of the Congo, where she had worked tirelessly for many years as a physician and teacher. She was highly respected and began many clinics in the lands beyond her hospital.

One statement she made I will never forget. Civil war broke out in the Congo. She was captured by soldiers who brutally beat her and abused her. They finally left her in an abandoned cabin in the woods, planning to come back to kill her. During the hours of fear and unbelievable anguish over her treatment, God spoke to Helen's heart and asked her, "Helen, will you trust me with this terrible situation even if I never tell you the reason why I have allowed this brutality to happen?" Helen struggled for a long time with the unknown "'why" question. She finally yielded and told God she would trust Him no matter what happened. God spared her life in a miraculous way. God greatly used Helen as she wrote about her experiences and travelled the globe telling her story and encouraging people to trust God, no matter what the circumstance, or if we never understand His ways, or get the answers to our "why" questions. In summary, Helen would say, "God never uses a person greatly until He has wounded him deeply. The privilege He offers you is greater than the price you have to pay." Helen Roseveare

Our desire to see healing and reconciliation happen with us and individuals of the church did not happen. Pete individually met with person after person, seeking to come to some understanding – some sorrow and repentance on the part of those who had betrayed us – some meeting of minds. The harder he tried, the more our realization came that we could not make people repent or reconcile.

Pete and I were torn and confused as to what more we could personally do. We knew the church was hurting and in turmoil, but all our efforts were of no avail. We forgave those who had betrayed us and falsely accused us. This was an ongoing choice for quite some time. Our forgiveness was not an emotion or feeling, it was a choice and it was in obedience to God's Word. Forgiveness is me not letting another person live in my mind or dominate my life. When you forgive those who have hurt you, you take their power away to make our mind captive to the wrong they have done to us. We heard Corrie Ten Boom speak on this subject. She puts it this way, "To forgive is to set a prisoner free only to discover the prisoner was me." How powerful.

We also guarded against having a bitter spirit toward those who had turned against us. We knew the admonition in Hebrews 12:15, "See to it that no one misses the grace of God and that no bitter root grow up to cause trouble and defile many". We knew how poisonous bitterness would be to our own souls and it would grow into the hearts of those we touched. We wanted no part of that.

We finally had peace about writing a letter to the church that would be read at a church business meeting. In a way this letter would be releasing us and the church from ongoing meetings and efforts to reconcile. Here is our letter a year after our farewell from the church:

Resting Our Case With God April 20, 1998

"What does this mean to us as it pertains to this painful church experience?" It means that we are placing into God's hands the unresolved issues and relationships of the past. We have longed for complete reconciliation and restoration, but that has not happened. We realize we cannot make it happen. With this growing knowledge, we place our pain, our losses, our confusions into God's hands, and we rest it there.

This does not mean we are closing the book on the church or its people. Rather, it means we are leaving the books open before God, asking Him to work in our hearts and in others' hearts to bring about complete healing and reconciliation. This miracle of brokenness and repentance is left in God's hands and in His timing. Only God can close the books. Only God can bring about complete healing. We pray and work to this end as much as is possible in our hearts, always open to God's further working within us.

In resting our case with God, we are seeking not to focus on our pain and losses any longer. We must move on to the ministry God has called us to, with a freedom from the past. We must let this church move on to the ministry God has in the future This does not mean we will pretend that everything is resolved and totally cleared up. To do this would be living a lie and not speaking the truth in love. If this false message, that all is reconciled, were to be presented to the church body, it would not bring the lasting healing we all desire, but would bring up the age old suspicion that everything is being ignored and swept under the rug, only to be tripped on at some later date. However, we realize that we, or the present leadership, can do nothing about the outstanding issues and relationships.

It is our desire to share our resolve with people who talk to us, encouraging them to also rest their case with God. We will not be part of negative conversation about the church. When criticisms of the church come our way, we will be quick to tell people they must not talk to us, but to the leadership about their concerns. We do not want to divide the church We want to bless the new pastor and the people, trusting that the church will succeed and prosper. This church was and is s a wonderful church with many, wonderful people in it. We believe it has a great future, as it walks in integrity and brokenness before God, staying true to the Word of God. We believe that God is sovereign, faithful and good.

We seek to follow Jesus' example, "For God called you to do good, even if it means suffering, just as Christ himself suffered for you. He is your example, and you must follow in his steps. He did not retaliate when he was insulted, nor threaten revenge when he suffered. He left his case in the hands of God, who always judges fairly" (I Peter 2:21-23 TLB).

We are trusting God to work out His promises in Isaiah 43:18-19, "Forget the former things; do not dwell on the past. See, I am doing a new thing! Now it springs up; do you not perceive it? I am making a way in the desert and streams in the wasteland."

We trust Him, in His way and in His time to work something beautiful out of the pain we have all experienced. Only God can take these ashes and make something beautiful! And He will. This is the heart of our desire to rest our case with God".

After presenting the church with this letter we were amazed at how this settled our minds. We made a threefold choice as we moved forward: no bitterness, an ongoing spirit of forgiveness, and resting our case with God. We decided that the past failures would not determine who we were. It would however be beautifully woven into the fabric of our lives. We rested in that knowledge and deep conviction. These powerful choices set us free!

We took bold steps to move towards God's next assignment for us, His servants. As we joined a whole new team called Campus Crusade for Christ, God was at work in ways we could have never imagined.

Chapter Ten

Surprised by God

Campus Crusade for Christ – Power to Change 1997-2013

The currents that determine our dreams and shape our lives flow from the attitudes we nurture everyday.

We finished out our three months with the church, seeking to be obedient to the leading of God in our lives. We knew that no situation that we had been through was outside of God's ability for restoration, reconciliation or transformation. God was not blind to what was going on and in our hearts. We knew He was in control of the whole universe, including our lives and the life of this church. We continually placed both in God's hands.

Before we officially began with Campus Crusade for Christ, God had a special blessing for us. A travel agency in our city had asked us to lead a tour group to the Holy Land of Israel in the beginning of April, 1997. We agreed, making this a part of our vacation for that year. We kept that commitment, so just a few days after our farewell Sunday, Pete and I were privileged to spend seven wonderful days in Israel, along with thirty other participants from various parts of Canada. Our only responsibilities were to be the chaplain for the group. Our expenses were paid for by the travel agency. This was God's gracious gift to us "for such a time as this." It was good to be away from the church turmoil back home, even though it was never very far from our minds. Every day was full of new sights to see and new experiences to enjoy. The tour went well. We were touched to walk where Jesus walked and to read God's Word at the very spot this portion was talking about. People were upbeat, happy, and satisfied. God gave us this little bubble of time to let us know there would be life after church conflicts and He had put this date on our calendar long before we even came to this church.

Our first meetings with the Campus Crusade leadership left us excited that we were joining a staff that was filled with such passion, endless possibilities, and dreams for the world and for Pete, once we were full-time with them. What a wonderful warm, joyous welcome. They didn't look at Pete and see an "F" for failure written on his forehead. They didn't see a man who had been beaten up, betrayed, and falsely accused. They knew him from the many times he had spoken to the staff and knew he was passionate about God's Word, as well as loving and working well with people and excited about bringing Christ to the world. They saw him with all the potentials and gifts they were looking for.

Campus Crusade asked us to get to know the heartbeat of this organization by taking a few trips with our new boss. Our first trip with them was to Ottawa, Canada's national capital in the month of January. God knew we needed a change of scenery and to be with people who would love and encourage us. We had never been to Ottawa before. We were surprised to see all the Scripture verses engraved in the dome at the entrance of our House of Parliament. I went around the building and wrote down all the Scripture references and prayed that once again our nation would return to its biblical roots. We sat in on a session of parliament and were amazed at the disorder of our governing body.

Soon we were sitting around the table with many of the leaders of Campus Crusade Canada. They talked of many things that went right over my head. I had a hard time transitioning so quickly from our resignation and the pain of the last year to this new group of forward looking, passionate leaders. We were well treated and welcomed warmly. During one of the sessions we were asked to think about what our goals were for the future and to write them down, to be prepared to share them. My mind was blank. I had no goals. My focus was on taking one step at a time and trusting that my grief and pain would soon abate.

When it was my turn to share, without pretending I said: "I'm in so much pain at this time that I cannot think of any goals for the future." One soft hearted, spirit filled man stopped the meeting and said, "This couple has gone through a very difficult time; we need to gather around them and pray for them." They laid hands on us and prayed for God's healing upon our hearts and lives. What a balm to our souls. Right after their prayer time another leader spoke up and said, "This couple, at sixty one, is going to have to begin raising all their personal support. Let's each one around the table ask God what we could do financially to support them for the first year of their ministry." Each one wrote down an amount. We were shocked and thrilled at their generosity; surprised by God's gracious hand of blessing, when we least deserved it.

The next day we flew on to Florida, where we were scheduled to attend a History's Handful Leadership Conference at the magnificent Marriott Hotel on Marcos Island. There were well over 200 business people and Christian leaders in attendance, from all across North America. All of our costs were covered by one businessman. It was quite an eye opener for us to see such an amazing passion for the lost around the world in the midst of such opulence. The speakers were great. The vision for global outreach as articulated by Bill Bright, the founder and president of Campus Crusade International, was nothing short of impressive.

We were awed by this mission, whose main focus was to reach people who did not know the Savior, and bring them into a growing relationship with Jesus Christ. Many arms of Campus Crusade did just that.

Our return flight out of Miami was over an hour late to depart. This meant that we missed our connecting flight in Toronto to Vancouver. The airline put us up at a nearby hotel for overnight. Our son Kim and his family were pastoring twenty minutes from the airport. They met us at the hotel where our meal voucher from the airline paid for all the dinners for six people. Then all of us went for a swim together in the hotel pool after dinner. In the midst of pain and struggle, God loves to drop in some delightful surprises in such lovely unexpected ways.

Everyone seemed to be so sure that we would have no problem raising our personal support. It was quite a bit more than we had ever received pastoring. We could live comfortably on less. We had some disappointments with those who promised substantial help in our support but never came through with anything. It was humbling to ask people to support us and more humbling to have them turn us down. It was especially hard on Pete. He said he felt like he was walking through his days with a tin cup on his sleeve, hoping someone would drop something into it. After forty years of having a set salary, we knew what we had to work with. We were often told that we were short checked for that particular month by the Crusade financial office. We finally told them it was okay. We were doing fine. Money has never been our focus but as we look back we are amazed at how God has taken care of us and given us enough and to spare. We began our marriage with always taking our tithe off the top of our smallest income. I believe God has honored that priority, allowing us in later life to do things we would never have dreamed possible.

We were scheduled to formally begin our ministry with Crusade on May 1st. That gave us almost a month of gap time between church and mission. Pete found it a great release to work on our new home during this gap month. Our contractor even paid him for his hours of work. We were soon busy picking floor coverings, appliances, and all things needed for our new home. By May 1, 1997 everything was finished and we had an open house with no furniture in place, or any of our belongings. We invited people to come and see our new home with our walkout basement that had a two bedroom legal apartment. This, we would discover, was such a help to us financially in the years to come. It was always rented out to wonderful people. As people wandered through our home I said, "Take a good look, it will never be this clean again!" People sat on the floor or on a few folding chairs that we had brought in. We had asked a dear former pastor to pray a prayer of dedication on this house that really belonged to God. We wanted to use it for His glory. We finished our little service with another dear friend singing the old hymn "Bless This House O Lord We Pray." What a glorious day to connect with such a large group of our choicest friends, who rejoiced with us and blessed us.

Two days after we moved all our belongings into our new home, our son Brent, with his wife Denise and their two kids, ages nine and seven, arrived from Italy to stay with us for an undetermined time. Oh, what joy to see them and welcome them into our hearts and let them settle into the basement apartment. They were hurting from the shattered devastation of their missionary dream in Italy.

They stayed with us for four months. We ate our evening meals together and often played games at night. God, in His mercy, knew how much we needed each other in the wake of our broken dreams and hearts. Neither they nor we had the capacity to hear each other's stories at this time. That would come later. Now we all were focused on living one step at a time. They, like we, became part of the wounded servants of God who, in time would forever minister with a limp, that revealed our brokenness on this journey to healing.

It was an ideal time for the kids to play outside in the mud and unfinished landscape around us. Few new houses were in our area so the kids had the joy of wandering and pretending. Brent made a "secret path," cut out of the woods behind our home. This path led to a burned down old house. This was to be a great drawing card of mystery with hours of fun for all our grandkids for years to come.

We officially became members of Campus Crusade for Christ on May 1,1997. Joining this mission was a mixture of high ideals, enthusiasm for new programs, and working with leaders who were passionate, single focused, and Godly. Pete's boss asked him to write his own job description, which he did. His title was Director of Pastoral Care and Church Relations. His mandate was to try to get in personal touch with as many pastors across the country as possible and listen to them, encourage them, and offer to be of whatever help we could be to them. His boss, always the visionary, told Pete he wanted him to be speaking in 2000 churches by the year 2000. That was a great goal, but Pete knew it was impossible. Churches were getting outside speakers less and less. If their senior pastor was away, they would have an associate pastor speak.

My husband moved into his new office, located in Langley, BC, just thirty minutes from our home. It was very opulent and stunning. Pete quickly made friends with the staff in offices around him and felt at home in no time. I, however had no office and no job description to even pretend to write out. Where I fit into this new ministry was a mystery to me. God would have to write that part of my story.

In July of 1997 we attended our first Campus Crusade annual conference. There were four hundred staff people at the Conference that was held in a beautiful hotel in Whistler, BC. Our official handshake, indicating we were now missionaries with Campus Crusade took place up the gondola to a large banquet hall overlooking the whole valley and Whistler Village. We were in awe at the opulence and the wealth that would support this kind of conference. We didn't know anyone except a few leaders and were surprised that we got to meet and greet Bill and Vonette Bright. We both thought Campus Crusade was a healing stop for us and in time we would go back to the pastoral ministry we loved so much. God had different, and much better plans for us. We were in God's "refining fire," preparing us for a work we could never have envisioned. There were weekly chapel times at the head office with all the staff, every Thursday morning. There was usually a speaker and then a prayer time. Pete often preached at these chapel times. The staff, young and old, so appreciated his passionate, from the heart messages. He has often said: "If you can't say it with passion, don't say it."

I was juggling a lot of changes in my mind. Things were going well for Pete at Crusade. For me, the battle of my heart was coming to terms with just how different my life was. In my mind we had lost a great deal. The realization of this often washed over me. I had never in my life, struggled with such a sense of confusion as to who I was and what I was to be or do.

It was a problem for us and for our former church, that we stayed in the city where we had our crisis. If we had accepted the call we had received from an Ontario church, it would have been much easier for us and for the church. Out of sight, out of mind. But no, here we stayed, built our new home and drove past our former church every time we went to town or to work. The church was ever before us and we were ever before them. In all honesty, we were not emotionally prepared to pastor another church right away. We needed time and healing. We thought we would be with Crusade for just a few years before going back to pastoring.

It was so hard on me simply going to get groceries. I feared who I would run into. What would they say? What had they heard? Why were they so silent? How could I avoid a few people who hated us? Pete felt this almost as keenly as I did.

One day at the grocery store a lady stopped me and said, "Could I just say something to you?" And then she started to tell me what Pete's ministry had meant to her personally and to her family. As she spoke I began to cry. The longer she spoke the harder I cried. She named the ways he had blessed their family, brought them to the Savior, and how they grew under his ministry. I kept crying and thinking: "Why have I never met you and why have you been silent all this time; why are you telling me these things now when it is too late?" That encounter kept me homebound for a couple of weeks.

I began to pray that God would protect me as I went shopping. That He would keep away people that would further wound me. How mixed up I was. I was wrestling with the ways of God, but I kept praying to my God for protection for the simple things of life. I believe God was not alarmed at either my wrestling or my prayers for help. He knew how wounded and fragile I was. It would be years later, before we would understand why God kept us in Abbotsford. He had a good purpose that we could have never imagined.

While Pete was away in Mexico City with a group, presenting the Jesus Film, I was home alone making curtains, hanging pictures, and making our house a welcoming home. In our guest bedroom I decided to hang pictures on the walls of our complete family. Each wall focused on one arm of our family tree. I think I needed to affirm the fact that I did belong somewhere. I had been blessed with a loving, extended, family.

There were many pictures of my family and me growing up, but few pictures of Pete's family. In fact, there was only one picture of his Unrau grandparents. I was able to get that picture from an aunt, halfway across Canada. Pete's parents were gone. There were photo albums with pictures, but no names and no dates. The next generation would find these worthless. With the help of siblings, I gathered together all the pictures we had and put them on the wall. I loved going into that family room.

I had previously written the stories of both of our parents' life journeys with names, dates and significant events. I believe God put it on my heart to make a Family Photo Heritage book for each of our kids and for the rest of the family.

It was a much larger job than I realized. The book ended up with two hundred pages of family pictures. All were named and dated. I also wrote an extended genealogy, plus a brief story of each family branch. It ended up taking me four years to finish this book, with the help of a laser printer. I had it hardcover bound, with beautiful embossed gold letters. If I had not gone through this transition time with no direction for my life, I would have never had the time or energy to create this book, which will be a forever keepsake. I'm thankful now that each of our children has this book, the value of which will only increase.

In the book introduction I wrote to our children, "Our family is one of the most precious treasures on earth. God puts us into families" (Psalm 68:6). This pictorial book is your heritage and your legacy. Through these pages you will rediscover your past. You will also get a sense of your roots, how you belong to a community of people called "family." Life changes. Family remains! I told my dentist about this book. After he had perused it he said: "Have you any idea what you have just done? This book it worth more than a million dollars to each of your kids." "Wow", I thought, " I will have to tell them that". (smile)

Finding A Church Home

I had always thought it would be exciting to visit other churches in our area and see how they were doing things, learn from them, enjoy something totally different. Well, let me tell you, it was no fun at all. One of the first churches we went to was a church where we knew and loved the pastor. After the service a church member came up to us and said, "What are you doing here? Are you lost?" My heart rose in anger. I wanted to say, "Yes, we are lost and does anyone care?" We didn't go back to that church.

We tried other churches and finally found ourselves in a local Alliance church. We sat quite close to the front. We were mesmerized by the strong preaching by Pastor Rick. At the end of the service he gave an invitation. He said, "In this large church, in this city, where everyone knows everyone else, are you willing to humble yourself and come forward in declaration of your commitment to say yes to God, whatever His plan is for you?" I poked Pete and said, "Let's go." He was more than ready. We knelt at the front of that church and I sobbed my heart out. Rick knew little about us, but was shocked at our brokenness. Pete said a few words and Rick prayed the most God breathed, anointed prayer over us. I honestly didn't care who saw us go forward, or what anyone thought. I figured our reputation couldn't be degraded any more than it already was. I cared only for the bottom line of our life. We were going to trust God, even in the midst of the storm and the crashing waves.

Thus began a beautiful, honest relationship with Pastor Rick and his wonderful wife Dianne. Rick was a powerful preacher of God's Word, but he was also a humble, honest man. After attending that church for a few months I told Pete, "I'm afraid for Rick. He is too honest. A lot of people cannot accept that level of honesty and vulnerability in their pastor."

Yes, we loved the music and how it ministered to my hurting soul. I began to get my song back. One Sunday we sang the hymn Holy Holy Holy, which I had sung most of my life. However, on this day, like never before, the words opened up a channel of understanding and validation of my wrestling soul, and I gained insight into the "call of creation" on my heart: all of this in one beloved old song:

Holy, holy, holy! Lord God Almighty!

Early in the morning our song shall rise to Thee;

Holy, holy, holy, merciful and mighty!

God in three persons, blessed Trinity!

Holy, holy, holy! All the saints adore Thee,

Casting down their golden crowns around the glassy sea;

Cherubim and seraphim falling down before Thee,

Who was, and is, and evermore shall be.

Holy, holy, holy! though the darkness hide Thee,

Through the eye of sinful man Thy glory may not see;

I had sung these words for years and this part of the song had never touched my soul like this. This hymn writer knew about the darkness hiding God. He knew of my human, sinful state and how at this time I could not see God's glory. Having the famous hymn writer, Reginald Heber, in the year 1826, articulate my heart today, put me in a state of awe. I felt a buoyancy of spirit that someone else had experienced what I was going through. I was not alone! That hymn and those words have stayed with me ever since.

Only Thou art holy; there is none beside Thee,

Perfect in power, in love, and purity.

Our old church had a seniors prayer meeting every Wednesday, early in the morning. They had been asking us if we would come and give them a report on what God was doing in our new ministry. They said they were praying regularly for us. and many were our supporters. I told Pete that I didn't think I had the emotional strength to face this group from our former church. He felt we should go, so I cried out to God for strength and went with him. I was to speak a few words before Pete gave our blessing report. The first thing this group would do was to sing a hymn. When they began to sing It is Well With My Soul, my tears began to flow. The longer they sang the more I wept. How could I sing or speak while pretending that all was well with my soul when it was not? Pete spoke well. People were warm and gracious after the meeting was over, but I was deeply disturbed.

When we got into the car I started crying again and said to Pete, "I don't know what to do. I just can't seem to get my life back on track with God." We were scheduled to meet with quite a number of the group at a restaurant for breakfast. When we got there the leader of the group, a tall kind man of God, put out his big arms around me and hugged me as I cried again. I said to him, "I am not doing very well."

He said, "Yes, you are. Just take your time and you will be alright." Oh what a healing balm to my soul this life long leader of the church was. Those simple words stuck with me and gave me hope of total healing some day.

God surprised me by opening up the floodgates for me to speak at women's retreats, special events, and banquets. Without any advertising on my part, invitation after invitation began to come to me. At the very beginning I set down a condition on which I would accept an invitation. We were living with one car and I didn't like to drive to unknown retreat centers or churches by myself in the dark. I would speak if they would have someone pick me up and bring me home. They readily agreed and I began a most blessed, anointed ministry time with women from many different churches.

I was surprised that God was opening a door to use me even in my state of brokenness and confusion. I would later learn that God is looking for broken vessels in which to pour out His love and light with honesty and brokenness on it's way to healing. The things that we think have broken us, become the very things that build our character and broaden our influence and affectedness with others. God never wastes our sorrows. I never talked about church problems but I did talk about relationship difficulties and the pain of not being able to reconcile with someone you love. I also talked about times of being disappointed with God and feeling His distance. I shared with the women how we need to give ourselves time, talk and tears. The problem of God disappointing us and the mystery of unanswered prayer touches us all eventually.

Their response was another God surprise. I felt so unworthy of what God was doing through my brokenness. Now I had a focus and someone who desired my wisdom and heart thoughts. Each weekend and special event required a different message, so this kept me quite busy. These opportunities also drove me back to God's Word as I prepared my heart to speak truth to these women. By the end of a weekend I would feel a deep connection to these women who had become real and honest with me and with God. When it came time to say goodbye I would often want to say, "Can I come back with you to your church family? You have something so precious that I am deeply missing: connection to a church home."

We were asked by Campus Crusade to get our training to become Family Life Speakers. These weekend conferences, called A Weekend to Remember, were held across Canada in grand, classy hotels. The conference would start on Friday night and finish Sunday afternoon. We would arrive on Thursday to get settled and have meetings with the team we would be working with. We would team teach with another couple for the speaking assignments. We were sent to San Antonio, Texas in September of 1997 for our training for this wonderful ministry. We wished we were scheduled to stay in this city longer to take in the unique sights and sounds of one of America's unique cities, with the river running right through the center of the city. We ate a meal right beside the river. There was lots of music and dancing and such a festive atmosphere! Our hearts were caught up in the lovely joy of it all.

Our training mainly consisted of attending an actual Weekend to Remember, which was in progress there at that time. We were to watch and observe how these teachers taught, and then we would meet briefly after the sessions to evaluate them. We were each given a set of tapes of actual Family Life sessions by different speakers, and were encouraged to listen to them. There was a manual with different subjects that we were to follow closely, not skipping any points. It was well-structured and good material. Our instructors and mentors were a wonderful couple who gave us much encouragement.

We came home loaded with manuals, cassette tapes, and a ton of work to prepare ourselves for our first conference, that would be in two weeks in Edmonton, Alberta. We worked hard and were excited about this opportunity. What a joy for a couple in their sixties to talk to younger couples, some just engaged or recently married, or married for many years. Every marriage can constantly be improved. If a marriage isn't growing, regardless of how long you have been married, then it is getting stale and dull.

We talked about the foundations of a fulfilling, happy marriage. We team taught which was a delight to us. We had done some of this type of teaching in our churches, to younger couples Sunday school classes and loved it. In keeping with our wedding theme, we were United to Serve!

Team teaching also helped our marriage. We saw growth in significant ways as we prepared and presented our talks It was good for us to work through some things, be fresh in our presentation, and use fun and real illustrations on how we had done it wrong and what we had learned through that. We never told a lot of our success stories. That doesn't help people. What they needed to hear was that we, throughout our engagement and marriage, had to work through the hard stuff. To be committed to both being heard and to come to conclusions we were both happy to live with. This was a refreshing new way for us to teach and for the participants to hear.

Our first Family Life teaching went so well. Right away we decided to teach out of our honest, healing hearts. We both were committed to No Pretending. We tried to teach the material with slipping in our own personal stories pertaining to our marriage and to raising four kids. We always said we had one of each when it came to our kids, because they were all different and all uniquely gifted. As we continued teaching these conferences across Canada, we became more relaxed and more free with our own struggles and victories. What a joy to see the response of the couples and to know that we were touching many different lives that would bless and encourage them and the next generations of married life.

We often taught in Victoria and Whistler, and various parts of BC. It was special for us to teach a number of times in my hometown of Kelowna BC. We went across our nation from Calgary, Winnipeg, Niagara Falls, Montreal, New Brunswick and many points in between. We never tired of this ministry. It was exciting and so rewarding to see couples come to Jesus for salvation, renewal, and fresh starts. I loved speaking to the wives and moms alone; cheering them on to be the best wives and mothers God intended them to be. It was actually fun for me to tell them the mistakes I had made and the lessons I had learned. It was also a special joy for us to teach with another couple and over the years to develop strong friendship ties with them that last to this day.

Some of the unique places and experiences stand out in my mind. We were asked to go alone to teach all the sessions in Whitehorse in the Yukon. We agreed, asking God for an extra portion of His Spirit and strength to be poured upon us for this big load.

We were also asked to speak on the Yukon CBC radio station This was a more difficult assignment than any I had to this point. The radio host had not written any questions. She said we would just wing it and see where we ended up. Her first question was: "You are celebrating your fortieth wedding anniversary. How have you kept it hot? I've been married for two years and things are cooling down already." We answered best we knew how and just found God putting words into our mouths when needed. The host was overjoyed with our conversation and we thought, "another new opportunity to share our hearts with people who might never have heard before."

Another great opportunity was to go to a First Nations Family Life Conference held in the far north of the province of Quebec in a place called Chibougamau. Once again we were asked, to teach the whole conference by ourselves to the Cree Nations people there. This proved to be a special highlight for us. They were so appreciative and responsive. At the close of our first conferences a former chief of the Mistissini Cree tribe got up and said this to his people, "My parents never heard this type of teaching and they surely didn't do it right. My wife and I have been married for over twenty five years, and we have never heard this type of good teaching before, and we have not done it right either. I'm going to make sure that from now on all of my people have the opportunity of hearing this and to learn to do it right in their marriages and with their families."

We taught these dear people for three years in a row. Each year we asked their leaders to give testimony or teach a certain section. We wanted them to learn how to do this teaching themselves. The response was almost like a revival. Those in charge took us to their reservation and we saw how neat and well kept it was. Some of the leaders of this group of Cree people were born again. They continue to have a great influence in their tribe. The men took Pete hunting and showed him their winter hunting house. It was a fascinating time. We still keep in touch with these dear people. What an honor to bring God's way into this group of people. Since then two of their own couples have been trained to teach this material. They have translated the manual into the Cree language. These couples are teaching this material in their own native language. We saw miracles happen right before our eyes and it warmed our soul. God was using our broken lives. He had given us a new vision and a new call.

One of our favourite places to teach was Victoria, BC on Vancouver Island, capital city of our beloved British Columbia. We stayed in the famous Empress Hotel. At one time we had eight hundred participants at the Weekend to Remember. I think this was one of our highest attendance at any of these conferences. Praise be to God as we saw couple after couple make things right with Jesus and right with each other. How He could take us in our brokenness and once again give us opportunity to speak into the lives of so many people. One of the side benefits that we found in traveling to all of these various cities to teach was that it often gave us the chance to see our son Kim and his family in Niagara Falls or Toronto, and our daughter Kathy and her family in Winnipeg. It also gave us the opportunity to spend a couple of extra days in those cities to make appointments with pastors and denominational leaders, since this was to be Pete's prime responsibility with Crusade. As Pete traveled to meet with pastors, I revelled in time to share with our kids and rock and play with our grandkids, who we saw far too seldom; surprised by God again!

Because we were traveling so much with Campus Crusade, we could hardly join a small care group. This resulted in a problem of not really feeling connected to our new church back home. We felt so connected to the pastor and his wife but we needed more. Because of our need for connecting with the body of Christ, Pete and I began to organize connecting point evenings with our supporters and friends to share with them the answers to their prayers and love. Dear friends arranged that we could use the clubhouse at their condo complex. We were surprised to see how many people came out. There were almost more than the Clubhouse could hold. We showed them pictures, told them stories, and shared our hearts. We laughed with them and cried with them. We connected with them as we heard about their lives and their stories. We held these Connecting Points for quite a few years.

In 1997 we accepted an invitation to minister with Word of Life Ministry at their youth camps and family life conferences in the Ukraine and in Hungary. We also spoke in local churches and had training sessions for camp counselors. We first arrived in Kiev on May 1st. It was cold and snowing. The whole city is heated by one central Kiev heating system which was turned off on April 31st each year and not to be turned on again till October 1st. Needless to say, we had many situations where the cold was almost unbearable. We had little time off but did have a good tour of each main city and a chance to go to the grand Opera House in Budapest to enjoy the Romeo and Juliet Opera. It cost us $3.50 a ticket. These countries were just getting free from the harsh hand of the Soviet Union. In Hungary we stayed in a grand castle where all the meetings were held. Our room was eighty eight steps up to the top floor. That provided good exercise but required a special care before we made the trek up to be sure we hadn't forgotten anything. What a glorious time in both countries, seeing God send many surprises of His profound work in so many lives.

In 1998 we were begged to come again to Ukraine, Poland, and Portugal. We made our way back into the arms of the people of Ukraine, who we had gotten to know and love so well. We still keep in contact with some of these people today.

This time Ukraine had the use of a run down camp for the summer. There was room for two hundred kids. The camp was overcrowded but well organized. The food was barely edible. We slept in a very cold cement building. Our mattresses were made out of straw. We did have our own bathroom. The rest of the camp had one shower for two hundred kids. But then there was the river and sports every afternoon, that gave the kids hours of fun and enjoyment. Pete often joined in on their games. The open hearts of the kids and adults made up for any inconveniences. The last meal, these kids were treated with an ice cream sandwich. The surprise and joy of these children at such an extravagant treat told us their story without the need for any words. We saw God at work in so many ways, in so many hearts.

In the fall of 1998, Pete's boss at Campus Crusade, read a news report in Christianity Today about a citywide, interchurch outreach program just completed in Charlotte, SC, called "Power to Change." He decided to fly down there with four other Crusade leaders, to see if they would allow us to refine and use their ideas to help evangelize Canada. The plan they used was to tape the testimonies of well known Christian celebrities in thirty to sixty second clips, on how they found power to change through Jesus Christ. They tried to saturate their metropolitan area with these testimonies on television. These ads included an 800 telephone number where people, who wanted to know more about how they too could find power to change their own lives, could call. Then someone who was trained on how to share their faith, would personally deliver a booklet that would further share with them on how they too could have a personal relationship with God. They apparently had an amazing response from the people of that city.

Pete's boss came back all excited. This was going be a means whereby we could reach into every home in Canada, and see literally millions come to faith in Christ. When Pete first heard about the plan, he was quite excited about the whole idea. His boss wanted him to join him in being one of his key lieutenants; especially in meeting with groups of pastors to inform them of the opportunity of getting involved, and to seek to motivate them. He also wanted Pete to be a key trainer on how to share their faith, and how to deliver the requested booklets to the homes of the people. Then there was the challenge to encourage the people who had requested the booklets to receive Jesus as their Savior. The person who delivered the booklet was also encouraged to hopefully get these new believers to become involved in their local church. It seemed to be a wonderful plan and Pete was enthusiastic about carrying out his part.

The testimonies that they used on television were superb. There was a famous Canadian hockey player, a mom, an Olympic gold medalist, a First Nations chief, and a teenager. All gave clear testimony as to the power of Jesus in their lives to bring change for today and hope for all eternity.

This campaign lasted for two years, spanning Canada from the West Coast to the East Coast

It seemed that Pete was constantly on the road meeting with pastors and teaching at the many training classes that were scheduled in churches. The goal in British Columbia was to train at least 15,000 people from six hundred different churches. They came fairly close to attaining that goal. The largest class Pete taught had close to five hundred participants. I was very supportive of this amazing opportunity to reach out to those who didn't know Jesus.

The Atlantic Provinces were the next to be trained and mobilized. This was a harder go than British Columbia had been, as many pastors had never heard of Campus Crusade. As always, there were significant relational times with the pastors. As Pete met with them one on one, he heard their story, often a painful story. He began to see how many wounded pastors there were across our nation and wondered who was ministering to them?

Pete was in Atlantic Canada often during that campaign. Two times I went with him. We took some days off and drove the Cabot Trail in the month of October. The autumn colors took our breath away. My camera was busy because my heart was so engaged with God's amazing creation. I so enjoyed the quaint little villages of this area. We went south in Nova Scotia and were stunned by the magnificent old stately homes and churches. Once again Pete met with many pastors and held training sessions in great and magnificent old buildings. Pete spoke in one church that was two hundred years old.

The next campaign was held in the province of Manitoba. That was a plus for me as I often went with him and stayed with our daughter and family in Winnipeg, which was his launching city. Once again he covered the area; reaching out to pastors, getting them enthused about this way to get the gospel of Jesus into the homes of millions of people Once again he met with many pastors who were weary, wounded, and just needed someone to talk to. The training session in each province proved so helpful to so many people as they were trained in how to share their faith and how to lead a person to accept Jesus as their Lord and Savior. There were also sessions on learning how to use the material to help people grow in their walk with God and how to follow up those who had showed interest in hearing more about Jesus' power to change. It really was a wonderful opportunity for people to become fully engaged in sharing Christ with neighbors, friends, and their city.

By now, he had personally met and talked to about four thousand pastors/Christian workers all across Canada during his almost three years with Crusade. The final response to this Power to Change campaign overall was disappointing. I knew one man, my man, who gave his all to fulfill his call to this outreach. We had to leave the results in God's hand. "We plant, we water, but God gives the increase" (1 Corinthians: 3:6, KJV). We would never know the long-term effect of these testimonies, all the training on how to share your faith, and the thousands of pastors he had met, listened to, and encouraged.

40th Anniversary Cruise

God gave our family a special reprieve during this heavy workload of the Power to Change campaigns, plus Family Life Conferences. We wanted to do something special to celebrate our fortieth anniversary. We decided to take all our kids and their spouses on a cruise. None of us had ever cruised before. It was time we all got together, with us living so many thousands of miles from each other. We phoned our kids and asked them, "How would you like it if we helped you to spend some of your inheritance?" They were puzzled until we told them that we would like to take them all on a Caribbean Cruise for one week in February. Not one turned us down. Now the anticipation and excitement began. We really had saved up and would not be taking this out of their inheritance. We just knew that a high priority of ours was quality time with our family and making memories that would last.

In February of 1999 our family was in flight from various parts of Canada and the USA. We met at a Hilton Hotel, in Miami, the night before the cruise. I couldn't believe it. Everyone could make it. The other grandparents or friends looked after the young grandkids. Our kids were giddy with excitement and freedom!

Boarding the ship the next day made me realize a long held dream of ours was coming to pass. I told God that if all our kids and spouses got on the ship, as it pushed away from the dock I would sing the Hallelujah Chorus. And I did! Pete had another reaction. As we pulled away from the dock he began to cry and cry. Our oldest son asked, "What's the matter Dad?" Through sobs Pete burst out saying, " I am overwhelmed with the goodness of God. I never would have dreamed that I would be on a cruise ship with all four of my kids and their spouses. I think of the dire poverty I was born into, the trials and shattered dreams we have been through, and today God's love and mercy flow over my soul." We were just so surprised and awed by God's ability to work all things together for good!

Before we left for the cruise, our kids asked us what expectations we had of them. We told them there were just two things we wanted. We wanted to all eat dinner together daily. We got a large table for ten and the best waiter and servers we've ever had. The boys couldn't get over the fact that they could order as much as they wanted and more. The other request was no surprise to the kids, I said, "On the last dress up night, I would like a picture of the whole family." On that night we were to meet in the solarium at the ship's center. Pete and I were early. One by one each couple walked down the winding stairs so handsome in their suits and so gorgeous in their long gowns. We both were pretty choked up with thanksgiving to God for the blessing and beautiful family God had given us.

The cruise was a time of unmatched family joy, harmony, and lots of fun. The kids embraced all the adventure of warm turquoise waters, enjoying parasailing, swimming, canoeing, snorkeling, seadoos, pingpong on the ship, the evening shows, and so much more. Our daughter told us after a couple of days, her amazement of this time. She said, "You have brought me into an enchanted paradise I didn't know existed."

From our beginning of extreme poverty, to raising our own support and not doing very well with that, God gave us the means to bless all our children by birth and marriage to experience this amazing time together. Surprised by God, for sure!

One of the most memorable times with Campus Crusade was when the complete staff of Canada and the United States joined together for a combined conference the summer of 2001. We stayed in the dorms of Fort Collins State University in Colorado. I asked Pete if these dorms would be air-conditioned? He assured me that they would be as all state university dorms would be. There were 4,000 Campus Crusade Missionaries in attendance and the dorms were not air-conditioned and it was hot and humid.

The wonderful part of the week was when we heard Joni Eareckson Tada speak. She was introduced and then there was quite a long waiting period. Finally Joni was wheeled out and she said, "I'm sorry I am a little late. I had an urgent call from my Mom. We talked a bit and then we sang. When we are in crisis we always have to sing."

Joni began to tell us a little of her life. As a result of a diving accident, she had been a quadriplegic in a wheelchair for thirty four years. She began to tell us how difficult her life had been. How she had sought for healing at special healing meetings with people who had the gift of healing. God had not answered her prayer. That was a huge disappointment. She told about being in Israel with her husband, Ken. He had carried her to the pool of Bethesda to see if God might move the waters and she would be healed. Nothing happened. And then Joni began to sing:

"Pass me not, O gentle Savior, Hear my humble cry;

While on others Thou art calling, Do not pass me by."

By now Pete and I had tears rolling down our faces. Here was a special child of God, sharing with thousands of young people the real stuff of life. There was no pretending with Joni. How refreshing to hear from someone who was honest, real and transparent.

She told us about her struggle in the mornings when she would hear the key turn in her door and she would know that her caregiver was there to dress her, feed her, brush her teeth, do her hair, do everything to prepare her for the day. Seventy five percent of the time she said she did not want to get up and face the day; she did not want to go through another day of pain and discomfort. So she sang. She prayed. She trusted God. As I write this my tears come. She has been trusted by God with a great struggle but she knows that God has put her on a platform and given her unbelievable opportunities to share Jesus because she is a victorious quadriplegic.

As I write this Joni has been in her wheelchair for over fifty years. I have many of her books. I thought I had most of them until I discovered that she has written forty five books, without pretending. God has used her in a multitude of ways because of her suffering and because she fought through her disappointments and anger with God, and came to the place where she would simply trust Jesus, even when she didn't feel like it.

She told us much that day. We were so touched; sobbing through her whole talk. We didn't take down one note. Who she was and what she had endured and what she said impacted us for the rest of our lives. We heard other famous speakers. I don't remember a word any one of them said, but I remember almost all of what Joni said. She opened her heart and let us inside. She was transparent, real and honest. That's what touches hearts. We will never know God's purposes this side of Heaven. All of us face different trials and struggles and to us they are the hardest. But, the God who is in control of all things is tenderly loving, and surprisingly watching over us and caring for us. He is not passing us by!!

Chapter Eleven

BEAUTY FOR ASHES

Abbotsford, BC 1998-2010

"Character cannot be developed in ease and quiet. Only through experience of trial and suffering can the soul be strengthened, vision cleared, ambition inspired, and success achieved." Helen Keller

A New Dream Is Born

My friend Susan, who had journeyed with me during all the darkest hours, took me out for a lovely English tea time. During our conversation she said, "Shirley, if you could dream again, what would you want to do with your life?"

Without hesitation I said, "I would like to work with pastors' wives or pastors and wives in some way, to encourage and walk alongside with them. I know this calling is often lonely and now that I'm older, I think I could bless some hearts and lift up some weary arms." Susan's response caught me off guard. She jumped up from her chair and said, "Shirley, you and Pete would be just the couple to do this kind of ministry. I have to show you something at my home. We have to go right now." What validation and trust she just gave me!

Well, we rushed to her home, where she showed me the brochure about SonScape. She said, "I have wanted to throw this out but I just couldn't. I have felt God's call upon my life to do something like this, as well." Her friend supported this work and had sent her a brochure. Now it was in my hand. SonScape, a Retreat Center, designed to specifically help those in ministry who were wounded, burned out or needing refreshment. My heart leapt. Now I got excited. At first I thought: "We could go there. This is where we perhaps could get some understanding and personal soul healing."

When Pete saw the brochure he, too was immediately drawn to this unique concept. Never had we heard about such a place. How we needed to go there, but they were filled up over a year in advance. We were put on a waiting list that went nowhere. The more we thought about a retreat center where ministry couples and singles could come for understanding, direction, counseling, and healing, the more our hearts were drawn to such a dream. Knowing you're not alone is so important to the process of healing.

Colorado Springs Trip

We asked the leader of SonScape if we could come to Colorado Springs to see their retreat center and to ask some questions that would help us start such a center in Canada. He was most willing that we come, and told us he would give us all the time he could and would help us in any way possible. We took the beautiful drive up the mountain near Pikes Peak to Sonscape. The leaders met with us for three hours, answered our questions, and gave us invaluable insights of lessons they had learned and how the retreats were run. They then prayed for us, asking God to lead and equip us for a ministry like this in Canada. What Godly, lovely men these were.

We had made appointments at other Mission Headquarters in Colorado Springs as well. Our burning question was, "What do you do for soul care for your missionaries?" We were pleased and surprised to hear how much they were doing for their missionaries and how important they felt this arm of their ministry was.

We had made an appointment with H.B. London at Focus on the Family. We had known him from our days in Oregon. He had pastored in Salem, Oregon, about twenty minutes from our home. He travelled the nation teaching on church growth. As we sat with him we told him the short version of our story. We wondered if he could be of any help to us. Soon he was telling his own story of his last church in California, and how deeply he was wounded and how his ministry had come to an abrupt halt. As he shared with us he wept out his own personal grief.

He encouraged us to take our time and to heal well. He also encouraged us in our dream of establishing some sort of soul care ministry for pastors and missionaries in Canada. As we left, he especially looked at me and said, "Shirley, take your time." We walked out of his office and down the hallway when he called to us, "Pete and Shirley, remember this will be your most important ministry and powerful legacy," as he held up a picture of our family we had given to him. As we exited the building I looked at Pete and said, "Who was counselling whom?" We were all wounded healers who also needed to tell our story to others and be encouraged on our personal journey.

We headed back home with a great deal of encouragement, tools, and prayers as we stepped into the next call of God upon our lives. Everything was both exciting and overwhelming. Where should we start? What would our ministry look like? Oh, how we prayed for God's great and clear guidance and wisdom as we took one step at a time. We gathered others to pray with and for us. "Unless the Lord builds the house we labour in vain who build it" (Psalm 127:1). We prayed for the constant anointing and guidance of the Spirit of God to hover over this ministry from its inception to its fulfillment. How wonderful to see people, too many to number, gather around the birth and growth of this new baby called Oasis Retreats.

Pete and I were still teaching Family Life and Pete was still on the road a lot with Power to Change. We did our dreaming and our praying in between other commitments. I stopped taking any requests for speaking at retreats or any function that would conflict with our overloaded schedule of team teaching.

Birthing Of Oasis

Pete told his boss at Crusade about our dream and his response was "Just don't cost us any money and don't embarrass us." We didn't feel like this was much of a blessing but we knew that Crusade's call from God was evangelism and big programs with big numbers. Oasis would not be that. We would have small numbers, little money, but great rewards as we would see the pastors and missionaries healed to do the work of shepherding and evangelism.

Right away Pete and I knew that we could never build a retreat center that could host Oasis Retreats. We had no money, no land, and no one who was offering us that kind of gift. We were planning on having six, five-day retreats a year; three in the fall and three in the spring. We couldn't have any in the summer as the Retreat centers were full of children and young people at that time.

We had often taught and preached at a retreat center that was in Washington state, about twenty minutes from our home in Canada. It was beautiful with miles of walking trails and many flowers. We talked to them about renting their facility from Sunday afternoon to Friday afternoon six times a year. They were very interested in our proposal and were willing to talk details as we got farther along in our planning.

Pete knew that to make a ministry like this become a reality, we would need the ground swell support of the denominational/mission leaders from across the country. They were the ones who had the pulse of many churches across their ministry field. They knew of pastors and missionaries in need of soul care.

Now we were beginning to understand the "why" of Pete's past involvement with so many different denominations/missions. We had served with four different denominations in our pastoral ministry. We had enjoyed our years with each denomination. Pete had been asked to serve as President of two of these denominations and on the boards of the other two. Thus he was well known among the denominational leaders. He had also served at Briercrest for six years as evangelist and professor. This gave him an even wider opportunity to have touched many lives. We had done camp work every summer for six years and met many leaders and campers. He was finishing major involvement with the Power to Change campaign under Campus Crusade, where he had met with hundreds and hundreds of pastors from across the country. All this to say that we had a ground swell of people from which we could draw from to encourage pastors and missionaries to come to a retreat setting for renewal and healing. Pete roughly calculated that during our short time with Crusade, especially in his travels with Power to Change, across Canada from Sea to Sea, he had met an estimated 5,000 pastors in large groups, small groups and one on one. We met pastors and people concerned for their pastors or missionaries, while travelling with Family Life. It was amazing to see how God was funneling all these opportunities to put us in a position of meeting and knowing so many people who would be interested in our new dream called Oasis Retreats. God had us under the umbrella of Campus Crusade; that gave us a known and respected mission to birth Oasis.

Denominational Leaders

We were now ready to invite fifteen different denominational/ mission leaders, to come for a working luncheon to Campus Crusade Headquarters, to be in on the ground floor of the birthing of this vital SOUL CARE ministry for their pastors and missionaries. In our letter of invitation, Pete made sure they knew that he was not asking them to get on board with something that was already finalized. We genuinely wanted their input and their recommendations. Pete told them in this letter that we were not even sure there was a need for a Retreat like this. If enough was being done, we wanted to get on board with whoever was already doing it in Canada. We didn't want to reinvent the wheel. Fifteen denominational/mission leaders accepted Pete's invitation to come, knowing that it would be a blue sky thinking and dreaming time together. He suggested several questions that they should come prepared to dialog about;

- What is available right now in a five day, limited numbers per retreat setting, with a multiple godly, professional staff, to minister to those who are weary and or wounded in ministry in Canada?

- Does more need to be done in this area?

- Can we be of help to you?

- If so, would the cross denominational aspect of being under Campus Crusade be of help?

- What hot button issues should be covered by the presenting staff?

- Do you have any potential adjunct staff in mind, that you could recommend?

- How much should we charge?

- In order to get the word out we would need to print a full colour brochure. Would you be willing to include your denomination/ mission name, as one that is recommending this retreat to those spiritual gatekeepers under your care?

- Would you be willing to get these brochures distributed to your pastors/missionaries?

- Would you be willing to serve on an Advisory Council for us to give advice and input, as we move forward in this ministry?

The leaders of these denominations who were present at that initial meeting, were unanimous in their consensus that:

- Yes, there is a real need for an Oasis type retreat for Christian workers in Canada;

- Yes, they would like you Pete and Shirley to be the leaders, who will plan and lead this ministry with our backing, and under the umbrella of Campus Crusade for Christ of Canada;

- In principle, they all agreed to allow the names of their denominations/missions to be included, on the proposed printed full color brochures.

Goals and Decisions

Our goal was to have the first Oasis Retreat, with a planned maximum of twelve participants (six couples/singles) at Cedar Springs, WA, within six months. This kind of overwhelming support from such a diverse group of denominations/missions, came as a total surprise, because we didn't have any staff in place, apart from Pete and me. We had no idea what to include in our curriculum; our program plan was incomplete, and we had wondered whether anyone would show up. Obviously much work was left to be done

Often in ministry, those who need help the most can afford it the least. We agreed to offer financial assistance for those who would not be able to come without help. We never turned anyone away, because of financial limitations, and we operated this ministry in the black for our fourteen years of our leadership. God provided.

We decided that we would primarily appeal to those in ministry, who were facing one or more of the four following issues:(1) Tragically, some face a moral Flame Out, where moral sins threaten to ruin their marriages and their ministries. (2) Others struggle with Burnout which has physical, psychological and spiritual ramifications. (3) Still others are facing the pain of being Turfed Out from their churches or missions. The pain of being "hired by God" (you feel the call of God upon you for this particular place and ministry) and then to be "fired by man"(you lose the confidence of the very leaders who so totally felt you were God's gift to them, such a short time ago) is a pain that few lay people fully understand. (4) Others will need, Rest and Refreshment through the teaching and counselling, or they need a mid-course encouragement, like a mini-sabbatical, while in the harness of ministry. They may not be in crisis of any kind. For them an Oasis would be more preventative than curative.

Mission Statement, Core Values, Brochure

Where does one begin with such a monumental task of laying the foundation for a new ministry? A godly missionary leader from Japan, Warren Janzen, played a vital role in helping us draft our brochure and our vision for Oasis. He was finishing his graduate degree with a focus on: "How to provide more effective Soul Care for missionaries." He offered us full access to all his research on this subject, including his thesis. God was at work. The Holy Spirit was hovering over the birth of Oasis.

Staff

Now we were looking for God to go before us and pick out the staff that would be committed to this new ministry and who would have a heart and a message for weary and/or wounded pastors /missionaries. God brought Dr. John Radford into our lives. He had recently moved to Canada from South Africa, where he worked on conflict resolution issues. Pete met with John and within fifteen minutes they both knew this opportunity was designed by God. John had dreamed of one day being of assistance to those in pastoral ministry. He chose to speak on "The Value of Hurtful Conflict." What wonderful, helpful insights he gave us at every retreat. A couple of years into Oasis he told everyone, "Oasis is the most important calling on my life. This was one of the main reasons God brought me and my family to Canada."

Ron Toews was a well respected, godly counselor in the Abbotsford area for a number of years. He, too, had dreamed of getting involved with an opportunity to help those in Christian ministry, but he never knew how to get them together. "If you had one morning to speak to a group of pastors/missionaries, what would you speak on?" His answer was, "I'd speak on the subject of forgiveness. "I Should Forgive...But!" Forgiveness is not a natural response to betrayal and false accusations. Both John and Ron also agreed to stay for Tuesday and Wednesday afternoons of each Retreat. They became our counseling team, to give each couple/single participant, a minimum of two hour long, totally confidential, personal counseling sessions.

We met Dr. Trevor Walters, the vicar from the Evangelical Anglican Church in Abbotsford at a retreat for pastors and had an immediate connection with him. He had already been personally burdened and was ministering to those who were weary and wounded and out of the ministry. He gave us great encouragement and help. Trevor handled the session on "Dealing with Burnout in Ministry." He himself had struggled with burnout and had great helps for those facing this very prevalent problem. He also dealt with "Struggling With The External Affirmation Syndrome." From personal experience, he could discern if a person had not received fatherly affirmation. He observed the tendency of such people to look for the affirmation of others all their lives.

Rick Porter, a pastor in Abbotsford became our own pastor. We knew how blessed we were under this honest servant of God and knew that he would be a blessing at Oasis as well. He loved coming to Oasis. He would say as he drove onto the campground that he could feel the Spirit's presence in a powerful way. Often he would sit before the group and just weep. He would see the openness, honesty, and willingness to be real among the Oasis folks. And he would wonder why that could not happen in his own church, or in any church? Why were most Christians so unwilling to say, "I was wrong. Will you forgive me?" Or, "I made a foolish decision and am willing to admit it." Just plain old-fashioned truth speaking - being real and open. He said that in most churches important issues are left untouched and swept under the rug until they fester and explode into unmanageable situations. Little would we know that down the road, Rick himself would go through much of what we had gone through in false accusations, betrayal, and feeling the pressure to resign. Showing the humility of Rick and his wife, Dianne, was to see them come to Oasis as participants rather than presenters, and sit under the teaching as a couple wounded, honest and needing healing.

Pastor Steve Berg from Abbotsford brought a different message. He told stories from his years in politics and in ministry. He said their church was known as the church that was growing in numbers. But he added "we were not growing in our love for Jesus, our love for each other or our love for those who didn't know Jesus. We really were not growing in what really matters." He was then willing to be vulnerable to the point that he told us about his burnout and nervous breakdown. He finally went to a Christian psychiatrist who listened to his story, and eventually put him on medication. He said, "I am still on it and may be for the rest of my life." No shame here, just honest real life stuff. If nervous breakdowns are often caused by prolonged and intense exposure to stress, we knew this to be a reality in many pastor's lives. The people of our churches will let us give as much of ourselves as we are willing to give. We are the ones who have to monitor our health, our days off, our boundary setting and our ability to say, "No." Depression and emotional fatigue is something most people will never admit to, and to have a teaching pastor admit to it was huge.

When Steve was well enough to get back into his pulpit, he and his psychiatrist shared the message together on, "What should a Christian do when they have struggles with burnout and emotional breakdown?" Steve said that no message has ever touched so many people or sold so many CD's. He gave us one that told his amazing story with such honesty.

Pastor/Missionary Brent Unrau, our son, took Rick and Steve's place when they had moved away. This was the last session of each retreat. Brent spoke on "The Power of our Story." He added a very powerful and unique component to the team, especially helpful to the many foreign missionaries as he and his wife served as missionaries to Italy for eight years after having pastored in Saskatchewan for five years. Their painful story from the mission field was so helpful to many others. Brent helped us to see that our own personal stories are good stories that need to be told, no matter how painful or messy. He told us of his own hard journey back to health with the help of professors at seminary who could handle his questions, his rebellion and anger. He earned his Masters in Counseling, which is his calling today.

He gave all of us at Oasis the gift of his story of innocence, tragedy, and finally hope. One of his key Scriptures was Hosea 2:14-15, "I will lead her into the desert and speak tenderly to her. There I will give her back her vineyards, and make the Valley of Achor a door of hope. There she will sing as in the days of her youth." In Joshua 7:26 the valley of Achor was where Achan and his family met their death because of disobedience to God's clear instructions. God can turn our places of death to our dreams into a door of hope and new beginnings, if we will trust Him and let Him work out His purposes. He ended his session with a tray of rocks just gotten from the shores of the Fraser River. He asked each participant to choose a rock that would tell the story of their week at Oasis. How unique the stones and the testimonies were. God was at work.

Hostess

We knew that we would need someone who would assist us during the retreats. Someone who would look after our evening snack time, get the coffee ready and give of themselves to the ministry of loving and caring for our wounded and weary participants. A gifted couple from our care group assisted us for the first couple of years. They were invaluable in the start up of Oasis. When they could no longer come, my friend Susan, who had already been deeply involved in assisting us in seeing our Oasis dream become a reality took over this ministry. Susan had both the gifting and the call for this role as hostess. She hardly missed a retreat. Her husband Warren encouraged and blessed her as he looked after the needs of the home and his medical practice during the weeks of Oasis. Susan's warm spirit and genuine love for God and for those in the ministry shone through so clearly. Her sense of humor and hearty ability to laugh was so infectious. She has such a gift of discernment when it comes to assessing people. She can sense phoniness very quickly. Beyond this, she is my special friend, who helped so much in evaluating each potential or real crisis at Oasis, as well as debriefing the whole retreat right after it is over. She also got special little gifts that she placed at the door of each of the participants each night, along with a personal note of encouragement. Her greatest gift to Oasis was the hours she spent talking with participants late into the night, hearing their hearts, praying and caring for them. When she had to miss an Oasis my other trusted friend, Diane and her new husband George, assisted in this area and other responsibilities. They have hearts of gold for this ministry and continue to this day to be the hands and feet of Jesus bringing their own gifts of love and care to the Oasis ministry.

Servant Team

Very early on, we felt the need to assemble a group of people that could act as our servant team. We needed help from people who would make up and provide the beautiful baskets that we placed in every room in advance of the arrival of each of the participating couples/singles. What an amazing blessing these baskets were to each participant. One lady did all our name tags, door names and the personal notes to accompany the baskets. She was a gifted artist and it showed her great care.

This servant team also provided transportation to and from the Abbotsford and Vancouver airports if needed. If a couple needed a place to stay overnight there was a home ready for them. These volunteers, largely retired couples, would hug them warmly at the airport, often took them out to lunch, and then brought them to the retreat by mid-afternoon, in good time for the beginning of each retreat. Many of them became lasting friends even with just such a brief time together. Some of these same ladies baked cookies and cakes for the evening snacks at the retreats.

Two couples also volunteered to be our official greeters and red caps at the retreats. They would meet the participants at their cars and offered to carry their luggage for them to their rooms. As soon as we saw another car arriving, Pete and I would always go out to them at their cars and hug them warmly, welcoming them genuinely to Oasis. This kind of personal treatment seemed to start to melt any ice or fears about coming to a place of safety. We realized that you can never make a first impression the second time and we only had a short time with each Oasis group.

Quite often we had ministry leaders who could not afford to come. There were a few business men and retired folks who were so sold on

Oasis and its need and effectiveness that they would pay the way for these participants to come. God saw all this work and labour of love behind-the-scenes and we know He will reward this faithful servant team.

We started charging only $750 per couple per retreat; singles paid $450. Our first Oasis was at Cedar Springs Retreat Center in Washington, USA. Because most people would have to cross the border it became increasingly difficult. In a few years we changed to Camp Hope near Hope, BC; a 45-minute drive from Abbotsford, BC, where we lived. Each couple had their own motel like rooms with full bathrooms.

We saw small and large examples of God's fingerprints all over this new baby, Oasis. We saw Him open doors, and lead us just to the right people through unusual circumstances. It often felt like we were standing still and watching God move, orchestrate, and guide. We believe God had given us a sacred task to be humble servants of God, handling this new ministry with the utmost of prayer and care. This was not our work or our idea. It was God's all the way through.

First Oasis

Pete and I were nervous before our first retreat began. We kept telling ourselves that it was God in us that would do the speaking. Many were praying for us. Quite a few of our servant team and staff had come to our first session. Sunday night Pete and I would tell our personal pastoral story. We knew we had only five days with these dear servants of the Lord, so we jumped in the deep end right way. In our story we told them a little of our family and then began to unpack the blessings, pain and disappointments that we had been through. We knew they wouldn't be impressed by our successes but would need to hear the difficult parts of our story from a couple who were over sixty. As we told our story, we would see the Kleenexes coming out as people identified with our betrayals, false accusations, and our sense that God was silent and distant. As we finished our story Pete would tell of his deep desire to be fully reconciled with our last church.

The Oasis participants came up to us with tears in their eyes telling us, "You just told our story. You just used different names." Already there was a sense of safety at Oasis. If we could be that real, so could they. As we told our story time after time I began to understand just a little as to why God had allowed me to go through such a deep time of wrestling with God, being disappointed with God, and feeling God's silence. If I had never tasted the depth of that dark night of the soul, I would not have been able to identify with most of these Oasis participants that had also been in this dark and difficult place. Many were in this painful place right now. We were seeing that God never wastes our pain or our sorrows.

A retired missionary couple, who we stayed with for two months while our house was being built, came to that first Oasis meeting. He was an elder at our last church and they did everything they could to help and encourage us. Pete asked them after that session if there was anything we had said that would have been an exaggeration or had we told it as they too had seen it. They said it was wonderful and they wouldn't change a thing. Their validation answered our question about how real we should be in telling our story. We wanted it to be without pretending, honest, real, and redemptive.

Growing In Times of Crisis was the topic Pete and I addressed on Monday morning of each of these fifty seven Oasis Retreats. We walked through some of the steps we had taken to get out of the pit of despair, through the wrestling in the dark and the wandering in the wilderness. Here are the key issues that we focused on:

Commit to a below the surface interpersonal relationship. Be vulnerable and honest. Admit to each other that it is OK to be in pain. "Pain insists on being attended to." C. S. Lewis. Pretend about nothing. That will only lead to deeper hurt. Honesty leads to healing. Learn the art of being a true repenter; take ownership of your own wrongs: readily use the words; "I was wrong, will you forgive me." Repentance with true forgiveness leads to true reconciliation. Who you are is far more powerful than what you say. We are human beings, not human doings. Loss is like an ambush. It attacks when least expected.

Find others who will listen with compassion and understanding. Don't open your heart too widely to too many. Test friends for safe hearts. We communicated openly with our grown children, who walked with us in integrity. Have people you can laugh and have fun with; play games with; or go for nature walks with.

Friends blessed us with their consistent prayers and encouragements. They gifted us by validating our losses without giving us simple answers. The vacuum of this huge need in our lives was what God used to put on our hearts the ministry of Oasis!

What Has Helped Us The Most?

We prayed together even when we didn't feel like it. Where could we turn but to the Lord? Often I simply prayed: "Jesus carry me. Holy Spirit, pray for me with groans that I cannot utter." (Romans 8:26-27). "Prayer doesn't change God but it changes me." C. S. Lewis. We trusted in the sovereignty and goodness of God, even when confused. We lived by God's promises not by his answer to our questions. We walked by faith, believing God was fair, even if life was not. All I could hear God say was "Trust Me!" "Stop asking why. That is a form of pride." (son Kim). We clung to the truth that, "Everything is Father-filtered." We chose to forgive others and ourselves, in the strength of the Lord. Jesus said, "If you forgive men when they sin against you, your heavenly Father will also forgive you. But if you do not forgive men their sins, your Father will not forgive your sins." (Matthew 6:14-15). "Forgiveness stops others actions from destroying your heart." Author unknown. Our hearts always wanted to be obedient to God. We drew upon our reservoir of God's hidden word, including lifeline verses that we had memorized. "When in the dark, remember what you have learned in the light." Joe Bayley. I had built up my reservoir in good times; now I was deeply drawing from it. We sought to readily affirm and praise each other where we could, and gently confront each other when necessary, always realizing that timing is essential. We focused on respecting and trusting each other. We sought to minister to each other instead of manipulating each other. We tried to carve out days off for dates, vacations, and mini-moons into our lives. We found healing as we continued to minister out of brokenness into brokenness. Many a well of joy has been dug by the spade of sorrow.

We found that our pain was transferable but our story was not. We could not tell this story at Family Life Conferences. That was another whole new world. God was gracious to give us both Family

Life and Oasis ministries. We thanked God that our lives were now touching and spreading into other lives in a greater way than would ever be possible as the pastor of one church. One lady told me at a camp, "Pain is pain. You didn't need to tell me your story. I knew you had broken hearts and I could trust you with my broken heart." God wants to minister out of our broken lives more than out of our gifts. We eventually began to help each other look forward, not always backward. We started counting our blessings instead of our losses. We stopped comparing our losses with others. We stopped talking about our pain. We chose to close the book on our past and rested our case with God.

At these Monday sessions at Oasis, I introduced the participants to the book by Jerry Sittser, *A Grace Disguised*. At first, we bought each couple/single participant a copy of this book for them to keep. We felt that strongly about the help this book would be for anyone facing loss and trauma. I shared a portion of the life-changing letter that Jerry had sent to me in response to my letter of deep appreciation to him. This letter tells of the horrific accident where three of his family members were killed: his four year old daughter, his wife, and his mother. What a terrifying loss. The book allowed us to journey with Jerry through darkness, questions, anger, and difficulty.

The letter Jerry wrote me gave me validation and understanding about my great sense of loss and confusion. He talks about being a pastor being part of who he is. It is not a job. It is a sacred call. He again validated the horror of being betrayed. That helped me see that it wasn't something insignificant that a simple prayer or Bible verse would fix. He gave encouragement for our ministry born out of suffering that will in time reveal God's redemption.

I am including a few of my favorite quotes from his book.

"A devastating loss never leaves you, but it will lessen in its ability to level you."

I could tell my losses were lessening in their ability to level me. That gave me hope.

" Catastrophic loss wreaks destruction like a massive flood. It leaves the landscape of one's life forever changed."

How insightful this quote is. How true it was of our lives.

I will forever thank Jesus and Jerry for this book and how God used his story to help me in the struggle of my story. That his letter came just before we started Oasis was not a mistake. God gave me clear evidence that He was at work and my response to all we had suffered was to simply trust Him and let God work out His redemptive purpose through our pain and losses. How very different this response was to my wrestling in the dark time.

As we continued on in ministry, Jerry and I wrote back and forth. Here was his response to this ministry that God had birthed in our hearts.

> Dear Shirley: I am very excited about this new door of opportunity, especially in your ministry to pastors who are often the most wounded believers among us. They have problems but do not feel the freedom to share them; they struggle with temptation but think they must project an image of invincibility, and they often feel lonely and isolated. You have much to offer.

> *Sincerely, Jerry*

How thankful we are for Jerry's encouragement, understanding, and blessing.

Why does God, in telling the stories of people in the Bible, give us such graphic examples of those who trusted God and went through great trials? I can't think of one story in the Bible that doesn't have some sort of suffering, disappointment with God, or trouble understanding the ways of God. Is that not life outside the garden and the pilgrim's journey through this cursed earth to heaven's glories?

I love the book of Ruth for this very reason. Naomi's life seemed full of death, despair and bitterness. But all along God is at work weaving a magnificent story of His love and grace, bringing Ruth a husband and Naomi a grandbaby, who is the great grandfather of David and is in the lineage of Jesus Christ, the long-awaited Messiah. Oh, how marvelous. How wonderful. If we could only learn to wait on the Lord. It is through suffering and pain that we come to this place of great blessing and peace with our God.

Jesus asked the man by the Pool of Bethesda, "Do you want to be healed" (John 5:1-8)? Is my identity wrapped up in my pain? Do I think of myself in terms of who I was, not who I am in Christ? What defines us? Is it our successes and our triumphs, or is it our failures, our pains, and our losses? Neither defines us. It is Jesus Christ only who defines us. We ended our session with me sharing what I thought were my losses.

We concluded by reading one quote from Gene Edward's book *Prisoner In The Third Cell*. Someone gave us a copy of this book that spoke to my heart in a profound way. It is the life story of John the Baptist, the cousin of Jesus. John had spent his entire life making himself ready to be the voice to prepare the way for the Lord. God gave him the awesome privilege of baptizing Jesus, the Son of God, and of seeing the Holy Spirit descending upon Jesus in the form of a dove. He heard the voice of God saying, "This is my beloved Son in whom I am well pleased" (Matthew 3:13-17). John's famous saying was, "He must increase, but I must decrease" (John 3:30-35 KJV).

The next we read about John the Baptist is that he is in prison because he confronted King Herod concerning his sinful lifestyle (Matthew 14:1-12). Now John is confused. His mind is in turmoil. He finally asked his disciples to go and find Jesus to talk to Him. His loaded question was: "Are you the Messiah or should we look for another" (Matthew 11:3)? Not only is John in prison; he is struggling with the ways of God. Jesus answers him by telling of the miracles He has done and then he says, "And blessed are you if you are not offended with me" (Matthew 11:6). John dies a horrible death without any answers.

Gene Edwards puts it this way: "A day like that which awaited John awaits us all. It is unavoidable, every believer imagines his God to be a certain way, and he is quite sure his Lord will do certain things under certain conditions. But your Lord is never quite what you imagine Him to be. You have now come face to face with a God whom you do not fully understand. You are going to get to know your Lord by faith, or you will not know Him at all. Faith in Him, trust that is in Him…not in His ways. The question is this: 'Will you continue to follow this God who did not live up to your expectations?' Blessed are you if you are not offended with me."

I had been offended by my God, whose ways I did not understand and who had not lived up to my expectations. My choice after my anger, wrestling and debating the ways of God was to fully trust Him through all the silence, the mystery and isolation, in all the suffering and storms of life. God's sovereign ways are good even if we may never see the good. He is in control and the knowledge of that brings my heart peace and my steps security.

Birkman Personality Assessment Tool

When we were setting the agenda for our Retreats, we were greatly helped by Bruce Gordon, who was the head of Birkman in Canada. Dr. and Mrs. Birkman lived in Texas and developed this amazing tool. It was designed to help you understand just how God has uniquely gifted and wired you, why you respond the way you do and how you fit into a team A powerful result will be that you will be able to minister effectively in your area of strength and hire staff to your point of weakness. Early on, Pete could see how helpful this could have been for him in ministry with his staff and with the church boards. When Bruce asked the Birkmans about us using it at Oasis, they were delighted. They had been praying that God would open the door in some way that the Birkman Assessment Tool could be used to help pastors and missionaries. They gifted us with the use of this tool at a significant discount off the going price. Brent eventually became our Birkman facilitator and did all the assessments for each participant at Oasis. Brent made Monday night a fun night by putting people in different groups according to their Birkman results and playing some games with that in mind. We began to see how unique each group was. After our heavy teaching and storytelling time, this was a good release for the group and a good chance to laugh, have fun, learn and get to know each other a little better.

What a joy it was so see Dr. John arrive on Tuesday morning. How glad we were to hand over the teaching morning to someone so humble, so godly and so gifted. The sessions were never long enough. Ron usually arrived in time for lunch. The staff met while we ate. Then John and Ron spent the next two afternoons counseling each couple for one hour each day. Many pastors and missionaries had never had a chance to sit down with a seasoned godly counsellor and share their hearts. God worked mightily through these two servants of God.

Before we had our story time on Sunday night, Pete would lead the group in a couple of familiar songs. They were songs most people knew. We always included my special song, "Heal My Heart." We used a lot of Brian Doerksen's songs with his permission. Brian says that a lot of the Psalms are laments. He wanted to write songs that touched the heart and changed our focus to God. One of our favorite of his songs is called Your Faithfulness and is found on his CD You Shine.

I don't know what this day will bring. Will it be disappointing or filled with longed for things? I don't know what tomorrow holds. Still I know I can trust Your faithfulness.

I don't know if these clouds mean rain; If they do will they pour down blessing or pain? I don't know what the future holds, Still I know I can trust Your faithfulness.

Certain as the rivers reach the sea; Certain as the sunrise in the east; I can rest in Your faithfulness. Surer than a mother's tender love; Surer than the stars still shine above, I can rest in Your faithfulness.

I don't know how or when I'll die. Will it be a thief or will I have a chance to say goodbye? I don't know how much time is left; But in the end I will know Your faithfulness.

We met with Brian a couple of times over lunch. We asked him if he would give us permission to put this song on a CD that we were sending home with the participants. With tears streaming down his face, Brian said, "It would be an honour to be part of this amazing ministry. I have wanted to be of encouragement to pastors for so long and this is one way that I can do that." Thank you God for giving us such softhearted servants.

Tuesday night was our first storytelling time for the participants. Each couple/single was told in advance that they would have the opportunity to tell their story to the group on one of the next three evenings. For most it was the first time they ever had a safe place to share their heart of pain and trial. Once they were done with their story, Pete would sit at their feet and love them, affirm their pain, give them an appropriate Scripture, and then ask the rest of us to gather around and pray for this couple, who had just emptied their hearts out to us. What a sacred beautiful time this was. These folks were not strangers anymore. They were fellow travelers. They had been playing volleyball together; sat in the hot tubs together, talking until late at night, and sitting around the tables at meal times sharing and caring for each other almost immediately. The one statement that we found to be true at each Oasis: "Those who get real get help and those who don't get real leave unchanged."

As we prayed together there were tears, words of wisdom, Scripture and mighty prayers. What a beautiful sight to behold. This wonderful story-telling time happened each Tuesday, Wednesday, and Thursday night. It was such a powerful, life-changing experience to tell your real story to a safe group of fellow sojourners and to be a participant, hearing each other's story. You knew you were not alone in this "Pain University" classroom. God would give the strength to carry on with hope and more anointed ministry born out of suffering. Give me a wounded healer any day.

The rest of the week was a wonder to behold, as each presenting staff shared their wisdom, answered questions, and gave time for application. What a joy unspeakable to see God at work at each retreat in amazing, different. and most blessed ways.

Redemption

As Pete and I sat through Oasis after Oasis, taking in all the sessions, taking detailed notes from our amazing God led staff, God was healing our own hearts. Oasis was not only a place of refreshment, healing, and validation for our participants, it was a huge major healing time for us. He had allowed me to go through such a deep wrestling of my soul, walking through the dark night of the soul, so that I could now share with other pastors and missionaries my struggles and how I came through it still trusting and serving God. Our painful experiences is what opened their hearts to be real and to realize God does not waste our sorrows or our pain. As Joseph said to his brothers, "You intended to harm me, but God intended it all for good to accomplish what is now being done" (Genesis 50:19).

Many times we would have participants thank us for birthing Oasis, for the pain we went through in that birthing and that we did not give up. We stood in amazement that God had brought us through the refiner's fire so that we could be the founders and directors of such a God-breathed ministry as Oasis.

There were unexpected times as we were saying our "goodbyes." Someone would ask if they as a group could pray for us. They publicly thanked us for pushing through the pain of birthing Oasis and what it had meant to them. They thanked us for our open, honest hearts as we told of our journey of blessing and betrayal and loss. We had never been prayed for like this. Our hearts and tears of thanksgiving were overflowing with praise and thanksgiving to God. Now it was time to part, and for most of them we would not see them again until Heaven. Pete and I were packed up, in our car to head for home. We always said, "There is no possible way to honestly share with anyone what just happened this week". It was overwhelming. Our hearts were so full of thanksgiving and joy, we felt like we were going to burst. Someone has well said, "If you can explain it, God didn't do it." We looked over the evaluations of the Oasis participants. Here are some of the remarks that were made:

> "We received much validation and affirmation of ministry in the context of loss. This concept of Oasis is critical to the church's current crisis in leadership."

> "It's the first time in twenty years of ministry that I have been able to tell my story of hurt without someone saying, "Yes, But....!""

> "Though we were in seminary for years, I don't think all our education could have taught us what we learned this week as a young pastoral couple."

> "It felt like we were given a life preserver and then given survival tools to go along with it."

> "I sensed a release of my damaged emotions in a safe and caring atmosphere."

> "We were able to break through old buried issues and pain. We

felt vulnerable and safe at the same time."

"A significant breakthrough in dealing with painful bondage from past hurts. A warm, and accepting team provided a safe place to be open and honest."

"I came hurt and closed, but by some miracle my spirit began to open within the first twenty-four hours."

"This week has been the most honest, helpful, soul-restoring event in twenty-five years of ministry."

Pete and I were in awe. To think that we had thought that we could not finish well! That our years of effective service were done. Just these testimonies made all the betrayal, loss, and wrestling with God worth it all. We thought of the hundreds of churches and missionary work our Oasis participants represented and how their renewed, refreshed, hope-filled hearts could continue ministering out of brokenness in a more effective way than they had ever ministered, before coming to Oasis. This ministry would ripple across our land and world in ways we would never hear about but God knew and God had been faithful to take our broken hearts, and "take our mourning and turn it into a joyful dance." (Psalm 30:11)

A Gift From God 2003

I had corresponded with Jerry Sittser a few times over the years. I told Pete if we ever get near Spokane, Washington, I would like to see if we could meet Jerry in person. That very day did come. We contacted Jerry and busy as he was, he made time for us to visit with him. Sitting in his office and immediately sensing his tender caring heart brought tears to my eyes. As we looked around the office there was plaque after plaque of Jerry being chosen: Most Appreciated Professor of the Year. How God had ever led me to be a small part of Jerry' life was nothing but a gracious gift from God.

As we visited in the office, eventually Jerry told us he was working on another book called *When God Does Not Answer Your Prayers*. Right away I told him I would sure be looking forward to reading his new book, as that was one of my deepest questions during my wrestling time. To my surprise, Jerry looked at me and said; "Shirley, would you be willing to write out your story for me. I would like to use something from a pastor's wife in my book." I told him I would be delighted to do that, "If God can use our painful story in any way to help others I would be thrilled." Our story is beautifully written by Jerry in this book.

Caution Detour Ahead

July 25th, 2003 Pete woke up with pain in his chest and in his arm. He recognized this detour sign and we headed for the hospital. After they put Pete on the treadmill the doctor said, "You have what we call a widowmaker, a silent killer, a heart attack waiting to happen. You have a blockage we will tend to right away." We were hopeful a stent could be put in but it could not, because his blockage was too close to the main aorta. He would have to have open-heart surgery for a single by-pass. And then the wait began. He was brought back to the Abbotsford Hospital and stayed there for twenty three days before he was finally given a slot to have his surgery.

The kids came and stayed and left. For the first time in my life, I was the one who was standing beside the bed and my husband was in the bed. On August 13 Pete came through the surgery well. The next day was our 45th anniversary.

Our family was facing a dilemma. We had made all the arrangements for our family of twenty to meet at our favorite spot on the Oregon Coast. I had worked hard at arranging a Blessing Tea for our two granddaughters. Our kids found another wonderful place, Harrison Hot Springs Resort. There was availability to rent a small cabin for each family. Five different hot spring pools, a beautiful lake with some of the nations best sand. Here our family spent five wonderful days of fun and sharing. They were close enough to take turns coming to see us at home. Pete was not doing well. He had pain, was uncomfortable and could not sleep. For the first time in his life he realized the challenges I face with sleepless nights. It was discovered that his medication had been wrongly prescribed and he was getting twice the amount of the main pill he was on. Once that was corrected he began to gain strength and health. Eventually he was his old positive perky self. Someone asked him, "Did they put an energizer bunny in your heart during the surgery?" That's what it felt like.

I had arranged for all the women of our family, to come into town with our two 16 year old granddaughters, for a lovely tea held at my dear friend Diane's beautiful home. She baked the scones. It was a lovely "blessing tea" to honor and encourage these sweet 16-year-old girls of the family. Each of the women prepared a page for a memory book for these girls. They had 8x10 pictures of themselves when they were sixteen. They wrote out their blessings to the girls and what helped them when they were that age. I gave each girl a small tea set. We all gathered around them and laid hands on them and prayed God's blessing, protection and guidance on their lives. It was a beautiful, sacred time.

The kids all came to our home for the last day of the reunion, Food and a cake for our 45th Anniversary was ordered in. Our kids had gotten together and gave us each beautiful new watches with the date of our anniversary and the words, "Still United to Serve" engraved on the back. Oh, what a blessing.

I was called the family paparazzi but never thought of taking a family picture until my friend Susan said, "You have to have a picture of this time." She ran over, we walked to our neighbor's steps and had our photo taken there. To this day that is one of my most precious family pictures. God had brought us through another crisis, filled with major health issues, pain, parties, and love. The stuff of life!

We ministered at Oasis for fourteen years. Through personal crisis of major surgery for both Pete and me, siblings deaths, illness and the challenges of life, neither Pete nor I missed one Oasis. That was God's precious hand of protection on the ministry of Oasis. We were so privileged to hear the stories of over 700 participants at 57 different retreats, coming from 63 different denominations/missions, from 30 countries of the world, 25 US States, and 8 Canadian provinces/territories. God had certainly started a new fire out of the ashes of what we thought was failure. God always has the final say.

Baton Passing

September 10, 2010, was a significant time for the ministry of Oasis. It was time for us, at 73 years of age to pass the leadership on to a younger couple. We had done much heart searching and fervent prayer as we asked God to direct us to the couple who would take over the leadership of Oasis. Bob and Penny Armstrong had been faithful servants of the Lord as pastors and counselors. They were drawn to the ministry of Oasis and felt the hand of God upon them for this calling. After much prayer and discussion on the part of us and the staff, we gave them a unanimous call. Our team warned us that things might change in the future. We would trust God in Bob and Penny and the staff to continue the vision of Oasis.

Many people who had supported this God blessed work of Oasis came for this changing of the guard. Family, friends, servant team, and staff came to support our finishing well, and Bob and Penny's beginning well. The President of Power to Change, was there with well-wishes and a beautiful bouquet of flowers. The staff spoke, our Pastor Rick was flown in to be a part of this evening, as was Brian Doerksen. The team honored us with gifts of blessing and appreciation, love, and thanksgiving.

When I spoke I said, "When we first started Oasis, God put in my heart these verses from Isaiah 61. That was our mandate for fourteen years. "The Spirit of the Sovereign Lord is on me because He had anointed me to bind up the brokenhearted, to comfort those who mourn, to bestow a crown of beauty instead of ashes, the oil of gladness instead of the mourning, the garment of praise instead of a spirit of despair. They (Oasis participants) will be called oaks of righteousness, a planting of the Lord for the display of his splendor."

I told Bob and Penny I was praying this same anointing on them, that the Spirit of the Sovereign Lord would be upon them. It is beyond any of us to accomplish anything in the hearts and lives of those who would come broken, weary and in despair. It is always the work of the Spirit of God using us as His vessels of clay.

The team gave us a lovely mantle clock with the pendulum swinging back and forth. What God began in us is rippling across the world in ways we could never have expected or dreamed of. He took the ashes of our pain and our shattered dreams and made something very beautiful.

For the child of God, suffering is not wasted. It's not an end in itself. Scripture reminds us, "For our light and momentary troubles are achieving for us an eternal glory that far outweighs them all" (2 Corinthians 4:17). In some way, God uses suffering to transform ordinary, broken clay pots into vessels that are strong in faith; vessels that are fit for His use; vessels that display His glory to the watching world. God redeems our pain and suffering as we trust the Potter to know exactly what He is doing. With God in control, our suffering, our sorrows, our disappointment in life are never wasted. It's such a comfort to know that God has a good purpose for all the pain, loss and wrestling we have been through. Oasis is a testimony to that truth.

Oasis continues to this day. Different, yes, but still ministering to the broken and needy servants of the Lord. We pray, we support, we cheer on and we stand still and watch what God will do with Oasis, our baby, our dream, now grown.

Chapter Twelve

RECONCILIATION – A MIRACLE OF GOD

Abbotsford, BC

"Wait for the Lord; be strong and take heart and wait for the Lord." Psalm 27:14

After writing our letter to our last church called, *Resting our Case With God*, we truly did leave the unresolved relationships with God. That letter was written in 1997. We stayed in the community, and had contact with many people who were dear friends from the church. It was these friends who became the core of our Servant Team and Prayer Team for Oasis. We did pray often for our former church and asked God that someday there would be reconciliation.

The Waiting Years Of Reconciliation

Seven years after our resignation from our church, we had a call from our dear friend, who Pete had led to the Lord in the early 90's. He was now the church moderator and was working closely with the new senior pastor. He asked if he could have dinner with us, as he had some things that needed some clarification regarding Oasis. We were delighted to meet with him.

At first the atmosphere seemed strained. The church moderator immediately asked us if we were giving the church a bad reputation when we spoke at Oasis. We told him that we were not. We shared how we tried to mask the identity of those involved in our betrayal, but never gave names and never put a bad light on the church. This relaxed him a lot. As we talked, he asked us to tell him our story of our experience of serving at the church from the beginning and of our ministry of Oasis. For two hours he listened as we poured out our hearts to him. He was quiet, contemplative, and thoughtful. What an amazing gift it is to have someone listen – really listen – to your heart, without interruption or clarification. At the end of our story he said to us, "This cannot be left unresolved. It must be reconciled, if there will ever be God's full blessing on the church and on your ministry." We were in shock. He pled with us to give him some time, and to pray that the Holy Spirit would guide him as he talked with the pastors and the board. He told us it may take a long time. He would contact us. And so we waited and waited. We knew all of this was really in God's hands and we often prayed for the church moderator and the church. Our prayers included pleading with the Holy Spirit to soften hearts and speak to those involved. Forced apologies never work. As the years rolled by, we thought there was no hope for reconciliation.

Life sometimes has abrupt changes. In December of 2006 while in the middle of our waiting and prayer for reconciliation, we were vacationing at our friend's condo in Arizona. My mother, now totally blind at 95, was not doing well. I got a flight home on Christmas Day, to be with my mother and sister, in Kelowna, BC, Canada. When I got to my mother's bedside all she said, over and over again was "Oh, Shirley, Oh, Shirley." Those were the last words she ever spoke. Kim was playing and singing to her as she entered a weeklong coma.

Pete decided to drive to my home, to join in the vigil with our mother. He was going right by our home, in Abbotsford, BC, on this drive, so decided to pick up the mail we had not forwarded to Arizona. To his surprise he opened an official looking letter from the church. When he arrived in Kelowna, he told me about getting a letter from the church, but little of that sunk into my mind. I was totally journeying with my dear mother, praying and releasing her into the arms of Jesus.

January 1st, 2007, as we sat with our Mom, to our surprise, she raised up a bit, opened her eyes more than wide, and looked up around the room with a look of awe and wonder. I rushed to her side and said, "Mama, are you entering Heaven? Is this your time to see Jesus?" My mother closed her eyes and peacefully died in the arms of Jesus. Oh, what a gift God gave all three of us to be with our dear Mom, the moment she entered Heaven. The awe and glory that she saw was surely a taste of eternity forever and ever.

The Hard Work Of Reconciliation

Later that night, Pete shared the letter with me. Below are some of the details of that letter, with the full permission, encouragement and blessing of the church board, I share it with you:

November 23, 2006

Dear Pete and Shirley,

Greetings in the name of our Lord and Savior, Jesus Christ, from your brothers and sisters! In Romans 14:19-20, the apostle Paul gives us the principle that we are to do everything we can to live peaceably with one another. Within the context of the passage, he urges us not to destroy the work of God for the sake of our own desires or interests. In recent months the Elder Council and Pastoral Staff have become increasingly burdened regarding broken relationships with former pastors, leaders, and missionaries of our church. We grieve these painful circumstances and therefore, would like to do all that we can to live out Paul's exhortation to live peaceably with one another. Before the Lord and each other, we would like to seek your forgiveness and the reconciliation of our relationship with one another.

We are, therefore, contacting all former pastors, leaders, and missionaries of our church to invite you to participate in this reconciliation process. It is our intention to contact all of you to ensure that no one, who might want to participate, is overlooked.

One way we, as the Elders and Pastoral Staff, believe that this area of pain can be addressed is during the weekend of January 27 and 28, 2007. We have set this weekend aside for the express purpose of reconciliation. Specifically, we see three components to this process:

> 1) A private meeting with you and your wife with three or four Elders and their wives, along with a member of our restoration team. The purpose of this meeting will be to allow you to express the wounds that we have caused and how it has

affected your life and ministry. It will also give us an opportunity to seek your forgiveness. Our intention is to acknowledge the hurt that you have experienced and to repent of the pain we have caused. This is not about adjudicating past disputes or grievances, nor is it our intention to assign responsibility.

2) A service of Communion will be held for the former pastors, leaders, and missionaries, with the Elders and their wives.

3) A public service titled, "A Service of Reconciliation and New Beginnings" will be held on Sunday morning, January 28, 2007. The purpose of this service is to publicly express our repentance and our sorrow for past actions and to ask forgiveness from you, our former pastors, leaders and missionaries, and from God. We will not be sharing details regarding past conflicts.

For some of you, the experience was many years ago and you may not want to revisit the pain that has been caused. For others of you, this may be an opportunity that you have prayed for. If you have questions about the weekend or the steps we have taken to get to this point, please contact the chairman of our restoration team and the Moderator of our Elder Council.

Would you please respond by indicating whether or not you intend to participate in this weekend? Also, we would appreciate any other comments or suggestions that you may have. We look forward to hearing from you.

In a spirit of humility, the Senior Pastor, the Church Moderator and the Chairman of the Board of Elders

Was this the letter for which we had been praying and waiting for ten years? Pete quickly called our friend, the moderator, and told him we had just received this letter and the reasons for the delay. He told him we were very interested in being a part of this reconciliation time. He told him we did have a couple of concerns and would share those with him. It was agreed that they could talk about these details after my Mother's funeral. Pete called the moderator later on and shared his heart with him. He was totally supportive of the initiation of the church to make reconciliation a high priority. "God has given us the ministry of reconciliation" (2 Corinthians 5:18-19). He appreciated the spirit of humility and the steps taken to make reconciliation a reality.

Pete said, "There is one sentence that does greatly concern me. When you wrote in your letter: '"This is not about adjudicating past disputes or grievances, nor is it our intention to assign responsibility." Pete said, "If no one is willing to take any responsibility for wrong done then there can be no reconciliation." The moderator said that they knew there were some things the church needed to make right with us and were willing to do so. He said they would have to ask us for additional help in areas we felt that we had been wronged by the church.

Pete told the moderator that he had just read Gary Chapman's book entitled, The Five Languages of Apology and was blown away with his clarity on asking forgiveness, admitting wrong, and saying the words, "I was wrong; will you forgive me?" Pete asked if the leaders of the church, that were involved in this reconciliation would read this book before they met together? The moderator was totally in favor of encouraging this.

We headed home, constantly putting our lives, our words, our thoughts, and our prayers for a deep total reconciliation to happen to the glory of God, the good of His church, and for us, His servants.

The moderator and the chairman of the elder board arranged a meeting with us in our home a few days after we arrived home. This meeting laid the groundwork for the whole reconciliation process. We immediately sensed such a mutual spirit of brokenness and desire to do this right. We expressed our blindness to our own faults and asked for their help for us by pointing out any wrongs that we were guilty of. They could not think of anything unresolved on our part.

Then they asked for our help in pinpointing the unresolved issues that we felt the church, through its leadership, needed to take ownership for and ask for our forgiveness. We wanted to major on the majors. We mentioned two things that lay at the root of the deep hurts still felt by us. One was the total mishandling of the staff evaluation process. The other issue that we both strongly felt needed to be flagged was the public meeting which was called for on a Sunday evening. The meeting was long and not handled well. People did not obey the parameters set at the beginning, and were not held to the clearly given guidelines.

Our friends seeking reconciliation left our home that night with a genuine commitment to get approval from the full elder board to move forward to complete reconciliation. What a blessed opportunity and relief it was for Pete and me to share our hearts with these men of God, and have them listen with such humble attitudes. They said they would write a letter of apology and mail it to us. I asked if they would be willing to come back to our house in person with this all important letter in hand. I felt that something of this magnitude needed to be done person to person. We needed to hear their hearts, not just their words. We needed to look them in the eye and feel their hugs. This was a momentous time, and needed to be treated that way. With joy, they totally agreed.

January 27th, 2007, was Reconciliation Sunday at the church. We were there. We wanted to cheer all attempts to hold high the values of people being reconciled among each other and the leaders. We believe the humility, the hard work, and the desire of this church to see reconciliation across the body of the church people, was something we wanted to celebrate with them. How beautiful are the feet of those who bring peace.

A huge white brick-like wall had been built on the platform, about four feet high. There was a door locked shut that no person could travel across this bridge over the water and the long path that the wall had made. At the finish of the service a large lumberjack of a man took his sledgehammer and eventually broke that door down. All who wanted to indicate they wanted to be reconciled or had just been reconciled, were to walk over the bridge and across the water on the path to the other side, indicating their willingness to reconcile with all people. We walked across that bridge with trust in the Holy Spirit who was at work. It was a grand celebration Sunday, ending up with a beautiful, tearful communion service.

For us personally there was something missing. We wondered if we should have come. Nothing was said about our presence or about the work of reconciliation that was in process with us. We left that all with God who was at work. Our time would come we believed.

Our Personal Reconciliation came two days after this public reconciliation Sunday, when the leaders of the church came to our home and asked for our forgiveness. sharing their beautiful letter of apology, with the naming of the things they felt needed our forgiveness.

Following is the letter that the moderator, the Senior Pastor, and the chairman of the board brought to our home to read to us. They told us we could use these letters as an example, a template, to share with anyone that could be helped in their work towards reconciliation. What gracious, humble, and teachable hearts these men of God had.

January 29, 2007

Dear Pete and Shirley,

The present leadership, on behalf of our church, would like to offer a sincere apology to you both for the hurt and anguish caused by decisions made at the church in the past.

We acknowledge that as a result of our decisions you were both subjected to pain, embarrassment, humiliation, and damage to your reputation, both within the church and in the community.

We also acknowledge that both your short term and long term financial status would have changed, and likely for the worse.

In particular we would like to offer an apology for:

The evaluation process that you were subjected to and any mishandling of that process.

The questioning of your integrity, which we acknowledge was later proved to be without basis.

The public meeting which was intended to

allow a structured discussion around issues, with both sides able to provide representation. We acknowledge that this meeting was not well facilitated and as a result you were subjected to a public assassination of your character without opportunity to respond.

Although most of the present leadership were not party to the events that we describe, we acknowledge that errors were made and there were times when decisions were wrong. Our church accepts full responsibility for all these events.

A number of years have passed since your departure, and as in all things God has been teaching us about our shortcomings and past errors in that time. As we have accepted God's leading and teaching, we can assure you that leadership at the church has strived to change procedures, governance, and processes. Through prayer, God has also taught us to be more patient and discerning when making decisions.

While it will be small consolation to you both, many of these positive changes were instigated as a result of our learning from the issues that arose prior to and after your departure.

We are thrilled that despite this chapter in your lives, God is blessing you both in your "Oasis" ministry, and we want to express our strong desire that God will continue to bless you both and that you will achieve even greater things with His guidance and prompting.

It is the desire of our Church to move forward and totally repair, and then continue to build on the relationship between yourselves and ourselves, whatever form that may take. For that reason, in the spirit of reconciliation, we offer this sincere apology and seek your forgiveness for the consequences of our actions.

In Christ's love,

Signed by the Senior Pastor, the Church Moderator and the Chairman of the Board of Elders

What a day of reconciliation! A day I will never forget! For them to use the word forgiveness meant the world to me. How can one simple word erase ten years of pain and sadness? We had experienced the working out of this verse, "Be kind and compassionate to one another, forgiving each other, just as in Christ God Forgave You" (Ephesians 4:32). It is God's way and it works!

Just before the men arrived at our home that day, Pete said to me: "To me, the ultimate sign of true repentance and reconciliation will be, if they ever ask me to come back to preach again." That too happened. After they read their letter, and we verbalized our full forgiveness, the pastor spoke up and said, "One more thing. I'd like to ask you to come back to preach for us in March." Pete lost it. He broke down and wept for joy and release. To be asked to preach is a sign of trust and respect which he had lost and it was now restored. We were all in tears and in each others arms as forgiveness was sought and granted. Experiencing the humility and detailed work these men had gone to touched us deeply. The joy of looking in each others' eyes and knowing the work of reconciliation was a work of God in all of our hearts. The above letter was shared two days after the church's reconciliation service.

Our Personal Public Reconciliation Sunday

The Sunday Pete came back to the church to preach was March 4th, 2007. All grievances and pain had been forgiven and put under the blood of Jesus. Before Pete began to preach, Our friend, the church moderator, got up and told the congregation the steps of reconciliation the leadership of the church had taken with us. He mentioned how they had come to our home and read a letter that had the things for which the church needed to ask our forgiveness. He told of the great amount of tears, complete forgiveness, peace, and celebration. Our prayers of ten years had been answered.

When Pete got up to preach, the first thing he did was to honor the pastor, the chairman of the board of elders, and the moderator on their humble and thorough work of bringing about this reconciliation. He looked right at the pastor and said, "You and your leaders did it right. You led your church in this grand reconciliation and we thank you and give God praise." Pete said he had never experienced such anointing from God as he did when he preached that morning. That Sunday there were many who came to the front to wish us God's blessing; a few asked our forgiveness, and many gave us the hugs and love we had so missed. After that service, we and our kids, Brent and Denise, went back to Warren and Susan's home for a lunch of rejoicing and relief.

We look back now and marvel at God's orchestration of the events of this time in our lives. God dovetailed the receiving of the first letter with my mother's homegoing to heaven. The timing was the working of our God of the details small and great.

We praise our Lord and Savior, that God led us to leave the door open for reconciliation on both our side and the side of the church. That was a key. All the pastors Pete has talked to in sixty years of ministry, traveling across Canada and the US, speaking to thousands of pastors, we have never heard of such a real reconciliation with a pastor and the church. I believe without the church moderator's hard work, reconciliation would never have happened. It takes one good man to be willing to stand up and say, "This cannot go on. This needs to be addressed." How this humbles us as we give all the glory to our God who "orchestrated all things to work together for something good and beautiful" (Romans 8:28 Voice). This truly blessed the church people, and us, His wounded servants. We ask God to do it again for the many unreconciled pastors and churches worldwide. Pastors and wives hear this story and weep for such a day in their lives. We weep with them because it so seldom done. Churches and pastor couples are suffering because reconciliation has not happened.

My dear friend Susan wrote about this reconciliation process for an assignment for her Master's Degree in Spiritual Direction at seminary. With her permission I add her unique evaluation of this Miracle of Reconciliation:

> "I have chosen to write about Pete and Shirley's experience because I walked very closely with them through the pain and agony of this time period. I have

told them that I believe their tenacity and unwillingness to just let it go (when there was immense pressure to do so) was a gift to the church. They were relentless in their desire for reconciliation and to truth-telling. They were unwilling to undervalue the immense pain and their losses as a pastoral couple. They were vocal about their desire to do what they call, "the work of reconciliation".

The process of reconciliation took about ten years, but in the end, this church decided to lift the carpet and take a deep look at what was underneath. For some time previously there were overtures and attempts at reconciliation, but for my friends, these felt more like trying to relieve the church's tension, than about expressing remorse and sorrow for the immense hurt that they caused.

Reconciliation Sunday was a beautiful day, ten years in the making, bathed in tears and losses, bathed in a will to lean into the pain, acknowledge loss, acknowledge guilt, acknowledge God's Spirit at work. They will to this day, speak about the day the church came back, to honestly deal with it's past. They acknowledge to the best of their ability that they are at peace with all men. They acknowledge that there are some of the original players which have remained strangely silent through the process, but they accepted the apology of the board and the church and offered forgiveness and reconciliation to them, holding hope that one day "all would be well". I look back on that whole experience and I feel as if God gave my friends just enough light for their way forward in a very dark night of their soul. I believe that their willingness to reconcile with God themselves, allowed them the space they needed to step back and let God open the doors toward reconciliation. They did their own work, were able to articulate their losses and offered them back to the church. The church in turn offered their acknowledgment of wrongdoing and held out their humble hands toward my friends. That day was a beautiful example of the restorative work of God in the church.

My love, Susan

As we look back on the miracle of reconciliation with this beloved church, we bless the Lord who worked in our hearts and in the hearts of the leaders and the people of the church. This miracle of reconciliation stands today as a testament to doing it God's way and receiving God's rewards on earth and for all eternity. The church has continued on and today is doing well. We were so gifted with this reconciliation and so was the church.

Our heart's of thanksgiving cry out to our God, praise be to our Savior and Lord who is called: " Wonderful, Counsellor, The mighty God, The Everlasting Father, The Prince of Peace" (Isaiah 9:6).

Chapter Thirteen

Retired Or Fully Engaged

Kelowna, BC, Canada 2008

Grow old with me. The best is yet to be.

The Next Step

Our daughter and husband phoned us in 2007 and offered for us to come and build a home on their farm once we retired. They wanted us to live nearby to enjoy proximity and also be available to help us as we got older. We couldn't turn down that offer. The city's stipulation was, our house had to be attached to their house, making a duplex-look. Our hearts were thrilled and we began to envision not having to put our shoes on to visit. What a blessing to think of living next door to our kids and three grandkids. Our son Kim and his wife Darlene with their three sons all live in Kelowna. This is where Pete and I were married. This would be the first time in our marriage that we would live in the same town as any of our kids and now to have six of our ten grandkids living near us. We would now be able to go to band and choir concerts, graduations, and connect with them on a more regular basis. Such a gift to us in our older years!

We had lived about an hour from Brent and Denise, Sara and Tristan once they settled in after Italy. We spent many happy times visiting them, making meals to eat with them when their schedule was too busy for them to come and see us. When we told our other kids of Bruce and Kathy's offer, granddaughter Sara spoke up and said, "We have had you for ten years. I think it is just right that we share you with the other grandchildren."

We put our beloved house that we had so enjoyed, up for sale. Our nephew, who was in real estate, encouraged us to try and sell it on our own. We sold it in one day. A whole story in itself. We sold when the market was high. The next month the bottom fell out of the market. Thank you God.

Daughter Kathy did all the planning of the new house on the orchard. It is 1,100 square feet with a full basement. She planned it to all be wheelchair accessible. Because our home sold so fast, we arrived in Kelowna before our home was completed. We lived with our kids for four months. All our belongings were in a steel box on the farm.

Our 50th Wedding Anniversary, August 2008

In the middle of the summer we planned to have a grand family reunion for our 50th Anniversary. We went back to Abbotsford to have our celebration in the church hall where we had been attending for ten years. We took formal family pictures and then we all ate dinner at Warren and Susan's house, prepared by my brother, married to Pete's sister, missionaries from Italy. How we all enjoyed this delicious meal. The kids set up a higher chair for me to sit on while we greeted people as they arrived at the church. My cancer leg will not take standing still for too long. We invited one person from each church or ministry we had served in to give a couple of minutes of testimony. This was very heartwarming for us to see how God had used these clay pots to bring people to Jesus and saw them growing in their walk with God.

Then our kids took over and gave us their blessing in many unique and beautiful ways. Our daughter had prepared a dance to honor us. Two of our kids sang a beautiful duet. There were fun and games with lots of laughter and joy. Our son Bevan gave a short devotional that deeply touched us. For the closing part of the program the whole family got up and sang To God be the Glory. The reception was lovely, a little like our wedding with strawberry shortcake. People came from long distances to be a part of this awesome evening. We were thrilled and humbled by it all. We then took our kids to Vancouver Island, where we had rented a lovely home, that slept twenty, right on a white sand beach. We had such a precious bonding time as a family. Watching our kids and grandkids organize their creative and fun ideas for play, was a joy to our hearts.

Back in Kelowna, our days were filled with building our new house and making a myriad of decisions. I remember the day the floor was laid. No walls were up as yet, just the floor. I asked our eight-year-old granddaughter to put on her tap dancing shoes and to tap dance her young heart out all over our floor. Once our home was built and we were settled into it, our hearts were full of thanksgiving and gratitude. Everything was so beautiful inside the house and our expansive view was breathtaking. We could see bountiful apple, cherry, and pear orchards. In the distance there were pastoral green lands with beautiful mountains surrounding our whole vista. What an unbelievable place our kids had gifted us with, for our senior years. We would never tire of this ever-changing gorgeous landscape.

We thought, we have the time and energy now, let's save resources and work hard to take each of our kids and their spouses, one couple at a time, on a separate cruise with us. Our daughter said, "You have always had the priority of relationships over money." I liked that our kids saw and experienced that heart focus of ours. We thought this would be a good time to cruise to some places we had always wanted to see, and who better to cruise together with than our kids. We did just that. We took each couple on four different cruises to the Panama Canal, an Alaska Cruise, flying into Anchorage and spending more time in the far north glaciers, a Baltic cruise and a Mediterranean cruise.

We felt that when we all meet as a group, as wonderful at it is, you never get too deep in conversation with anyone for an extended period. With these cruises we would have dinner with just one couple and talk about things that really mattered to us. Our kids were thrilled and that made us so blessed and thankful for the great harmony in our family. Yes, there are differing views on a number of issues, but on the major life issues we all agree and we leave the differences with God. One son put it this way, "Mom and Dad, it's good to remember that in our family we have some no-fly zones. There are subjects we just leave alone." Yes, my son, you are a wise man.

Eye Stroke 2010 Just before the Baltic cruise I had a stroke in my left eye. It happened in church. It felt like something flew into my eye. When we got home I covered my good eye to see if I had a detached retina or something else. I saw very little out of that eye. It was like a curtain had been pulled down over the eye and just a little light shone through at the bottom. We went to an ophthalmologist, who froze my eye to see deep within and said to me, "Mrs. Unrau, you have just had a stroke in your eye. It happened suddenly. There is nothing anyone can do to repair this eye stroke. This condition is irreversible and permanent. You will learn to live with one eye. Lots of people do. There are a lot of one-eyed drivers out there."

Well, I had never heard of such a thing as a stroke in the eye. I was admitted to the hospital for a multitude of tests, but no one could see where the clot had dislodged from to give me the stroke. The picture of the eye clearly showed the little clot in a vein, but beyond that vein there were no more veins. One doctor said it could have been far worse if that clot had gone to my brain, for then I would be dead or paralyzed on one side of my body. Another doctor called this "a shot over the bow of your ship." It was a sign and I must pay attention. Blood thinner pills would be the norm for me for the rest of my life. After more tests, procedures and the final exam I was cleared to go on the cruise.

Our second stop on the cruise was a beautiful day in Helsinki, Finland. Our son wanted to take a picture of us on this hill with the city in the background. That meant we would have to look into the sunlight, which has always been hard for me. I told our son to count to three and then I would open my eyes. Before he started counting a searing red-hot pain pierced through my eye leaving me doubled over with pain. I crouched, immobilized for a while, allowing the pain to decrease. Soon I was getting up and before long the pain was gone. We continued our tour of this beautiful city. Back at the ship I once again put my hand over my good eye and that curtain had lifted. I could see out of my left eye.

We told our son and daughter-in-law about it at dinner and Bevan said, "I prayed that this pain would be a healing touch from God; not further damage." Oh, thank You, Jesus. You have given us both blessing and sorrow but through it all, you are SO good.

When we got home, neither ophthalmologist or optometrist could believe what they were seeing in the damaged eye. Before the cruise I couldn't see the eye chart on the wall, now I could read three or four lines down. One doctor said, "This just doesn't happen. I can't explain what has happened that your eye is clear." Pete asked, "Could it have been be a miracle?" The doctor said, "Whatever." The last time we saw the picture of the eye the doctor was once again amazed. Beyond the clot, new veins had formed, bringing me better vision now in my damaged eye than my other eye. It surely is true that one never knows what a day will bring forth." We are in God's hands at all times.

Family Reunion on Orchard Hill Farm, Kelowna, BC 2011 Daughter Kathy had a dream to host a family reunion on their farm. The whole family arrived, bunking in with us, our son Kim's home nearby, and Bruce and Kathy's home. We have learned with nineteen active kids and grandkids that we and our kids have to plan in advance so that there will be participatory and exciting activities for all.

We decided to make one day a water fun, play day. Kelowna is surrounded by a myriad of beautiful lakes and beaches We rented a boat, a couple of Sea-Doos, round tubes that three or four could get on, pulled by the high-powered speed boat. The grandkids were all just the right age to enjoy this day at the waterfront extravaganza. There was also time to sit on the beach, play volleyball and visit with each other. Soon it was time to head back to the farm, enjoy tasty meals, the swimming pool, hot tub, ping-pong and other table games on the go.

The next day was Pete's 75th birthday celebration. I asked a friend to cater this meal. Tables were set out on the patio with lights strewn around the edge. I saw my daughter sitting there with her sisters-in-law, her friends, and just glowing with satisfaction. Her dream had come true.

Pete thought, "I am the patriarch of this family. I have the privilege, responsibility, and relationship with my family to share my heart with them during the evening gathering." He did just that. It was a hushed sacred moment while he shared the following.

Pete's 75th Birthday Challenge

Today, August 5, 2011 is a dream come true for Mom and me. All twenty-one of you have made the effort to be here in Kelowna for our family reunion. Just this past week as I was anticipating your arrival, it hit me, "Pete, you're about to be 75 years old; that's three-quarters of a century." I was inspired to speak the following words of wisdom to all of you.

1. Never give up on responding to and following Jesus. He is still the way, the truth and the life. May every response to every

choice that you face always be, "What would Jesus do?"

2. Never ignore the Bible. It is still God's authoritative and reliable book of instructions for all people for faith and practise. May your ultimate question in response to any message or voice that you hear or read ever be, "This is what she/he says, what does the Bible say?" That will give you a solid anchor in life.

3. Never give up on the church. It is still God's agency for mutual fellowship, spiritual growth and character development, the celebration of the ordinances and missional outreach to those outside the family of God.

4. Never minimize the value of the family. It is still the God ordained haven of rest, safety and lifelong care. You will ever be welcome and loved regardless. You can never stop us from loving you and praying for you.

Dad and Mom

After the reunion was over Pete gathered all the pictures together, and made a wonderful computer book with pictures of all our activities, including his birthday. At the back of the book he wrote out this "Birthday Challenge." We gave a copy of this book to each individual in the family for Christmas. We would have never imagined that this would be the last time our whole family would be together on this earth.

Heartbreak Call 2011

We were on vacation in Florida, December 31st. 2011. New Year's Eve, we received the most difficult and hardest phone call we have ever received. Our son Kim was on the phone. He told us that our 14-year-old grandson, Jordan, had stage four bone cancer in his right leg. It had already metastasized to his spine and to a place on the arm on the opposite side. We could not believe what we were hearing. We just had had an early Christmas with the Kelowna families and everything was full of happiness, health, and fun. Now Jordan was at Ronald McDonald House, in Vancouver, BC. This was a special home for kids and their parents in trauma and crisis near the Children's Hospital. The doctor told Kim right away, that he didn't have much hope that they could save Jordan's life. They would do their best. This could not be happening, I thought, cancer on the same leg as mine thirty years ago. There are no words that can explain our shock and grief.

We had planned a cruise out of San Juan to sail to ports in the Southern Caribbean. We sure didn't feel like cruising now. How can you sit at a table of strangers with a rock in the pit of your stomach? We were scheduled to have ten days of ministry in Puerto Rico with our dear friends who had come to Oasis. We wondered how we could minister to others when we were so hurting and broken ourselves. We told Kim that we would cancel everything and come home right away. He said, "Don't cancel your plans. There isn't much you could do at this point that you can't do elsewhere, mainly pray."

Jordan was the youngest of Kim and Darlene's three boys. He was a beautiful blond haired happy boy who loved Jesus with all his heart. He had a very tender spirit. He was also inquisitive and full of questions. One of his favorite things to do when we would take him out for a treat or a special birthday breakfast, was to hurry around to my car door and open it for me, wait until I was in and close it. What a little gentleman he was. He was also very bold about talking to people about Jesus. When in the hospital he would ask a doctor to pray for him before a procedure. When the doctor said that he didn't pray, Jordan asked if he could pray for him? Wow, what a testimony he was. When in a wheelchair he would wheel up to someone else in a wheelchair and ask them, "Do you know Jesus?" or "Do you mind if I pray for you?" His love and faith in Jesus just poured out of him. Now all family, friends, prayer warriors, and those who heard of Jordan's situation were called to join in fervent, believing and continual prayer.

When we were in Puerto Rico there was much prayer going on for Jordan. We had come to minister. God turned it around so that we were the ones being ministered to. When we got home, our first time with Jordan was sad and short. What do you say to your 14-year-old grandson, who you love with all you heart and now he is in such pain? Jordan had some periods of remission. One day we were at his home visiting him and the ever questioning Jordan asked, "Grandpa and Grandma, if you could go anywhere in the world that you have already been to, where would you go?" After thinking for a bit we said "Hawaii. We love that place." Jordan said: "I love Hawaii too." A few months later Jordan was able to "Make-A-Wish", as to what he would like to do during his remission. He immediately chose Hawaii with his whole family. Oh, what precious memories for the family.

There were weeks and weeks of unrelenting pain. Jordan kept his eyes on Jesus. Eventually nothing could relieve him from the pain. "Oh Jesus heal him," we would cry and pray. At one time the doctor wanted to amputate Jordan's cancerous leg. He said it would give him about three months more to live. Jordan said, "No, do not amputate. Either Jesus will heal me or take me to Heaven." His last request was to have communion with his Mom and Dad. Oh, how precious! What a testimony to loving his Jesus even when healing was not coming. After communion he slipped into eternity and into the arms of Jesus he loved so much.

Christmas came a few short weeks after our farewell to Jordan. In time I wrote this to my Facebook friends, "It is true. You can balance both grief and joy in your heart at the same time. Jordan's home going to Heaven and Christmas are bleeding together, whether I want it to or not. I have a basket full of cards of sympathy and love and another of Christmas cheer. We have our little Christmas tree up and the flowers from Jordan's celebration are still blooming. It all boils down to this: Christmas is Emmanuel, God with us. Jordan is with Jesus. Jesus is with us. Either way we both have Jesus with us, and that brings peace and joy in heaven and on earth. Oh, what a Savior."

A friend from Pete men's group, is a businessman and a poet. He wrote this poem for Pete. It represents a letter to Pete from Jordan in Heaven:

Letter to Grandpa Pete
I wish I could hug you, To put your mind at ease;

I am more than content, I'm free from my disease.

No more suffering, My new body's strong;

I woke up in Heaven; Singing a happy song.

Nothing could be sweeter; His promise has been kept:

Brought home to His garden; No more tears to be wept.

I'm living my new dream; Now I'm able to run.

This is the beginning; I can't describe the fun.

One day I will show you; But this is not the time.

Live your life with purpose; Be confident I'm fine.

Rick Lamoureux

Life continued on for our family, each of us bearing this grief and pain in different but real ways, forever. Death leaves a heartache only God can heal. Love leaves a memory no one can steal. Pete turned to God's Word and read through his Bible two times in six months. It led him to a deeper, wider prayer life. The circle of family, pastors, and friends he prayed for grew, as he prays a different verse each day over those on his prayer list. The thought was, "Why not send these people the Scripture I am praying for them, blessing them not only with prayer but with God's Word." Thus, his unique prayer texting ministry began. As I write, the verse Pete has sent out today is "'You have tasted and found the Lord to be good' (1 Peter 2:3 Voice). I'm praying for you right now that you will bask deeply in the goodness of God all day. Your spiritual bodyguard, Pete." This prayer time takes up several hours of his time each morning Monday through Friday: Another beautiful fruit that came out of a difficult heartbreaking time.

15-Year Award July of 2012.

We were invited to an upscale hotel in Vancouver for the annual staff conference for Campus Crusade, now called Power to Change. They wanted to give us a reward for fifteen years of service with them. Pete and I were the most surprised people that we had been with Crusade for that long. It was almost twice as long as we had been anywhere else. God had led us to a mission that would give us the opportunity to teach Family Life Conferences across our nation and beyond. It also gave us the freedom and a protective umbrella, if needed, for the birthing and the directing of Oasis Retreats. That superseded all of our varied ministries in its redemptive healing nationwide. Only God could have orchestrated such a myriad of events that had brought us this beauty and redemption. Being used of God is an adventure you don't want to miss.

Retirement From Power To Change

We had the passing of the Oasis baton to new leadership in 2010, but we continued serving with Power to Change. Our retirement came in November 2013. We had been with Power to Change for sixteen years. Looking back we could see what the hand of God had brought us through. These were all a necessary part of our learning, and our brokenness. "Unless a kernel of wheat falls into the ground and dies, it remains only a single seed. But if it dies, it produces many seeds (John 12:24). This dying to self embraced our own ambitions and our vision of what finishing well would look like. In His time, God brought forth new glorious fruit, that we never would have dreamed possible. We could have stayed in the pastorate and seen God bless there, but Oasis would have never started. God brought death to our reputation, our connections with a loving church, to our hopes of finishing well, and brought forth new life to His glory and praise.

Power to Change put on a lovely farewell for us at the headquarters building. The president and the vice President both gave humbling words of appreciation, respect, and thankfulness to us. They asked us to speak to the staff of mostly young people, on the subject: "What have you learned in 58 years of Ministry?" Pete immediately changed the title of his farewell speech to "What are we still learning after 58 years of ministry?" We never stop learning. I spoke a few words, then Pete gave this slice of his heart.

What are we still learning after 58 years of Ministry?

Here are the anchors or core values that have been our foundation for our years of marriage and ministry:

1. God Always Has The Final Say

As we learn to embrace and rest in the sovereignty of God, it always results in increased humility. As we look back over our years of life and ministry, we can see the weaving of God in our lives for good, when we thought our dreams were being shattered or our life would soon be over.

John the Baptist said, "He must increase and I must decrease" (John 3:30). That is a lifelong struggle to let God be God and not to want or insist on our own way. Jesus prayed in the Garden, "Not my will but yours be done" (Luke 22:42). If we could moment by moment follow the example of John and Jesus, we would not struggle so much when life does not go our way, and our plans are aborted.

2. God's Word Always Has Final Authority

Our life's pivotal question is, "Is it Biblical?" If the Bible says it, I will believe it and stake my life on it. We all choose the voices that we will listen to, the books we will read, the authors and speakers we respect and trust. I want a God who is bigger than my brain. He can be trusted.

3. No One Gets Through Life Unscarred or Unscathed by Pain

Then what? The most frequent response to shocking news is, "Oh God, why?" God never wastes pain; it will make you either bitter or better. Sooner or later pain gets stamped into your passport, unplanned and unwanted. The driving passions in our culture are avoiding pain and finding pleasure. "We celebrate in seasons of suffering because we know that when we suffer we develop endurance which shapes our characters" (Romans 5:3 Voice). God is more interested in our character being developed, preparing us for eternity, than making this short life pleasurable.

4. All Of Life Is A Struggle To Move Us From The Tight Fist Of Control To The Open Hand Of Surrender

Herein lies the root of all conflict, division, wars, hatred, crime, violence, jealousy and family strife. Jesus, the Prince of Peace, came to earth with the message: "Peace on earth, good will toward men." God's ways are often so different than our ways. We heard Corrie ten Boom speak. She said, "It's much easier when I open my hands to God because it hurts so much when God has to pry open each finger." Our choice is to commit ourselves each day to have the attitude of open hands of total surrender to our God.

At the close of the chapel we were presented with the most

beautiful bowl filled with a lovely floral arrangement. We were given gifts, hugs of love, and prayer for God's next steps for us. It felt like God's smile of approval on us. In our hearts we believed we had finished well with Power to Change in Canada.

What Does Retirement Mean To Us?

Pete and I had never really talked about retirement. We actually don't believe that is a Biblical calling. At our wedding, Pete's brother Henry gave the message. He spoke about the parents of John the Baptist, Zechariah and Elizabeth. The Bible says: "They were both righteous, good and just people, in God's eyes and were walking in integrity, careful to obey all the commands of the Lord" (Luke 1:5-6). They were still serving God in their old age. That was the challenge Henry gave us. "Be righteous, be obedient to God, and serve God all the days of your life."

We joined a church and are encouraged and challenged each Sunday by receiving the solid preaching from the Word of God. We are also blessed with the connection we have with our community of believers. It has taken time, lots of initiation on our part, but it is so worth it. We want to be refreshers, not depleaters as we connect and communicate with people from all walks of life. Pete began making appointments with the staff of our church to hear their hearts, to encourage and pray with them. Pete also began meeting with young pastors of our city. His desire was to listen, encourage and be a spiritual body guard for so many pastors who had no one to share their concerns and challenges with. If we hadn't been broken and put through the refiner's fire, we would have little to offer other pastors and church leaders and participants. This was another evidence of blessing out of pain.

We are part of what we call our fun group. Four couples meet once a month at rotating host homes. The host chooses what restaurant we will meet at for dinner. When done, we go to the host home and gather around the table for a rousing game of dominoes It's always men against women with lots of healthy rivalry and laughter. We then have dessert made by the hostess and have an honest, caring, sharing and prayer time. This is a wonderful evening. We need a lot more laughter in our lives We need to connect with others We need to care and listen to each other and pray together These friends have been so caring and safe. We all feel the liberty to send out a prayer S.O.S. and to pray for needs as they arise. God put this group together and we are so blessed by each member. Try it. You'll like it.

Almost In Heaven December 2013

Our kids from Kelowna all left right after Christmas for a family vacation. Pete and I decided to take a vacation. Where? Hawaii, of course! That conversation with Jordan stayed with us and we thought, "Let's book a trip to Hawaii in Jordan's memory and rejoice in the Lord and turn our mourning into a Hawaiian dance". Everything was booked, with all the tickets purchased and a condo rented right on the beach. We could hardly wait.

I awoke on the morning of December 27 with a pain in my left side. We headed right for emergency. One look at my blood pressure and they rushed me right into ICU with doctors scurrying around me. I had an infected kidney stone that was poisoning my entire system. This is called septicemia. The doctor couldn't operate because all my vital signs were off the chart. My body went into shock. I was so cold, and shaking uncontrollably. I couldn't form the words for prayer, but I remembered a preacher telling us if you can't pray, just say the name of Jesus over and over again. I did that. It brought peace to my heart but my body was failing. "In the multitude of my anxieties within me, your comforts delight my soul" (Psalm 9:19).

I awoke from this state with seven doctors surrounding my bed talking about how sick I was. And then, God performed a miracle. I passed the infected kidney stone along with all the septicemia infection. I would survive. Recovering from this physical trauma would take time but step by step, day by day, I did recover.

God had given me another miracle! Why does He choose me? I have no answer,

"I am not skilled to understand what God hath willed what God hath planned. I only know at His right hand stands one who is my Savior." by Dora Greenwell (1821-1882)

As we grow in the Lord and in His Word, we grow in our marriages. At our 50th anniversary, I gave Pete a plaque that says,

229

"Grow old with me, the best is yet to be." It lays perfectly below our TV. I meditate on that plaque often. When I gave it to Pete, I was not well. I determined to give him that plaque in faith, believing that with God all things are possible. "Learn from yesterday, live for today, hope for tomorrow." (Albert Einstein) I have made the choice to be fully engaged wherever I am and to let God lead my days and my opportunities, to bless and encourage others.

Now, ten years later, I have weathered more trauma that could have easily taken me to heaven. But God has left me here with Pete and our family. I count each day as a blessed gift from God. Of course our marriage and our family has it's human struggles. We fail, we disappoint each other. There are times when I am not grateful and find things to complain about. I have begun to bemoan the fact that I still have to cook three meals a day, and I am tired of doing it for 60 years. Then I hear about Ruth Graham who had a plaque in her kitchen that says, "Divine service conducted here three times daily." I am convicted and want to look at everything as an opportunity to do all things to the glory of God, even in the kitchen. (1 Corinthians 10:31) I want to be more grateful that I have legs that I can walk and stand with, a mind that can think, money to buy groceries, and a beautiful kitchen to do all this in, plus a husband who helps me so willingly. In our marriage we choose daily to be fully engaged with each other, listening, sharing, laughing and working together. Yes, this does feel like God has granted us the very best years; the Golden Years.

For a number of years we had taken the time to pray together first thing in the morning and the last thing at night. These prayer times have brought us closer to each other and closer to our family, as we prayed for each individual in our growing family by name and the needs and blessings in their lives. We also pray for those of our friends in crisis, and always the missionaries whom we love and support.

In the morning we pray Romans 8:28 from The Voice translation of the Bible. "We are confident that God is able to orchestrate everything to work toward something good and beautiful when we love Him and accept His invitation to live according to His Plan". During my wrestling time this was the verse I could not embrace. Now, we have memorized it and it has become my anchor I cling to.

Our evening prayers end with the prayer God asked Aaron to bless His people of Israel with. God told Aaron if he prayed this blessing over the people, God would add his blessing. We alternate the lines as we pray this blessing over each other. "The Lord bless you and keep you; the Lord make his face to shine on you and be gracious to you; the Lord turn his face toward you and give you peace" (Numbers 6:24-26). What a lovely way to end a day.

This journey to our heavenly home is often difficult with sorrow, loss, pain and heartbreak. God is at work within us to develop our perseverance, our character, our love, and our hope. It is out of our wounds, our failures, and heartbreaks that God can use us to His glory and to the encouragement of His people. People are not interested in our successes, it is our wounds that are healing well and the scars we bear that give us admission into others' hearts.

It's hard to look back on a life of sixty years of ministry and marriage, without tears coming to my eyes. Tears of humble thanksgiving to a God who always keeps His promises, and who loves me unconditionally even when I am so unworthy of His love. I marvel at God's patience with me, when I was wrestling with the God I love and serve. It doesn't make sense to me, but the trauma and our catastrophic loss, did wreak havoc on my soul. We feel we have done all we could have done to reconcile with people in our past. I have purposefully omitted certain details of our most painful church experiences and kept them as unspoken thoughts. We are seeking to follow in Jesus steps "who did not retaliate when He was insulted, nor threaten revenge when he suffered."(1 Peter 2:23) Jesus carried us through that time, people prayed for us, as did the Holy Spirit, and in time we were gifted with healing. With the healing came beauty and redemption out of the ashes of pain and loss. As I look back I realize it was God who was writing my story. Life always has its challenges mingled with great blessing. I have finished this book limping my way along. Five months ago I came down with a bad case of Vertigo. While recovering, one morning I blacked out, fell backwards, broke my wrist and got a light concussion. My arm was in a cast for six weeks. My wrist has healed but the mild concussion has left some challenges. So I write through the difficulties and know God is going before me and giving me strength just when I need it.

I am amazed that I do not struggle with God anymore as I did when I mistakenly took that polio vaccine when I was in my twenties and was sick for so many months. Neither do I struggle with the different and mysterious ways of God. I have stopped wrestling with God. Period. It has taken me time and suffering to learn these lessons of faith. In the refiners fire I have learned to have a deep settled peace that my God who loves me is in control. Nothing will happen to me that is not Father-filtered. All that touches me comes from the heart of the One who loves me the most. This assurance has helped me have calm in the storms of life, in sleepless nights, in mysterious falls, and in the disappointments of life. God is love and He is a good, good Father! Simply trusting Jesus in every situation of life, is my stronghold.

For God's child, suffering is not wasted. The Bible tells us, "For our light and momentary troubles are achieving for us an eternal glory that far outweighs them all"

(2 Corinthians 4:17). In some way, God uses suffering to transform ordinary, clay people into vessels that are strong in faith, fit for His use, and displaying His glory to a watching world. Let's not waste our sorrows.

A few months ago our church had a lovely celebration, for all those in the church that were celebrating either their 50th or 60th Wedding Anniversary. My friend Susan, flew up for this occasion, while friends Diane and George drove the four hours to be here. Our kids and family that live here also attended. We were given a beautiful rose corsage and boutonniere and a bouquet of a dozen red roses. To our surprise our kids, Kim and Darlene, were asked to speak at this Celebration. Twelve couples were honored and interviewed. What a fun, happy time. We feel so blessed to belong to a church that so wonderfully honors the longevity and permanence of marriage. We got a card with children posing as an older couple. From the back you see his arm around her, she's leaning into him. The caption says: "Looks like you are still having and holding".

When God gave me back my song, He gave it to me in abundance. I wake up in the morning with precious songs in my heart and mind. The song stays with me all day or it may change. Oh what comfort the songs of my heart bring to me. And yes, I can sing It Is Well With My Soul, with no pretending.

It's good and healthy to have things to look forward to. We have put a high value on getting the whole family together about every two to three years. We will soon have six little great grandchildren to love and cherish. We are now, with the help of our kids, planning our 60th Wedding Anniversary Family Reunion. Yes you guessed it. We are having it at the end of this summer at the Oregon Coast. Not all can come. With jobs, sickness and unknown situations, we write all our plans with a pencil, and give God the eraser!. He knows what is best for us and for each member of the family. For those who can come, we will have a great time. We will build memories and relationships as we play, talk, eat, and walk on the beach. "Write your hurts in the sand. Carve your blessings in stone."

I cling to the verse in Isaiah 46:4, Even to your old age and gray hairs I am He; I am He who will sustain you. I have made you and I will carry you; I will sustain you and I will rescue you." Oh, what a Savior! Similarly, Psalm 71:18 declares, "Even when I am old and grey, do not forsake me, O God, till I declare your power to the next generation, your might to all who are to come." That is my deepest desire, that God will use me in our family to encourage, bless and pray for the next generation, as I declare God's mighty power to the generations that follow me. I love the following verse which blends the suffering here on this earth, as we await the glories of Heaven, for all eternity. "You should greatly rejoice in what is waiting for you, even if now for a little while you have to suffer various trials" (I Peter 1:6, Voice).

I often bathe in the words of this Fanny Crosby hymn, that is my testimony and my comfort.

"All the way my Savior leads me. What have I to ask beside?

Can I doubt His tender mercies? Who through life has been my guide.

Heavenly peace, divinest comfort. Here by faith in Him to dwell.

For I know whate'er befall me, Jesus doeth all things well."

As you have journeyed with me through this book, walked with me and learned with me, I pray that your faith will be stronger and your love deeper in the One who has made us, given us breath, and a life to live for His glory, as we await our call to our heavenly home. I pray that as you struggle with life's difficulties, my story will help you to realize that you are not alone! In the situations where I have failed, may it help you to not go down that path. I tell you my story to encourage you in your life of faith and trust in God, the Sovereign Lord of Heaven and earth. God's Story in my story is intended to change your story.

I heard this real life experience of a missionary who had gone to Africa to serve God there. He was disappointed in his assignment. He had so wanted to live near the ocean which he loved so much. At the end of the first semester, he shared with his students his longing to go to the ocean, to pick up a seashell and to be refreshed by the beauty. A few days later one of his students came to his home with a seashell as a gift for the teacher. When questioned how he had gone to the ocean and come back with a seashell. The student told him that he had walked to the ocean, got the seashell and walked back. The teacher was in awe at the long distance he had walked. The student said, "The long walk is part of the gift." I believe that is the same with my no pretending journey. The long walk of 60 years of being a pastor's wife, the pain and blessings I have shared with you, is part of my gift to you. The gift of the long walk in the same direction, of trusting God, regardless of the cost.

"Now to him who is able to do immeasurably more than all we ask or imagine, according to his power that is at work within us, to him be glory in the church and in Christ Jesus, throughout all generations, for ever and ever! Amen."

Ephesians 3:20–21

Notes and Permissions

Introduction

Carol Kent, (When I lay my Isaac Down) NavPress, 2004

Steve Saint Director of ITEC USA, itecusa.com

Chapter 2. Church Planting

Billy Graham, fking@bgea.ca, Billy Graham Evangelistic Association Canada 1-800-293 3717

Chapter 3. In God's Waiting Room

Tim Hansel, You Gotta Keep Dancin' (David C. Cook Publishing Co.,1985) p 55,123

Chapter 6: It's A Whole New World

Max Lucado, An Angel's Story, (Thomas Nelson, 2004) Introduction

Chapter 8: God Is Not Finished With Me Yet.

Kevin Miller, The Pain of Betrayal (Copyright © 2002 Christianity Today)

Chapter 9: Wrestling In The Dark

Helen Roseveare, Living Fellowship,(Hodder & Stoughton, Great Britain, 1992) p 166

Jerry Sittser, A Grace Disguised, (Zondervan, Grand Rapids, 1995) p 9,16,34,92,104,125

Chapter 11: Beauty For Ashes

Brian Doerksen, Song Your Faithfulness, Today CD Released 2004

Helen Adams Keller, Helen Keller's Journal:1936-1937, (Doubleday, Doran,1938) p 60

Gene Edwards, Prisoner in the Third Cell, (Tyndale House Publishers,

Inc.1991) p 79-80

Jerry Sittser, When God Doesn't Answer Your Prayer, (Zondervan, Grand Rapids, 2003) p 21, 190

All persons identified in Chapter 11 have given permission to use their name and information.

Chapter 13: Retired, or Fully Engaged

Letter to Grandpa Pete by Rick Lamoureux, Kelowna, BC

All Hymns are Public Domain

Made in the USA
Columbia, SC
25 February 2019